Blood, Sweat & McAteer

A FOOTBALLER'S STORY

Jason McAteer is a former Premier League footballer from Birkenhead. He is now a sports presenter and pundit.

Blood,
Sweat &
McAteer

A FOOTBALLER'S STORY

Jason McAteer

HACHETTE
BOOKS
IRELAND

First published in Ireland in 2016 by
HACHETTE BOOKS IRELAND
First published in paperback in 2017

Cataloguing in Publication Data is available from the British Library

ISBN 9781473636057

Typeset in Palatino by redrattledesign.com

Printed and bound in Great Britain by Clays Ltd, St Ives plc

Hachette Books Ireland policy is to use papers that are natural, renewable
and recyclable products and made from wood grown in sustainable forests.
The logging and manufacturing processes are expected to conform to the
environmental regulations of the country of origin.

Hachette Books Ireland
8 Castlecourt Centre
Castleknock
Dublin 15, Ireland

A division of Hachette UK Ltd
Carmelite House, 50 Victoria Embankment, London EC4Y 0DZ

www.hachettebooksireland.ie

For my two boys, Harry and Logan

Contents

Foreword

I t's the first thing that comes to mind for most people I suspect. Jason McAteer and Holland, Lansdowne Road back in 2001 and the goal that defined a career – the goal that almost brought the old East Stand crumbling to the ground.

Of course, that goal will always be the defining moment of Jason McAteer's career, if not his life. It's the most natural thing in the world to remember him for that goal, and why not?

We will all be remembered for something in our lives, won't we? So wow, what a memory if that defines your professional football career or even just your time with Ireland.

As a player, I will be remembered by some as the one who committed the most fouls at the 1990 World Cup finals. As a manager, I might be remembered for other things connected with 2002.

But for me, personally, that goal against Holland was a defining moment because it meant so much for all of us in our bid to get to the World Cup finals having missed out on the previous European Championships when we should have been there.

I saw Jason's goal again when I was researching my Paddy Power blog ahead of the recent European Championships and I enjoyed every minute of the YouTube video, not least because my good mate Bob Gibbs was caught celebrating by the cameras.

What struck me all these years later was the commentator making the point that picking Jason was a big call, the only big decision to be made ahead of the game. When I heard that, I remembered that there was a bit of a movement in the press to get Jason out of the team, a bit of anti-Jason feeling.

He would have hated that because he was such a loved character within the Irish game going back to the 1994 World Cup in the States.

Everybody in Ireland instantly fell in love with his larger-than-life character so for his place in the team to be questioned would have hurt him.

Me? I paid no attention to it. He had always done well for me as Ireland manager and there was reason in the world for me to leave him out that day. Boy did he repay me in spades. Not that I was surprised.

The first thing I was asked to do for this book was to describe Jason in one sentence. That's something that requires some thought, quite a tribute to the man in itself.

To sum him up though, I'd say that Jason McAteer is a lovely, open, refreshingly honest person and a really good character. It's been a pleasure to know him and a pleasure to work with him down through the years, both with Ireland and with Sunderland.

I may have met Jason briefly before the 1994 World Cup finals in America but that was the first time I really got to meet him and I liked him. He was the new kid in the Ireland squad alongside Gary Kelly and Phil Babb and I was out in America working with Dublin's 98FM and enjoying the World Cup in a new role as a pundit.

I was only thirty-five at the time but when I saw the Three Amigos buzzing with energy on the training ground and around the team hotel, I really felt like Old Father Time himself. They were chirping and cheeping about the place and I had an instant liking for Jason.

I only spent a couple of days around the team on that trip – I remember the hotel was bonkers in Orlando with everyone in it – but I did take up Jack Charlton's invite to go to one of the training sessions and that's where I properly met Jason, Gary and Phil.

They were full of beans and a breath of fresh air when the Ireland scene needed some youth.

I didn't come into the International game until I was in my mid-twenties when Eoin Hand picked me and even under Jack in the early days, Niall Quinn was the closest thing we had to a youth policy.

America in '94 was the start of the changing of the guard and Jason was one of the players at the heart of all that. He was all action, full of energy and I loved the way he played and the way he trained.

I'd go so far as to say he was the perfect right-sided player in a 4-4-2 formation and when he played right wing-back for Liverpool, he was a different class as well.

A couple of years after that World Cup, I got to work with Jason as his Ireland manager and that was an absolute pleasure. He is a real touchy, feely kind of guy and while a lot of people will find this hard to believe, strangely enough, so am I. You always got a hug off Jason and I like that in people.

He responded to that sort of relationship, he responded to being liked and to being trusted and to being thought well of, which we all do. Some people can cope without that but Jason needed it, he needed that reassurance.

He was a player who liked to have a good relationship with his manager and wasn't afraid to have one. He loved to have a chat with his manager and he was never embarrassed to talk to his boss.

Not all players are like that. Some steer clear of the boss, some don't want to let anybody see them talking to the manager. Not Jason.

I doubt he coped well at clubs where he didn't have that relationship. Of course he wanted to please, we all do, and there is no harm in that. He wanted you to like him and to show him that you liked him and I liked that quality in him. The players did as well. He was good fun to be around and from my view of him, the lads loved having him around the place.

We did have our moments mind. He got injured in that Izumo friendly against Hiroshima right before the opening game at the World Cup finals in 2002 and I knew from looking at him in training that his knee wasn't good.

He wasn't anywhere near right for the Cameroon game and he only lasted forty-five minutes of it before I took him off at half-time and put Steve Finnan at right-back. Gary Kelly went onto the right side of the midfield where Jason had been and Gary did so well for the rest of the tournament that he was my outstanding player in that World Cup.

Jason didn't take his demotion too well. He threw a bit of a strop and threatened to go home which would have been the most stupid decision of his career. We talked him round and he got another ten minutes in the third group game against Saudi Arabia as Gary's replacement but he just wasn't fit enough.

We had words again in my second season at Sunderland, at Gatwick Airport after I had taken him off at half-time in the first leg of the promotion play-off against Crystal Palace. Jason wasn't happy with the decision and he was even less pleased when I made it clear that I wanted to start with the on-loan Carl Robinson for the return leg at home.

He came to see me and bent my ear to play him, promising he wouldn't let me down. I made it clear I wasn't convinced he should play but we needed that conversation. I put him back in the team and, again, he didn't let me down.

I did let him go at the end of that season. His legs were starting to go and he was on a fortune compared to the sort of money we were starting to pay players coming to the Stadium of Light. He won't have liked that conversation either but I am sure he knew where I was coming from and why I did what I had to do.

Jason did end up doing some coaching himself at Tranmere after Sunderland but management wasn't something I'd have seen in him. I know he loved his football but there was always that flippant side to him as well, the come-a-day, go-a-day, here comes Sunday banter.

Coaching would have suited him better than management because there is a deeper side to Jason McAteer than the side that he gives off in public. He is a lot more thought-ful about a lot of things than he lets on to be.

I don't see that much of Jason these days but when we do meet, I can tell straight away that he hasn't changed and never will. I have a real soft spot for him as a person and I always liked him as a player.

He was great for me as his manager, with Ireland and with Sunderland. You always knew what you were going to get from Jason McAteer. He would run all day, work hard and commit. He would never let you down intentionally. He might make a rick but I can look at myself as a player and as a manager and say honestly that I never let anyone down intentionally. I might make mistakes but we all make mistakes.

Jason was my type of player and my type of person – open, honest, friendly, committed. And nice. Always nice. That's most important of all.

Mick McCarthy
August 2016

Chapter One

The Germans are pinned down in the corner. They've nowhere to go. We're crouched low. I release the pin from the grenade. 'Throw it up in an arc, not straight, it has to fall from a height,' he says.

I let it go.

'Good shot.'

It lands right behind the television. The Germans are goners. 'You throw a good grenade,' says my granddad from our bunker behind the couch.

It's Friday night. Nan has gone to bingo. Grandad's telling me his war stories again and showing me how to throw grenades – with a rolled-up sock.

'The fighting McAteers, one of them, are you? You're big around here so. Is Les your uncle? And Irish Pat the middleweight? Is one of them your auld fella? No? So you're the son of the youngest fella, right. What's his name again? Never boxed, did he?'

My dad is William, known as Billy by the way, but growing up it's the McAteer surname that means something in Birkenhead. Not who I am or where I am from. It's all about the name.

I'm a McAteer, one of the fighting McAteers, and I am carried around on a Saturday morning on my uncle Les' shoulders, like Rocky in the meat market in Philadelphia. I'm a somebody from up on Town Road in Tranmere, the McAteer who lives on the top of the hill they use as the vantage point for all the photographs, the spot where you can see everything from the Cammell Laird docks, where my auld fella works occasionally, across to Merseyside and Liverpool itself.

Look down from the top of that hill and my life is laid out in front of you. There's the Grange Mount Maternity Hospital where I was born, the famous Birkenhead Boys Club and the market, where they offer their hero Les everything from free bananas to raw steak, fit for the champion he is. I'm sitting on the shoulders of a giant.

My dad's dad is of Irish stock. The McAteers came over from County Down in the north of Ireland looking for work, and never went back. We're Wirral Scousers now and proud of it.

They're hard men – hard and tough, each and every one of them. My dad says they get it from his father, who ruled their house with an iron fist. He was strict with his kids, never afraid to give the boys a clout when they deserved it and sometimes when they didn't. Growing up, my dad and his brothers learned about life the hard way. They learned discipline and honour and determination, and they say that's running in our McAteer veins. There's a toughness and a steeliness about us. That's what they say.

The funny thing is that, as a kid, my uncle Neil was the best of the fighting McAteers in the boxing ring. He gave it all up for life in the police force and a rise through the ranks in the CID. Another 'uncle' – who was really my dad's cousin, and who we knew as Irish Pat – had left for the States before I was born, but not before he'd become British Empire and European Champion at middleweight.

You've met Uncle Les already. He's the hero of the brood and is loved everywhere he goes on Merseyside. My dad reckons he's royalty round our way, after he followed in Pat's footsteps and won the British Empire title at middleweight.

My dad's the youngest of the five boys and one girl, and he was never that much into boxing, if truth be told. He did all the training and the hard hours in the gym and on the road and he fought in the amateurs, but he never quite got out of boxing what the others did. He'd been happy to hang on to their coat-tails when he was a nipper, but was happier still when he was playing football. That's all he wanted to do, play football. And thank God for that.

Just the name meant he was invited to all the parties, met all the right people and all the nice girls, but he never had to take a punch to get there. Pat and Les looked after all that – he just tagged along. That's how he met my mum.

She is from a family of bakers across the border in Wales. My nan has a bakery in Bebington and all my aunts work there with my mum and my granddad. She'd been engaged to another bloke when she met my dad on a night out in Birkenhead. He was a good-looking bloke back then, a Steve McQueen lookalike with the charm to match. And, typical of my dad, he had her eating out of the palm of his hand that night. She didn't want to fall for him, or that's what she says, but she did. She had to end her engagement to go out with my dad but that's exactly what happened, and the rest is history.

I'm the oldest of their three children. I've a sister Beverly and a brother Sam. We live in Town Road now, but that's not where I was born. I was brought home from Grange Mount Hospital to Rhyl Street, just around the corner.

Boxing is still a big thing for the family but, like my dad I suppose, it's not for me. Like him, I'm quite happy to be carried on the shoulders of my uncle Les' fame, but I've never been into the sport – and I've had all the chances. There were boxing gloves and punch balls and boxing balls at Christmas and birthdays, which were great, but I never think of them as being important.

Boxing's never been pushed on me and I've never gone looking for it. I've never felt the need to. Unlike my dad, I've no punch. One night he hit the boxing ball in the kitchen so hard that it fell off the stand. I can barely move it!

Judo is my first sporting love. I'm about seven years of age when they start lessons after class at Mersey Park School. I fancy trying it, and I really like it at first. My partner's a school mate called Richard Long and we're getting good at it. We train Tuesdays and Thursdays and then compete at weekends. We're going up through the belts and we're winning things, lots of things.

We've been area champions for the northwest of England and we've been to national championships as contenders as well. We are the reigning northwest under-ten champions – but my dad is starting to take control of it. I don't like that. My mum's an encourager. She wants me to enjoy it and she never pushes me the way he does. She only encourages me to do my best and insists my best is all she will ever ask of me.

My dad's different. As soon he sees I'm good at something, he wants me to win all the time, become the best. He saw that winning mentality in his brothers and his cousins – and they'd never have become British Empire and European Champions without it. He grew up in a house full of winners. For them it was win at all costs or not at all, and he wants it to be the same for me now. I'm afraid, afraid of the failure and afraid of letting him down.

I'm standing there before competitions with my pumps on, feeling like a bag of nerves. I've just cried my eyes out to my mum. I've told her I can't do it anymore. I have to stop the judo.

I've started to do cross-country running at school and even though I'm the skinniest kid in the class, I'm good at it. I know I am. I've got an appetite for running and I've found a niche for myself.

So I stop the judo and concentrate on running. I'm soon the best at school and then the best for my age on the Wirral.

Every year, four times a year, they bring the best kids from the ten schools in the area to race against one another. I win the first race by miles – at least it seems like miles to me. Then I win the second one and the third one. Nobody has won all four races in the same school year in something like seventy-five years. This is big news locally.

I'm a judo champion and an athletics champion and I'm about to make history. My dad is in his element. He wants me to win it, he wants to see the McAteer name up in lights in Birkenhead once again.

I win the race, almost in spite of him, but I don't enjoy it. I don't relish the achievement of winning all four Wirral races in the same season. I can't enjoy it.

I finally snap when I get to run at a school sports day at The Oval in Bebington. It's the track they used when they were filming *Chariots of Fire* and it's not far from where we live. All the schools from the Wirral are there again, and I'm entered in the 1,500 metres, the longest race you can run in my age group. After winning the four cross-country races I'm the favourite in everybody's eyes, especially my dad's.

I can't sleep the night before the race. My mind is running faster than my legs with the thoughts of *having* to win. It's all down to me. I've no one to share the pressure and expectation with. I'm a bag of nerves again and jumping with adrenalin at the start of the race – at the end of it, I only place eighth.

That's it. I've had enough. I sit down with my mum when I get home and I tell her I can't do it anymore, any of it. I bawl my eyes out.

My mum knows where I am coming from. She and my dad have been arguing terribly about it for ages. Then there would be tears and arguments and stress – for all of us.

My mum supports me, and that's all I need for now. I won't have to compete in any sport again unless I really want to, and that's a big weight off my mind.

All I need now is another sport. I'm sure I'll find one – or it will find me.

Chapter Two

I'm upstairs in my room, crying my eyes out. My mum has made me a full Liverpool strip on her sewing machine. It's red and it has a big Liverpool badge on the chest, but it's made of curtain material. I tell her it's great, the best present ever. Then I run up the stairs and bawl my eyes out. I can't be seen in this in public.

It's Sunday morning, and the coolest kid on the block is running up and down the street. He has a ball at his feet and is holding a piece of paper with the key to the future on it. It's a registration form to play football on a proper team, and he knows it's an offer that every boy will find hard to refuse as he works his way up and down Town Road.

It's a typical Sunday on the Wirral. The women spend the mornings in the kitchen getting the lunchtime roast and the Yorkshire puds ready, the dads are either in the khazi or down the pub.

The cool kid is my mate at Mersey Park School, Chris Reilly. He's the one with the trendy clothes and the nice shoes. We call him 'Little Chris' because his dad is Chris Reilly as well. Big Chris works on the buses with the Merseyside Public Transport Authority.

The Reillys live across the park from us on Town Road. Chris and me are in the same class at school, and he's always calling. So it's no surprise that he's at the door this Sunday morning. The surprise is what he has to tell me.

His dad is really into his football and wants to start a team for Little Chris and his mates. Little Chris wants to know if I'm interested in being part of it. I don't even need time to think about it. I'm straight into the kitchen to tell my mum and she's fine with it, she tells me just to talk to Little Chris' mum or dad and let them know.

I get back to the door and tell Little Chris I'm in. By the time I get to ask him what we'll be doing and when, he's already knocking on Alan Rimmer's door to see if he wants to play as well. Little Chris is a kid on a mission to bring football to Town Road, and nothing's going to stop him.

This is how the Reillys get a team together, by Little Chris running through the streets, knocking on doors and letting us all know about Transport Juniors. Big Chris had spoken to his bosses on the buses and persuaded them to sponsor the team's kit, and other bits and pieces.

I'm eleven years old and I can't wait to get started.

I love the idea of being on a team where there's other people to share the pressure and the burden of expectation. It's not all about me, and I'm fine with that.

I've loved football all my life. Like every kid in the schoolyard, I play football with our jumpers down for goalposts, but now I'm getting to play with a team. I want to be Kenny Dalglish. He's my hero.

I got to see him once. My mum's sister's husband, or my Uncle Mack as we call him, has season tickets for Anfield and he brought me there once as a special treat with his son, my younger cousin. We were in the lower level of the main stand, right on pitch level at the halfway line. Dalglish was on fire that day, straight in front of me. It was like he knew I was there and he was putting on a show just for me. Me and King Kenny. He was so close I could have reached out and touched him.

Whatever about liking Liverpool before that game, I was in love with the club after it and King Kenny was the greatest footballer of all time.

My mum knew how much I wanted to be Kenny Dalglish. We were skint at the time, and she was working about five jobs to keep food on the table and make sure we wanted for nothing. She did everything from cleaning to babysitting to working in the family bakery.

To save a few bob, she used to make our school uniforms on her sewing machine. So she made me a Liverpool kit when I got back from that game at Anfield, a full Liverpool kit made from some curtain material she'd picked up in one of the local shops.

She was a good seamstress so it was easy for her to put it all together – the red shirt and red shorts – she even got me some red socks as well. She bought a big Liverpool badge and sewed it onto the jersey. We still have the photograph, me standing there with my arms folded in my home-made Liverpool kit with this bloody big badge stuck underneath my shoulder.

It may have looked a bit ridiculous but that was me mum all over. She wants me to be happy and she wants me to have the same Liverpool shirt that I'd seen King Kenny wear.

I wasn't happy about it though. I cried my eyes out in my room the night she gave it to me because it wasn't the real Liverpool jersey, but I didn't tell her. I was cute enough to know not to hurt her feelings. She had done her best and that was how we got by.

It's 1981, and times are tough round here. My dad is in and out of work at the shipyard and hand-me-downs from Uncle Neil's family are the norm.

I may be young, but I know enough about what is going on in the real world. My dad is a spark – an electrician – in the shipyards with Cammell Laird, and Maggie Thatcher is trying hard to wipe out his trade and his industry. Shipbuilding is dying and he is part of the cortège, both at Cammell Laird and then at the McTay Marine, one of the spin-offs.

His work is never consistent and he's always doing foreigners – what we call nixers – odd jobs for neighbours and the like. He's always trying to take me with him and get me to hold the hammer or the screwdriver or whatever.

It's boring. It bores the arse off me, and I know I never, ever, ever want to be an electrician. It's all 'hold these screws,' 'pass me those screws,' 'get this, get that,' and it's not for me.

The lack of regular work puts real pressure on my dad, and it puts real pressure on the family. My mum makes sure we never want for food and she insists we have a proper family meal every night around the kitchen table, whether my dad is working or not.

She works hard, and when my dad is out of work, she

works even harder. She's a proud woman and she takes pride in how we look and how we behave. She ensures we are never scruffy and warns us never to do anything that might damage the family.

Life is tough on my mum and dad and, as I get older, I start to realise what is going on around me.

My escape is to head off to my nan's out in Bebington at the weekends. They live beside the municipal golf course called Brackenwood. The golf course is a cash cow. I sneak out there in the fading light, find a few Dunlop 65s and sell them back to the players. Then it's in for me cooked tea and back into the loving arms of my nan and granddad.

I go there as often as I can. My nan picks me up on a Friday and I work with my granddad and her in the bakery on the Saturday, then they bring me for a family tea on the way home that evening.

I'm their first grandchild and they spoil me rotten. They even buy me my first pair of Patrick Keegan Kid football boots. During the school holidays I try to live there full-time – that's how good it is. Even when my nan goes out to bingo on a Friday night I'm happy to sit there for hours listening to my granddad tell his war stories. He tells the same ones every time, but I love it. I know all about how he won the war all on his own and sent Rommel packing in the African desert.

Saturday mornings I'm down the bakery with him, baking the bread and the cakes and just enjoying the routine and the normality of it all, enjoying this substitute life for the one I don't have at home. I love the cakes. He has me pasting the egg yolks and mixing the butter cream and he turns a blind eye when I stick my finger into the mix and lick it up.

I want life to be like this forever, but it can't be. It's soon going to be time to move on to secondary school and, truth is, I'm not the most academic kid in the world. I'm bright rather than smart, and I'm sporty. I'm always out in the park, playing football or hide and seek – 'alleyo' as we call it – and messing around. I'm up and down the hill on Town Road so often that I'm as fit as a fiddle. If anyone round these parts ever needs stamina training, just buy a house on Town Road. You'll spend your life going up and down that hill and you'll be fit in no time.

Part of the reason for my constant running up and down the hill is that my best mate, Gary Preston, lives at the bottom. We're up and down like yo-yos, always calling for each other, always looking to get to the park, always on the lookout for the next great adventure.

The year I leave Mersey Park, the other pupils elect me head boy. I suppose I'm a bit of a loveable rogue as far as the other students are concerned, but I'm also well behaved. My dad wouldn't have it any other way, to be fair to him. I'm small for my age and the headmaster at Mersey Park has always taken a shine to me.

I think he enjoyed the attention the school got when I was winning all those cross-country races, so he approved when I was elected head boy. I'm head boy and Elizabeth Smith is head girl. We get to wear special badges on our uniforms every time we represent the school at various events, like scout badges I suppose. I still have mine, it's a real badge of honour.

I'm going to Rockferry High School, and my mum has her sewing machine out again. She's insisted on making my blazer and is making my trousers as well, all from this horrible material she's picked up. When she's finished, I cry my eyes out again, but in front of her this time. I look like the bloody Michelin Man. My blazer is so different to the one that everyone else is going to be wearing and I cry about it so much that she goes out and buys me the proper one.

The slight problem with Rockferry High is that it's a rugby school and I don't fancy rugby much. It's far too physical for someone my size and I don't like the rough and tumble of it at all. So that's something I'm not looking forward to. Thankfully I meet a teacher early on called Mr Lloyd and he's a big footie fan. He knows there's a gang of us from Transport Juniors who've all just started at the school together, and he promises to get a school team going.

Basically the school side is the same one that turns out every week for Transport, the same eleven kids who Big Chris Reilly, with the best of intentions, piles illegally into the back of his Vauxhall Viva every weekend to go down to the local playing fields at Borough Road.

It's a good job the school gets a team together because Transport Juniors come to an end not long after we start secondary school. Big Chris and a load of his mates have been let go by the transport authority, and there's no more funding for the team. Without the money and with no job, Big Chris just can't keep the team going.

There is another local team called Victoria Park Rangers, from one of the local parks where we spend all our time, and a gang of us move there after Transport Juniors falls by the wayside. Their manager Billy Prescott knows us because his young lad Wayne is on our school team.

We're a decent side. We christen ourselves Vicky Park Rangers and, by the time we get to the under-14 age group, we're doing quite well for club and school – so well that a number of us get called to trials for the Wirral Schools ahead of their annual match against the Liverpool Schools.

This is a big chance.

The Liverpool Schools side has some of the best young talent in England, never mind Merseyside. There's a kid called Steve McManaman playing on the wing, a striker from Toxteth called Robbie Fowler and a big centre-back from Kirkby Schools called Alan Stubbs.

We know all about them from playing in the club leagues, and both me and John Norman the other kid sent for trials, know that this is a really big game for us.

Colin Harkness is the coach in charge of the team and he must have hundreds of kids to look at in the trials. I do okay, or so I think until I open the pages of the *Wirral Globe* the following week and see the list of successful trialists printed in black and white. John Norman has made the squad, but there's no sign of any Jason McAteer.

I'm devastated when I read it, absolutely devastated. The only glimmer of hope is an add-on at the bottom of the article which says that anybody who thinks they should have made it and didn't can ask for a review of their situation. My dad's eyes light up when he sees this bit and he's on the case straight away.

He knows what this chance means to me and he does me proud. He writes to them and explains how he thought

I should get another chance. They're good about it when they get the letter and they invite me down to a training session so that Colin and the coaches can have another look at me. We get there expecting to find loads of kids in the same boat but it turns out I'm the only one. My dad was the only parent to go to the trouble of writing the letter, and fair play to him. I get a second trial and I do really well, so well that the guy in charge comes up to my dad straight after we finish and says they might have made a mistake after all.

He offers me the chance to carry on training with the squad and assures me that even if I don't make the team for the game against the Liverpool Schools, at least I will be in and around the place with eighteen of the best young players on Merseyside. He promises me and my dad that it can only improve me as a footballer no matter what comes of the experience.

That's good enough for me, all I can ask for after the second trial. I go to see the headmaster at Rocky High and explain to him that I now need time off every Tuesday to go and train for the Wirral Schools with John Norman. The head is great about it to be fair, says it is brilliant that we made it through to the squad and agrees to let us skip double biology every Tuesday to go and train at Ridgeway.

Something clearly gets lost in translation, however, because a few weeks later he stops me after assembly one morning and asks how my cricket training is going. He says he's big into cricket and is chuffed that two of his pupils have made it onto the Wirral Schools cricket team. He's none too pleased at first that it's football we've been recognised for.

Eventually we get recognised by the school itself for our achievement. Tradition at Rocky High has it that any pupil who brings honour to the school is presented with a special braid that they wear under the school badge on their uniform. There's a grading system in place. Anyone who represents the Wirral gets a light brown braid, if you are picked on a Merseyside team you get a dark brown one and if you get as far as national honours with England you're awarded laurels, which are sown into the blazer, directly underneath the school crest.

It's quite a distinction to walk around the school with the braids but, so far in my two years at the school, no one has received a laurel. My first braid arrives when I get picked to play at right-back for the Wirral Schools, despite my size. And the more I play with them, as per the promise, the better I get.

Soon enough I'm being offered trials with the Merseyside Schools and that's the big thing for any player round our way. The trials are to be held at a school in Liverpool called Savio and they're on the same day as Bob Geldof hosts Live Aid at Wembley Stadium.

John Norman and me are again sent for the trials together and we both get into the team, me at right-back, because the guy they really want is injured, and John at centre-back. Cue another braid for the blazer.

We need an England call-up now to get the laurels and we get close without ever actually getting there. The FA has started a scheme to get the best schoolboy footballers in the country enrolled on their apprenticeship course at Lilleshall. The idea is to bring the best English talent together to work with FA coaches in a bid to nurture them for the clubs and for the national team.

John Ebbrell was one of the first kids from Merseyside to get picked for the scheme and everyone says it is the way forward. For our chance to get selected, both John Norman and myself play in the North England v. South England trials. We do well in the early stages, so well that we make it all the way to the final trial, but then it all goes pear-shaped and we're out of the running for Lilleshall – and the laurels on the school blazer.

The scheme at Lilleshall is an apprenticeship in football, and I really want it. I could make it at Lilleshall, get signed by a big club and play for England after coming through their academy. Imagine that.

My mum and my nan know how upset I am when word comes through. My nan books me onto a Bobby Charlton soccer school in Chester as a surprise to help me over the disappointment. And, typically, my mum goes the extra mile to make it up for me.

Christmas has always been a big thing for us and she knows how much presents mean to me and my brother and sister.

When the Lilleshall trials don't work out, she pushes the boat out again. I don't even know that she's off out to a testimonial dinner for the Liverpool and England defender Phil Neal one night, but she goes there knowing how much I love Liverpool FC and how much I idolise Kenny Dalglish.

Nothing would do her that night other than to get Kenny's autograph for her eldest son. She gets Kenny and

Phil to sign the dinner menu and, when I wake up the next morning there's King Kenny's autograph staring up at me from my bedside locker. I can't believe it. This is like gold dust to me.

It's a bit of a family tradition to leave gifts like that on the bedside locker. My nan went off to the Canaries on holiday one year and the next time I stayed in her house there was a Lacoste shirt waiting for me when I woke up. Anything special goes on the bedside locker – just so you can check you weren't dreaming.

I'm not dreaming the morning I wake up to King Kenny's autograph and I pinch myself just to make sure. The memory of that signed menu card – and the card itself – will stay with me forever.

Chapter Three

I'm still waiting on that Jimmy Saville to get back to me. I wrote him a letter weeks ago, like he suggests on his telly show. He says he can fix things for people, so I've asked him to fix me up with a trial for Kenny Dalglish's Liverpool FC. That's what my letter to Jim'll Fix It *said. And he still hasn't got back to me.*

There's a club called Manchester United who want to have a look at the cut of me on the football field. Well, that's what I'm telling my other fourteen-year-old friends and anyone else who'll listen to me – a starry-eyed kid with dreams of life as a professional footballer.

The Lilleshall disappointment is behind me. I don't have time to dwell on it because the rumours are flying. We keep hearing stories about scouts from Chester, Tranmere, Everton and Liverpool coming to look at every match I play in, be it with the school, with the Wirral or with Vicky Park Rangers.

The scouts are easy to spot. They stand out like sore thumbs on the sidelines in their big, long, sleeping-bag coats, padding down to their ankles with the badges on them just in case we don't know they're working for this club or that club. They try to keep their presence low-key, but we know who they are. Some of them are regulars, like Mickey O'Brien who always turns up in his Blackburn tracksuit and is never afraid to have a word or two with my dad. He's a decent bloke and my dad reckons he probably does the scouting for nothing more than petrol money and a few tickets. He tells my dad he likes the cut of me, but that's as far as it goes.

Every other decent kid, including John Norman, is being told the same thing, of course. The clubs around us are too astute not to constantly monitor every kid kicking ball on Merseyside. They always have and they always will. But, in my mind at least, the scouts only have eyes for me, even if my size – or lack of it – is a big disadvantage, particularly because John is so tall and skinny and jumps like a gazelle.

I do feel like I am always competing with John anytime we go out on a football field, and it's not a good attitude to bring into a game, particularly when important people in puffed-out jackets are watching.

United and Liverpool are probably the best equipped to scour the area for talent. Both clubs operate three-day trials every year over the Easter holidays for the best youngsters in the northwest and a handful of us are invited to attend a training camp at United.

They put us up at the local university halls of residence, with all the training and assessments at The Cliff, and Joe Brown is the man in charge of the programme.

It's brilliant. Everything is done on the Astros at The Cliff at the same time as the first team are training on the pitches nearby. We're actively encouraged to talk to the players, to meet them and greet them, to ask them questions in the dressing room. They want us to bond with the likes of Mark Hughes and Bryan Robson. I can't believe it. We're so close to the players that I can see that Bryan Robson's feet are black with bruises when he gets off the training ground.

United bring us down to the club shop and give us all posters with pen pics of the first team. Mark Hughes signs mine for me and I'm made up. He even gives me his training top. That's heading to the bedside locker.

Ron Atkinson is the manager, and he is larger than life, just like my dad said he would be. The first time we see him is in the car park. He has the boot of his car open and these three different suits are hanging on it, out in the open for the first team to have a look at. Manchester United are playing Everton in the FA Cup final in a month, and these are the potential suits the players and staff will wear to Wembley. They're dead smart.

Kevin Moran is there with Atkinson and he's really friendly. He's a big hero at the club and he says hello. Remi Moses is there as well with his big Afro hairdo and he's priceless, cracking jokes and making us all laugh.

United really push the boat out over the three days, but reality bites soon enough when I get home and the letter arrives to say I'd done really well and that they'll 'monitor' my progress but that I was 'just not right for us at the moment' and 'thanks very much'.

Everton aren't even that involved. I keep hearing stories about them watching the games but they never offer me as much as a trial. I do get to play a few games for Chester's youth team just so they can have a look while United are 'monitoring' my progress.

There's also a trial on offer at Tranmere, my local club, but there's something not right about their interest, and it quickly becomes apparent that it's all a bit of a stitch-up.

The club is broke, same old story, and they've been tapping my uncle Billy, who's really my dad's cousin, for a good few bob. In return he gets the run of the social club at the back of the ground, but what they really want is access to my uncle Pat, Irish Pat, out in the States. They know that Pat has built up a really successful business empire in the construction game over there, and it's his endorsement that Tranmere are really after. If they can get Pat and my uncle Billy to rubber-stamp them, they're made.

They want to keep the McAteers sweet, so I get invited down for a trial one Saturday morning not long after my time with United. It's May now, but it is still freezing with the wind whipping in off the Irish Sea. Nothing happens in the game and it strikes me that nobody really wants anything to happen. There's no interaction with their coaches, no encouragement or guidance. Nothing.

They've ticked the box, had a look at me and done their duty. They can approach Pat now having had a look at his nephew and I will have to wait for my big break to come from somewhere else.

I'm nearly fifteen and I am starting to panic a little bit. All I can think about is football and a career in football but there's no sign of it happening for me.

Chester are handing out YTS apprenticeships but I don't get a look-in. Liverpool and Everton have gone cold on me. Tranmere have done with me. Maybe my size *is* an issue.

Life choices await and I don't want to face them. School is only an afterthought but I have decisions to make with my CSEs and O Levels next on the agenda. I've to pick three subjects from twelve for O Levels, but art is the only one I care about, the only one I have any passion for.

That's the one subject that comes easily to me. The rest I could happily do without. The school pushes me towards Geography because they think I have a chance with it. They're wrong.

I pick French as my third subject for one reason and one reason only – I have a crush on the teacher. She looks and sounds like Vicki Michelle from *'Allo 'Allo!* And I am convinced she has a soft spot for me to boot. Then she goes off and gets married and moves to the Isle of Man and leaves me to face that bloody French exam all on my own. *Merci beaucoup.*

I am struggling academically, but I'm not bothered, even though the teachers and my parents are telling me I should be. The careers teacher tells us to write down a list of the three things we want to do after school.

One of my mates puts professional snooker player at the top of his list, so I put down professional footballer at the top of mine. I'm struggling for a second career option, never mind a third one. In the end I put down PE teacher in second spot and lifeguard third. They're both loosely connected to making a living from sport but I only write them down to finish the exercise.

I am going to be a footballer and nothing is going to get in my way. I'll get knocked down but I will get up again, just like a fighting McAteer.

Things are moving at pace in my life, too fast really. John Norman gets a YTS contract from Tranmere and that only fuels my suspicion that my lack of size is the real problem when it comes to football. He's not the only one from my football family to get a contract offer: Barry Geress gets taken on at Liverpool and Stuey Griffiths gets into the Everton academy. The Vicky Park gang is starting to break up.

I'm fifteen now and I don't like what I see in front of me. When the other kids were busy doing their work experience, I was using that time to go on trials with football clubs and to train. Now I have nothing to show for it, but they've experienced life in the real world. They know they have options after school. I've given everything to football and got nothing back.

All I have away from the game is a part-time job at the Tranmere Rovers Social Club at Prenton Park. My uncle Les runs the place and he hires me and my mate Paul Jenkins as glass collectors, and we have the life. We're down there on Saturdays and Sundays and it's an eye-opener, listening to all the auld fellas, getting their tips for the horses and cashing in. There's a bar and function room and we work the function room first and then the bar. We hang around, cook the pizzas for the functions, listen to Les' mates tell all their stories, grab tokens for the fruit machines and keep any money we win for ourselves.

Les is still a big name round our way, and we get some of his old mates from the fight game in from time to time. Joey Singleton is a regular and Brian London has been in for a big dinner night. There's a buzz about the place and I'm making the most of my name and my status as Les' nephew. I suppose it's a bit like my dad hanging on Les' coat-tails when he was my age.

The money's not bad either, twenty quid most weekends is a nice few bob, plus whatever we can make on the fruit machines and from any of the hundreds of tips for the horses that we hear and take seriously.

It's a life of sorts, and it might be the only life open to me the way things are going. But it's not football. And football is all I want, even if football doesn't seem to want me.

Chapter Four

There's no way my mum is going to let me sign on the dole.
Instead she signs me up for a job interview with McDonald's.
They're hiring at their Birkenhead restaurant, the perfect spot
for a sixteen-year-old fresh out of school to start life in the world
of the employed. I apply and get an interview – and that's it.
Nothing more from Ronald McDonald other than a rejection
letter. No happy meal for me. Even McDonald's don't want me.
What hope have I left?

My CSE results are OK but my O Levels are a disaster. Geography is a fail. French is a pass but only just. Art is a pass with flying colours, pun intended, and it is definitely the only thing other than football that I am any good at. The school knows it, my mum knows it and I know it.

There's no point even thinking about staying in secondary school for another two years and doing any A levels. It would be a complete waste of time for all concerned.

My mum is the realistic one in all of this. She tells me straight out that I haven't done anything worth talking about in my O levels and that I have three choices, though only two in reality – there's no way she is going to let her eldest child sign on the dole.

The first of the two remaining choices is to go and get a job, a real job, and not one collecting the glasses down my uncle's bar and function room. McDonald's are hiring at their Birkenhead restaurant and that seems like a logical choice for a sixteen-year-old kid looking for a start in adult life. I get an interview but not the job.

College is the other option. I'm out of choices with my O level results, but my mum knows of an art school called Withens Lane that's running a graphic design course I could try to get on. My grades aren't good enough for the actual college course they run but there is a foundation course, a year-long B Tech National Course, and that will get me enough qualifications to get onto one of the courses I really want to do.

It's a second chance and it's my only chance. If I can get through this foundation course, then I can apply to study graphic design for real or have a look at something like jewellery design. This time, though, I know that I have to start putting the work in and make the grades.

I get through to the interview stage of the application procedure and everything clicks. I'm in. It's like I've gone on a trial all over again but this time I've been accepted. It really is going to be the best thing for me.

As it turns out, there's a bloke working at the Withens Lane College called Alan Molden who will play a big role in my life. He's a bit of a local football hero, is Alan. He was a contender as a kid but never made it, and spent most of his playing career with Wallasey. He's well respected in the game round here, though, even now that he's in his mid-thirties, and he can still play a bit. He can also identify with what I've been going through for the past couple of years as I try to bridge that gap between contender and achiever.

We get talking football early in my time at college and I tell Alan all about the path from Transport Juniors to Vicky Park and then with a team called the Young Lions for a very short time when the Vicky Park side broke up.

I've moved on to Shaftesbury Boys Club by the time I start college, but the whole set-up there is a bit posh for me. They've an indoor pitch and a tuck shop and all that nonsense but they also have a fella in charge and I get the feeling he doesn't like me.

I'm still playing with the Wirral Schools but this fella at the Boys Club doesn't fancy me at all, something he makes very clear from day one. As I'm approaching sixteen he tells me that I'm not good enough for his precious little set-up anymore. I'm sure he thinks he's in charge of United or Liverpool or something.

Ian Doran and Johnny Lucas, a couple of my mates in Rockferry High, who I know locally, play every Monday with the Birkenhead Boys Club on their indoor pitch, so I start going down to train with them. It is far removed from Shaftesbury Boys Club, SBC. It's a tough area and you have to be tough to survive, but they can play a bit as well.

The club has a reputation for winning the national five-a-side competitions. The year ahead of us has Ian Woan on their team along with a lad called Paul Nelson and the Reeves brothers, David and Alan. They won the national five-a-side last year and we're going to defend it.

It's a bit rough and tumble, but I love it in Birkenhead. They make me really welcome, and I need that after all the kickings I've got from football. We get to the national finals in Bradford again and retain the trophy, beating a team from Northern Ireland in the final. To win a medal that's all about the team and not just about me, like the athletics and the cross country, is a brilliant feeling. But, more importantly, my time with the Boys Club rekindles my love for the game.

I've got a new job as well to keep me in money for college. Ann Green and her husband Derek, friends of my nan, have a pub called The Sportsmans Arms in Tranmere, a stone's throw from the ground. They need a glass collector and they know I have previous in that department, so Auntie Ann, as she will be forever known, hires me.

She all but mothers me in the job, but she teaches me a few life lessons. Ann takes no prisoners. If you cross the line, you are out – staff or customer. As a result, her pub has been winning awards for years, it's as clean as a whistle and her staff are loyal to her, which is not that common in the industry.

I've seen her take a pool cue to two blokes when a fight broke out. She whacked one of them with it, stopped the fight and then barred them both. I was frightened just looking at her. It's like a cross between *Prisoner: Cell Block H* and the *Road House* movie at times.

Another day she barred my dad for arguing when I was working there – and she knew exactly who he was!

It's also time for me to find a new football team to play with at the weekends, and the Poulton Vics are my next port of call. Their pitch is not far from The Sportsmans Arms in Wallasey, and I get a few bob for expenses, even though I'm starting off in the reserve team.

I'm sixteen and things are looking up at last. I'm getting about seven quid a week in travelling expenses from the Poulton Vics for playing on a Saturday morning, a regular income off me Auntie Ann in The Sportsmans, where I'm surrounded by good-looking young barmaids, my nan has given me a load of cash to get me started at art school and my mum is still spoiling me rotten at home. What's not to like?

Even the forty-five-minute bus journey to college in Wallasey at eight every weekday morning is a pleasure, simply because the bus is packed with good-looking young girls on their way to work or school.

I'm starting to see that there is a life for me beyond football, even though I'm still convinced that the only life I want is football. I just can't have it at the minute.

Working with those pretty barmaids in The Sportsmans does help make up for any footballing disappointment. One of them – slightly older than me, closer to forty than thirty if truth be told – fancies me as much as I fancy her. She makes that clear the night she has a party back at her house and invites all the staff. She kisses me full on the lips when I'm leaving, and it's a proper kiss, my first proper kiss. I shit myself and run straight home. I don't know what to do about the kiss but I know I like it. I'll try that again, thank you!

Life is starting to make sense now, with girls offering a bit of a distraction and cash in my pocket. I work hard enough to pass my exams at the end of the foundation year and the college offer me a place on their three-year graphic design course. I'm made up and my mum is dead proud of me for finally knuckling down and achieving something that doesn't involve kicking a ball around a field.

That's still important though, so I sign for a Sunday league team called Parkside, run by Chrissie and Paul Traynor, who drink in The Black Horse, the big rival pub in Tranmere to The Sportsmans Arms.

Parkside is a proper football team, built around Steve Craven, who used to play for Tranmere, and it's a tough, tough environment. They play to a decent standard and I feel I'm in with the big boys now. I thrive on it.

We start playing in college as well, during the dinner break, out on a big field at the side of the main building. Alan, the caretaker, joins in with us and he can see that I am miles ahead of the rest of them as a footballer. He starts to take an interest in my football and I start to look on him as a father figure, as someone who can give me the advice that I'm not getting at home. He's a gentle soul and the next best thing to my dad. I really look up to him and admire him, the whole college does.

We've a disabled group studying in the college and Alan looks out for them too, he makes sure they are okay in the canteen or out around the yards.

There's one autistic kid there, and he's like Dustin Hoffman in *Rain Man*. He'll ask you your name and, as soon as you tell him, he gives you your date of birth: 'Jason McAteer, eighteenth of the sixth nineteen seventy-one, eighteenth of the sixth nineteen seventy-one.' He reads the register and he has everyone's date of birth right off. He's amazing.

This is what I love about college. The environment they've created at Withens Lane is great, and I love the mix of students that art school attracts. We have everything from the Goths to the grungy types studying art, to the luvvies doing drama and all the trendy kids in graphic design.

But even here I'm still happiest when I'm out kicking football at lunchtime, and happy that I have Alan and his wife to talk to when I need it. That's quite often, as it happens.

As I grow up, emotionally as well as physically, I can see the increasing strain on the relationship between my mum and dad.

He grew up as one of the fighting McAteers and had a privileged life as part of a respected family in Birkenhead. Then the boxing stopped and it all stopped, for him quicker than for Les or Pat.

Nobody cares anymore that he was once the younger brother of a British champion. He has to stand on his own two feet and take his own count every time life sends him crashing to the canvas. He was once a fighting McAteer, now he is just a McAteer, and it is hitting him hard.

I'm trying to get through college, trying to play football, trying to cope with my own issues, all against the backdrop of my parents' failing marriage.

My dad will get a contract down one of the shipyards and we'll be fine for a while, all happy families and lovey-dovey. Then the work dries up, and he's back on the dole.

Every time he loses his job, we know what's coming next, and I'll be there trying to protect everyone else from the inevitable hassle that follows.

Their marriage is never going to survive this strain. They can't go on as they are.

Chapter Five

My cousin John is going to the FA Cup semi-final at Hillsborough tomorrow. So are our mates, Chrissie and Kevin Traynor. They've tickets for the Leppings Lane end for the match between Liverpool and Nottingham Forest. I'd love to go, but I've got to work in the pub. It's going to be chocker all day.

Saturdays are the busiest day of the week in The Sportsmans Arms but today promises to be busier than ever because Liverpool are playing Nottingham Forest in the FA Cup semi-final at Hillsborough, Sheffield Wednesday's ground.

Ann has us in at the crack of dawn, and the place is jammers from early on, with lads getting ready for a full afternoon's worth of racing on the telly and footie on the radio with bets going down on everything that moves.

Merseyside is buzzing with talk of this game. My cousin John is going down for it. The Traynor brothers Chrissie and Kevin – Chris and his other brother Paul run my Sunday team Parkside and young Kevin plays with me – are going down with a car full of mates.

All day, as quick as the lads behind the bar can pull the pints, we're collecting empty glasses for the next round. Everyone's in good humour. It's one of those Saturdays full of expectation, with summer around the corner and Liverpool on the verge of winning something again. As the match kicks off, the pub quietens down to listen to the radio commentary.

Then someone says the commentator is talking about a crush at the Liverpool end of the ground.

The mood changes in an instant.

We've only just got over Heysel when all those Juventus fans got crushed to death in the European Cup final against Liverpool. It can't be happening again.

The pub goes eerily silent. Everyone is hanging on every word. The commentator is getting more sombre with every passing second. It's clear something isn't right in Hillsborough. And it's the Liverpool fans he's talking about.

The minute he starts to talk about fans dying, about dead bodies crushed at the Leppings Lane end, the pub clears. They can't get out the door fast enough.

The few who are left behind are queuing for the payphone to ring home, to ring for news of their loved ones, any news. My dad's in the bar. He's not sure if my cousin John went in the end. He's good mates with the Traynors and he knows for certain they were travelling with a big contingent of Liverpool fans, all with tickets for Leppings Lane, the very end they were talking about on the radio.

The television news programme is on now and it's all about Hillsborough. There's live pictures coming in from the ground. The teams have been taken off the pitch and into the dressing room. We can see Liverpool fans behind the wire screaming for help. Others are being carried across the field on advertising hoardings.

None of us left in the pub can believe what we're seeing on the screen in front of us. Each and every one of us standing there is in shock, we all know someone at the game. Each and every one of us is praying that they are okay, that they escaped the madness we're watching.

But in our heart and souls we all know the likelihood is that they are in the middle of that carnage. Terror fills the air. Shock turns to worry, and then to anger and rage.

There's no end to the nightmare on the screen. People start to make plans to get to Sheffield, some to try and find their loved ones, others just to try to help. My dad's mate Steve Hughes is best friends with Chrissie Traynor, so Steve and my dad leave for Sheffield.

The *Liverpool Echo*'s 'Pink' football paper comes into the pub, as it does every Saturday of the season, but this time the darkest of stories fills the front page. We know there are dead Liverpool fans lying on that pitch but no one knows how many. We won't know for hours.

My dad and Steve arrive back from Sheffield in the early hours of the morning. The news is mixed. My cousin John had a ticket for the Leppings Lane end but we know he's safe.

Steve and my dad scoured the ground and then the hospitals in Sheffield looking for Chrissie Traynor but they couldn't find him. Kevin Traynor is missing as well. Nobody's heard from either of them. We all fear the worst.

We're back in the pub on the Sunday morning when the call comes through that the Traynor brothers are dead.

It's horrible. Their story and our reaction is just typical of what so many families on Merseyside are going through. An entire community goes into mourning.

The lads go down to Sheffield to collect Chrissie's car, a red Ford Escort. They put the keys in the ignition and the stereo jumps into life. Deacon Blue's 'Dignity' is playing, the last song he heard as he parked his car in Sheffield.

It's the first time I've really been touched by death since my granddad died from throat cancer. I went to see him every day I could in hospital and it was terrible, looking at his life slip away.

This feels the same and I don't know how to cope with it, even though I'm not alone. We all know someone who died at Hillsborough. I go to the Traynors' funeral to pay my respects and there are hundreds there, including John Aldridge and some other Liverpool players. Paul Traynor hadn't gone to the match and he is in bits as he buries his two brothers. The whole church is in tears. I look at Paul and I realise just how lucky my cousin John is. He was in the Lepping's Lane end. He could be dead now.

Of course, life will carry on. Liverpool Football Club will continue to play football. But it will never be the same again for the families of the ninety-six fans who lost their lives that FA Cup Saturday in Sheffield.

Chapter Six

The manager at Marine is a well-known character on Merseyside. Roly Howard is a window cleaner who counts Kenny Dalglish amongst his clients. He fancies himself as a boss, but he doesn't fancy me as a footballer. He makes that perfectly clear when he picks me for the first-team squad and gives me nothing to do other than pick up the jerseys in the dressing room after the match.

My mate Alan Molden has friends in high places – big friends, important friends. Literally. He's running a team called The Oak in the Wallasey League, a pub team, as you might have guessed by now. He wants me to leave Parkside and the Birkenhead League behind and play with him every Sunday morning. The bonus is that the Liverpool midfielder Jan Molby knows the lads from the pub and is their biggest fan. He runs another pub team in the league and is regularly at games.

Alan tells me I'll get to play in front of the Danish legend most Sunday mornings if I sign. He even promises to pick me up from home and get me back in time for my Sunday afternoon shift in The Sportsmans, the job that is still funding my college life.

It's an easy call to make. I value everything Alan says to me, and he's right when he says it's a decent team and a decent level of football. I sign the transfer form and it pays off – we win the double in my first season and Jan Molby makes it along to the party that night for a beer.

Alan's pushing me to step up my football alongside my studies. He says I can play at a higher level if I really want to without it interfering with my graphic design course.

There's a bloke who comes into The Sportsmans Arms regularly called Paul Mechan who plays with the well-known, non-league side Marine, a semi-professional team in the HFS Loans League. He's good mates with Chrissy Holmes and he gets chatting to me about football one afternoon in the bar. Paul says he's heard only good things about me from the lads at Poulton Vics and The Oak, and adds that Marine are interested in having a look at me for their reserve team, who play in the Lancashire League against the A teams from the likes of Liverpool, Manchester City, Manchester United and Bolton.

It's an easy sell for Paul. He says there'll be money for travelling expenses every week, even though he is offering to drive me to training every Tuesday and Thursday. He'll be with the first team on one half of the pitch and I'll be training with the ressies on the other half, so it's a perfect opportunity for me to take that next step up in the football world and edge closer to that dream breakthrough.

My first game for Marine reserves is against Morecambe. I'm up against a guy called Gary Williams. His main claim to fame is that he scored the goal that kept Tranmere in the

Football League a couple of seasons ago. He doesn't score this time, but he does stand on my hand and break my finger. Welcome to the real world.

Dave Ramsden is the reserve-team manager with Marine and he's a hard man to please. I quickly refer to him as Angry Dave because even though he's a really nice bloke off the pitch, around the game he is always shouting, always animated. He's very aggressive, more aggressive than any coach I've worked with previously, and very, very strict. But that's exactly what I need in my life as I get serious about my football again. Dave is soon a big, big influence on my career and a big help with my ambition to make something of myself in the game.

Marine have me down as a right-side midfield player, and that suits me fine as I get stuck in against the likes of Blackburn, Everton and Man City's A teams. I'm in with a load of other kids looking for a second chance in football and I'm loving it. We're a decent side. Many of those playing beside me have got further up the ladder, but never quite made it at league clubs. A good few of them have been YTS players with the likes of Liverpool and Everton but never got beyond that stage. Others, like me, are still trying to convince the scouts that we're young enough and good enough to take a chance on.

There's a good standard in this league and I'm made up when we play Liverpool and their team sheet includes the great John Barnes, on his way back from an Achilles injury. I don't get to mark John directly, but I do get to play on the same pitch as him and that is quite the honour for this Liverpool-mad football fan.

If that's a highlight, the prospect of telling my dad that I've crashed his Rover on the way to training fills me with dread. He'd got the money together to buy the car not long before I got driving lessons for my eighteenth birthday and passed my test at the first time of asking. Being the cheeky sort, I ask him if I can borrow it to go training and he agrees, but only on condition that I don't crash it.

So what's the first thing I do? Crash the car, the first time I drive through the Mersey Tunnel on the way to Marine. A guy comes across me on the roundabout at the end of the tunnel and I go straight into the back of him. He's caught Scouser whiplash and everything. He's out of the car, screaming at me and threatening me with all sorts. If anything, I'm more scared of telling my dad. I ring my mum from a phone box on the side of the road. She says she'll pray for me but to go on to training and we'll sort it out with my dad when I get home.

There's a bit of damage to the car all right, but less than I thought and my dad is okay about it. All he does is tell me to forget about borrowing his car again and 'get back to that Paul Mechan fella' about lifts to training!

Even when Paul can't carry me, I never miss a training session. It's a walk down to Birkenhead Central, a train into Liverpool and then another train out to Cosby and a walk to training from there. But this is my chance, and I'm not going to waste it.

There's other lads here in the same boat. Joey Murray played for the England youths but got released by Liverpool. He eventually gets a second chance with Wrexham. Vinny Maskell played with Steve McManaman at all the underage levels but also got released by Liverpool. Dave Walley was on the books at Everton before Marine. These kids can all play, but the big thing for me is that none of them are any better than I am. They don't look any different to me when we play Liverpool at Melwood or Everton at Belfield.

I'm comfortable enough now with who I am as a footballer and my physical stature as well – so comfortable that I am ready for the Roly Howard treatment. Like Dave Ramsden, Roly is a hard taskmaster. He finds it hard to praise me, even when I lob the keeper in front of 250 fans against Witton Albion, the highlight of my time at Marine so far.

Roly has a decent first team at his disposal, so he can afford to be choosy. John Roche is the mainstay of the team and he has a good centre-half called Keith Johnson, a keeper called Kevin O'Brien, who goes on to work with the Everton academy, and a good lad called John Gourtry. My favourite player is the Marine winger Eddie Murray who used to play for Tranmere and is known as Fast Eddie by the fans.

I know Roly's seen a good bit of the reserve team in action, but he doesn't seem to be that interested in me as a player. By the time I'm twenty I do get into the first-team squad, but my only role is to pick up the kit and clean the dressing room after his players. Maybe he's trying to teach me a lesson about working for my chance, but it seems clear to me that Roly Howard doesn't rate me.

It's the same story when I finally get four or five first-team games. His verdict is a familiar one. I've shot up in height now but he still reckons I'm too light and not up to the physical demands of first-team football. I'm growing up but I'm not filling out. I'm still a light-skinnyweight in boxing terms!

He does admit that I'm quick and agile and can throw crosses into the box from the right wing all day long, but Roly says that's not enough for the modern game. I'm just too small to impose myself on matches and too small to make it.

His timing couldn't be any worse. My three-year graphic design course is coming to an end. I really don't know what's next. I've passed my final exams at art college, but I've failed the Roly Howard test at Marine.

I'm back to the drawing board, literally most days, and it is time to make some life decisions. Again.

Chapter Seven

I'm signing autographs every second week now, down the dole office in Birkenhead. It's humiliating and I hate it, but I've no choice. I hate this shit life. My mum knows this and she decides it's time to ring Uncle Pat in America, see if there's anything he can do for me out there.

Decisions, decisions, decisions. I graduate from Withens Lane Art School in the summer of 1991 with a B Tech Higher National Diploma in Graphic Design to my name. It's something I should be proud of, having shunned my studies in favour of football for so long, but I'm a twenty-year-old at his wits' end.

I've finished up playing with The Oak on Sundays and the season is over with the Marine reserves. Football's gone back on the long finger.

There are other things to do. I'm seeing a girl called Maria – there's a song in there somewhere – and I've applied for a few jobs and a few more courses. Maria wants to continue studying art and she's applied for an art course at Wrexham University.

That sounds good to me, so I throw in an application too. I apply to Chester Teaching College as well. Wrexham say no thanks without even seeing me, but Chester are good enough to invite me down for an interview, which I think goes well until the rejection letter arrives at the house.

I'm going nowhere fast and I'm really struggling, so it's back to the option my mum told me never to even consider when I first left school – the dole. I'm down at the social in Birkenhead signing on every fortnight. It's humiliating. They give me buttons every second week. I can't carry on doing this. Something has to give.

I tell Marine I'm taking the summer off to get a job when I can find one. The son of my mum's best mate is the manager of the Foot Locker outlet in the Grosvenor Precinct in Chester and he gives me a start. He even brings me to work when we're on the same shift.

I'm grateful for the chance and delighted to be off the dole, but it's not what I want from life. I hate it – there has to be something better out there for me than selling trainers.

My mum knows how unhappy I am. She makes a call to my uncle Pat out in America and has a long chat with my dad about my future. Uncle Pat has been out there for years. He has his Green Card now and he's doing well for himself in the construction industry and he's making a fortune.

My uncle Gordon has been over with him for about ten years now as well, and Pat and himself offer to get me started on the American dream. Gordon's daughter is coming over to England for a holiday and everyone agrees I should go back over with her and have a look around and see if it's for me.

I don't need much persuading to get the three-month holiday visa that will get me into the States. There's nothing happening for me at home – America can't be any worse.

Pat and Gordon live close to the US Navy Academy at Annapolis, which is near Washington, D.C. They welcome me with open arms and look after me. Irish Pat says he can introduce me to a few people who are big into soccer, as they call it, and who will see if they can get me a trial for a scholarship with some of the local colleges.

What starts out as an extended summer holiday becomes a test to see if I can settle in Washington and transfer my football dream – sorry, soccer – to the USA. So I start to play with a local side called the Washington Stars and I do well. I score in a couple of games and the word starts to get out amongst the college scouts. Irish Pat gets a couple of calls, and the coach with the Stars says the universities are talking about me.

Tiffin University in Ohio are the first ones to step up to the plate with real interest. A guy called John rings and offers me a scholarship, studying sports science and playing for the college team. They want me to start when the new academic year kicks off in March, and everything will be paid for. They'll even sort my visa when I go back to England before my current holiday visa expires.

The only thing I have to do is pass their SATs, the assessment tests used for entry to American colleges, and I can even do them back in England before I return next year.

It's all too good to be true and I can't turn it down, even if I am desperately homesick. My uncle Billy, the one who invested in Tranmere, has me working with his company knocking up these wooden houses. A real Bob the Builder I am, and the craic with his lads is great, but I do miss home something rotten.

Our family dog, an Alsatian called Tina, dies while I'm Stateside and I'm heartbroken. I bawl my eyes out down the phone when my mum rings to tell me.

It's only when I get back to England in December that I really understand how much I've missed the family, my mum and my brother and sister – even my dad. It's going to be a wrench to leave them all again and emigrate to Ohio in March, but it is something I have just got to do. I cannot carry on as I am, and much as I want to make it as a footballer in England, no club in England seems to want me to make it.

Tiffin John rings just before Christmas and says he has me booked to do the SAT exams in Manchester in January. He says he'll book my flight to Ohio for March and, knowing how homesick I was in Washington, the college have agreed to get my mum a house so she can move the family over with me and give me a real family life in America as well. That's how good the college is to me! I'm made up when he tells me.

John asks me to play some football while I'm back home, to work on my fitness and keep my eye in. I tell him the logical thing would be to go back to Marine reserves for the winter and see if they'll take me. He agrees it's a good idea, and I promise to ring Dave Ramsden and set it up. And Dave is as good as gold when I call him. Even though I'm only going to be around for a few months, he's happy to have me back and says he'll definitely play me before I get that flight to America. That's all the encouragement I need and, before I know it, I'm pulling on the Marine jersey again.

One of my first games back with the ressies is against the Bolton Wanderers A team. It's an away game and it's being played at some shithole ground on the edge of the town that they use for such matches. As far as I'm concerned, though, I'm back playing in England so I don't care what the ground is like. It's all about me repaying Dave Ramsden and Marine today for giving me another chance.

I end up having the game of my life – the absolute game of my life. Getting the offer from America has, it seems, lifted a weight from my shoulders and I can do no wrong. Everything I try comes off. Every pass finds it target and every cross makes the box. I'm on fire, and Dave is dead chuffed with me.

He's not the only one. On the way home he tells me that the Bolton first-team boss Phil Neal and his chief scout Mick Brown had a chat with him after the game. They were there to keep an eye on their own players, but it seems they were really taken with me.

He says they wanted to know everything about me, so he explained that I'm from Birkenhead but I'm just back from America and that I'm only playing a few games with Marine to stay fit before I go back out there in March to take up a soccer scholarship in Ohio.

Spotting the need to act quickly, Dave says Phil Neal wants to know if anything could be done to stop me going back to America.

Wow. This has come right out of the blue.

Dave says he told them he'd see what he could do and gives them our home phone number. He also says he told Phil that he'd want to speak to my mum and soon if he is serious about keeping me from that scholarship and a new life in the States. He also tells me to keep his conversation with Phil Neal and Mick Brown quiet. I'm not to breathe a word of it to anyone other than my mum and dad because I've no contract with Marine.

A few days later Dave rings and says we're to expect a call from Phil Neal. The only time my mum had spoken to him was to ask him for his autograph for her football-mad kid, when she was out enjoying his testimonial dinner. Now it seems he has plans for me. He might even ask her for my autograph – on a contract!

Dave tells my mum to listen to everything Phil has to say, but not to commit to anything. That will do for me. Straight away I start thinking that I have a chance, but my mum is level-headed enough to remind me about all the false dawns we've had over the past few years.

But before Phil Neal rings, Marine have another reserve game, and it turns out that Phil has asked Bolton's reserve-team manager Steve Carroll to have a look at me. He assures Dave afterwards that he likes what he sees as well, and when Phil does get on to my mum he tells her Bolton want to invite me to Burnden Park to train for a week with their reserve team, to see how I get on.

There's no talk of a trial or a contract or anything of the sort yet, but this really is too good to be true, though a part of me is still thinking, *Here we go again, I'll slug my guts out for a week and then they'll say I'm too small and won't make it*. But another part of me recognises the trouble they are going to when I already have an offer from America in the bag. I have nothing to lose and everything to gain with Bolton – Ohio will still be there for me if I need it.

I go training with Marine the following night, which is

a Tuesday, and it's clear straight away that someone has let the cat out of the bag and told Roly Howard a thing or two about Bolton's interest.

Dave pulls me aside before training and says that Roly is planning his own move. Just a few months after telling me I was never going to be physically big enough to make it as a professional footballer, the Marine first-team manager is preparing a contract for me. Funny, that.

He's as good as told Dave that he's going to offer me a contract worth a hundred quid a week to become a Marine player. Dave knows exactly what's going on, and tells me not to sign anything that night. He says I've to tell Roly that I have to bring the contract home to my parents before I can even think about accepting it. I have to buy myself some time.

Sure enough, Roly asks me for a word when training is over and brings me into this big boardroom where the guy running the club – I think he's the chief executive or something – is waiting for us. As Dave predicted, Roly puts a contract offer on the table. He says he is offering me a hundred pounds a week straight off and promises to play me in the first team. He then says they'll even look for a part-time job for me and will make sure that I am okay away from football.

How the times have changed. I'm now a player that Kenny Dalglish's window cleaner rates and wants to sign. I'm a bag of nerves standing there in front of him, but I remember what Dave told me, and I tell Roly that I have to bring the contract home with me and go over it with my mum and dad.

He agrees to that but insists that I have to sign it when we train again on Thursday night – and then throws in that I'll be training with the first team that night, by the way!

I've bought myself a couple of days. Dave is waiting outside the office and he says to go home and talk it through with my parents. If we need any advice, he's on the end of the phone.

My head is spinning now. My parents have a look at Roly's contract and tell me not to do anything until we see what Bolton have to offer. I can't just sign the first contract Marine put under my nose. If I do, then Bolton will lose interest very quickly because they'll have to pay a transfer fee for a player they hadn't heard of less than a week earlier. Bolton know I have no ties to Marine as things stand and am also free to go back to America in the morning.

I chat to Dave before training on the Thursday night, and he says that honesty might be the best option. His advice is to come clean with Roly and tell him that I've had a call from Bolton and I'm waiting on them to come back.

We both know in our hearts and souls that Roly knows this already. Sure enough, when we meet that night, the first thing Roly says is that he's aware of the interest from Phil Neal and Bolton. Then he says to forget about their offer to train – because I'll never make it there. He's back on the old Roly charm offensive again.

His bizarre logic is that Marine is where I want to be, not Bolton. It's his contract I should sign instead of taking up the offer to train for a week with the Bolton reserves. A few months earlier he told me that I'd never make it into his team, now he's telling me that his team is better for my football future than an offer from a professional club in the Football League. As he sees it, I've more chance with Marine than I have with Bolton Wanderers.

He's up to something, I know he is. I just don't know what.

I want to buy some more time, so I tell Roly that I'll get the game at the weekend out of the way and then have a proper think about it with my mum and dad. We'll sort the contract at training next Tuesday.

He tells me again that when I sign his contract he will put me into his first team, but I've got to stay with Dave and the reserves for now, and that's fine with me.

I play for the Marine reserves on the Saturday. Steve Carroll is there to have another look for Bolton and again I do well – really, really well.

Phil Neal rings the house on the Sunday. Roly Howard's been on to him and said that Marine want ten grand for me. He's told Phil that I'm under contract to Marine and they're entitled to a fee. Phil knows it's rubbish. My mum has been on the phone with Phil a few times and has made it clear to him that I don't belong to Marine, that I was only playing with them to keep myself fit before I go back to America.

Bolton are skint and can't afford the ten grand, so it is vital for Phil that I not sign any contract with Marine. He still wants me to come down for the week-long training session with their reserves so they can have a proper look at me and he certainly gives my mum the impression that Bolton have done their homework.

Phil doesn't say it out straight, but my mum's of the opinion that he's going to sign me for Bolton as soon as I get through that training week without any problems.

All I have to do is explain to Roly that, as a non-contract player, I am entitled to go and train with Bolton and there's nothing anyone at Marine can do about it. In the end they get a bag of footballs and five hundred pounds which pays for a new roof on the social club – which must be one of the weirdest transfer fees ever.

I ring Roly and say just that to him. I'm not going to sign any contract with Marine until I compare it with what's on offer from Bolton. I'm shaking as I phone him, but I make it clear that I know there is nothing he can do to stop me going to train with Bolton. He's not happy but there's nothing he can say other than to tell me to go ahead and to wish me good luck with it. At least he did that much.

The week at Bolton can't come quick enough. On the Monday I get a lift up to meet Steve Carroll at Burnden Park and I go off training with the reserves. I'm nervous but it goes okay and Steve tells me to relax, I'm doing fine. There's seasoned pros out here, but there's young kids as well and I don't feel like I'm out of my depth.

I get the train up to Bolton on Tuesday and all goes well with Steve and the reserves. The third day, we train together at the stadium, first team and reserves, and they keep me back for shooting practice with the strikers and midfield players from the senior squad. I'm in with the big boys now and I do okay, even managing to chip the keeper. Everything I try is coming off for me and I can't believe it. A trial – and this is a trial in everything but name – is finally working out for me.

I get called in to see Phil Neal in his office after the training session on the Thursday. He tells me that everyone on the coaching staff has been impressed with me, with my ability and my attitude, and they want to offer me a contract until the end of the season. He asks if I'd be happy with that, and I have to stop myself shouting 'yessssss' at the top of my voice.

I'm only going to be earning a hundred quid a week, the same as Roly offered me at Marine, but Phil promises me that if I do well, then he will reward me with a proper contract at the end of the season in May.

He lets me ring my mum on his office phone – she's chuffed for me.

The next thing Phil does is call Sammy Lee and tell him he's going to be my chauffeur for the rest of the season; he's the man charged with getting me from Liverpool to Bolton for training every day. This is the same Sammy Lee I used to watch in a red jersey. He is now going to be meeting me every morning at Lime Street Station and driving me to Burnden Park. Wow.

When I get home that evening we have a big family party. I've a few people to call and thank as well. Dave Ramsden is first on the list. He was good enough to let me play with the Marine reserves when I got back from Washington and he was quick to point me in the right direction when Bolton first showed an interest.

The Marine situation isn't quite over. In the middle of all this I suddenly get an offer – via Marine – from Howard Kendall to go on trial with Everton. Someone says he is mates with Roly, but nobody at Marine can really tell what the deal is with Everton. Is it a trial match or a week's training with their reserves? What is it? If I go to Bolton will Everton withdraw their offer? If I go with Everton will

Bolton forget about me? Will Everton make me sign the contract with Marine then buy me for ten grand?

I don't know enough about Everton but, after four days with Steve Carroll and Phil Neal, I know Bolton is the right choice for me. I've finally got the chance I've waited my whole life for. I'm not going to blow it now.

There's one other thing I need to do before I sign for Bolton, and there's one man who will know better than anyone how to do it. I have to call Tiffin John in Ohio and explain to him that I won't be coming out in March to take up the scholarship offer. The irony of course is that it was John who suggested I go back to play with Marine to keep my fitness levels up – look where that got him!

The best man for this job is Alan Molden. He'll know how to handle it. I've already been to have a chat with him about the scholarship and he urged me to go to America in the first place when my mum spoke to my uncle Pat last summer.

He fully supported my return to the States to take up that scholarship, but he also understands what I've been going through with Bolton and Everton and Roly Howard. Even as an Everton fan he urged me to take a chance with Bolton as I am more likely to get a break there, with a Third Division team, than I am with a First Division club like the Toffees.

Alan tells me that the only way to do this right is to ring John in the States and tell him straight what's happened over the past fortnight and explain that I just have to put a professional contract in the English game ahead of a scholarship with an American college. So that's exactly what I do, and John takes it like a man. I thank him for everything he's done for me and my family and he is magnanimous about it all. It's one of the easiest conversations I've ever had.

He can't promise they'll keep my scholarship offer open for me if it doesn't work out at Bolton, but he will do his best – and he hopes he never sees me in Ohio. Ever. Fair play.

Phil Neal is true to his word and gets the contract to my mum on the Friday so everything is ready for my first day at work as a professional footballer, on Monday. I place the contract on my bedside table – where else? – and my shiny new Adidas boots down by the bed. I set two alarms and I've memorised the train timetable to make sure I'm waiting for Sammy Lee at Lime Street.

I can't sleep. I'm as nervous as can be again. I've got here at last but I'm too tense to enjoy it yet. I can still feel the pain of rejection after all those trials. I can see the face of every coach who stood in front of me and told me I was too small, too weak or too skinny to make it as a professional footballer. Maybe they were right. Maybe when I was sixteen I wouldn't have coped with the mental and physical demands of an apprenticeship if it had come my way. Or maybe that McAteer determination, the desire that turned my uncles into champion boxers, would have got me through as my dad had insisted all along. Maybe that drive to succeed that he'd tried to instil in me for judo and athletics would have stood to me as an apprentice footballer.

I don't know. I'll never know. But I want to drag them all onto the train tomorrow morning, all the doubters and the 'no' men, and let them watch when Sammy Lee collects me in his big car, make them see me sail off into the sunset with a Liverpool legend on my first day at work as a professional footballer.

The envy I felt when John Norman and all those other lads got YTS contracts has been replaced by a sense of achievement. John's been let go at Tranmere but I'm about to start a new life with Bolton Wanderers.

Things could have been so different.

I could have been the one signing for Chester or Tranmere or even Manchester United at sixteen and could be the one coming to terms now with rejection after my YTS contract expired. I could be counting down to America and a sports science course wrapped around a soccer scholarship, whatever that entails.

It's all ifs, buts and maybes as I try to get to sleep with all these thoughts going through my head and keeping me awake. Who knows what might have happened in any other set of circumstances? Who cares? It hasn't been easy getting here. I've worked bloody hard for four years to get to this point and I'm not going to throw it away now.

Tomorrow is the first day of the rest of my life. The first day of my new life as a professional footballer. God help anyone who gets in my way. The fighting McAteers are back.

Chapter Eight

I'm finally earning some decent money at Bolton, so I treat myself to some trendy gear. Nothing too mad, mind, just some Ralph Lauren polo shirts and jeans. We've not seen much of Ralph Lauren round our house. My mum is a bit puzzled when she washes them and the backs of the shirts come out longer than the front. She reckons she's shrunk them so she cuts the back to match the front and stitches them up on her world-famous sewing machine.

It's like there's a light bulb goes on the day you sign as a professional footballer. Maybe it goes off the day you leave – I don't know – but I'm shaking with the excitement. I'm about to meet Sammy Lee outside Lime Street Station to cadge a lift up to Burnden Park in Bolton and start my new life, the life I have dreamed about for the past ten years.

The bulb is as bright as a floodlight as I wait in front of the station with my kitbag over my shoulder. It's taken me a long time to find the light switch and my meter runs out at the end of the season unless I prove myself.

Sammy's all chat as we drive, but I can barely take it in. There's too much to think about, too much to get excited about, too much to fret about. This is it. This is the chance. It might be the only one I get.

As I look around the reserve-team changing room when we get stripped ahead of the minibus drive to the training ground, I realise I'm not the only one relishing their chance. There are a few faces I know from knocking around the various Merseyside leagues and schools games. Most of them are just like me, young and hungry to prove themselves, desperate for the contract that can lead to a better life away from the mundane and the misery of not knowing what the future holds.

Andy Roscoe was once on the books at Liverpool. So was Stuey Whittaker. Sat in the corner is Alan Stubbs who played for Everton youths. So did Darren Oliver and Neil Fisher. Nicky Spooner is a local lad from Bolton, but I'm sure I've seen his face at the various trials up and down the northwest over the years. Looking at their faces is like looking in a mirror.

This isn't football's version of *The Young Ones* by the way. It's not all whippersnappers calling the shots as the banter flies around the dressing room, all jockstraps and testosterone, the smell of Old Spice and Brut, and the whiff of brute force and ignorance. There's a few old fellas here as well, guys who've been around the block long enough to be cynical about any new kid in town. There's the usual few first-team players looking for the form that got them into that team, a few recovering from long-term injuries, a few who know their careers are coming to the end of the line, even if they won't admit it.

We're all in this together, the last-chance saloon. Technically we're all playing for the same club, for the same badge. In reality we're alone. We all have that most personal and greedy of ambitions driving us on. And there's a bit of desperation added to that hunger. We need to have that. *I* need to have that – if I don't, the guy sat next to me will eat me for breakfast.

Young and old, we have to be better than the lad sat next to us. I want his jersey. I want his future. I want to be on Phil Neal's team sheet every Saturday. I want a contract. I want to stay. Greed has to be the nature of the game now.

Steve Carroll is the reserve-team boss. I know him from talking after games when he came to see me with Marine. He was relaxed then, a man on a mission. In here, he's his real self, a man in charge in his natural domain. He's tough as nails, that much is clear from the off as he leads me around the dressing room and introduces me to the lads.

We're up against the first team in a training game. I'm straight in at the deep end. It's a Shankly thing that Phil Neal has brought up the road with him from Anfield, first team against reserves, men against the boys (and the men).

Sammy Lee is still the big name. He's getting on a bit now but he's still a great player. The goalkeeper is called Dave Felgate. There's Dave Reeves from Birkenhead Boys Club up front with Tony Philliskirk. The main man in the middle of the field, despite what Sammy thinks, is Mark Seagraves. Mark Kane and the skipper Phil Brown are the men at the back. The lads tell me Brownie is the karaoke king and he has the most amazing tan, which I can tell you now is not from Bolton!

We pile into the minibus for the short drive to the training ground, which is in the grounds of the factory that produces all those Halls throat lozenges. Ah the glamour of it all, the lure of professional football.

I'd thought I was ready for this at sixteen but the chance never came. Now I'm twenty and I'm not going to let it slip. You can see from some of those who've come up through the ranks as apprentices that they can take football for granted. It's all too easy for them because the system has groomed them for this moment. Not me. I know there's a privileged lifestyle ahead of me if I can make this work.

I could be clocking on at Foot Locker in Chester today. I could be packing my bags for Ohio. But I'm not. I'm in a minibus on the way out of Burnden Park to a sweet factory. I've won the golden ticket. It's not Wembley, and it's certainly not Anfield, but I don't care. This is where I belong.

They make lozenges to clear your throat and nose at the Halls factory, but I could do with a blocked nose when we arrive. The factory stinks. The good news, the lads tell me, is that I'll be getting a big bag of lozenges to bring home to my mum. Happy days.

And there's more. There's free bread and free hot-cross buns from the club sponsor Warburtons as well. Privileged or what?

But first there's training and then that match against the first team. Steve Carroll is shouting at us. He's battering us – but he's a great coach. The best I've worked with. Ever. He's running us to death but he tells me it's for my own good. He's hard but fair. I'm one of his boys now and he makes it clear that he's the gaffer. He's proud of his boys but he demands respect and loyalty in return. That's the rule. I promise him I'll do whatever he tells me, no questions asked.

The session ends with the practice game. I doubt anyone is going to kick me on my first day in the office. They won't risk injury in a training routine. Wrong.

Two minutes into the game and Ziggy Seagraves goes through me for a shortcut when I get on the ball and go to turn in the middle of the field. As soon as I twist, he whacks me. 'Welcome to Bolton Wanderers, son. And don't think you're here for an easy ride.'

I'm not. Steve keeps me back at the end of that first session for some extra work to bring me up to speed with the rest of the lads. They're over halfway through their season and way ahead of me. It's not a problem. I want to learn. I want to train. I want to be coached. There's energy in my legs that's been stored up for years, waiting for the chance to get out.

I love everything about Bolton Wanderers from the minute I step into the dressing room. It's a real football club, a real community, a club that belongs to the people and the town who support it. BWFC is about morals and passion and character – real morals, real passion and real character. This is Lancashire and these are northern football folk with a proper club to call their own. I'm one of their own and I want to stay that way. I know the life that exists outside this world and I'm not going back to it.

To play for Bolton, though, I need to get to Bolton for training and matches. Pretty quick into my new life I realise I'm going to need a car of my own. Sammy Lee is under instructions to drive me to training, but he's with the first team and I'm with the reserves, and our schedules don't always match. He's a great guy, is Sammy, but he's not going to give up his day off just to drive me to training!

For some strange reason, my dad's not keen to give me the Rover again after the Scouser whiplash incident. And my hundred quid a week isn't going to buy me a car, not even in the weeks I get the fifty quid reserve team appearance bonus. So I pick up the courage to go and ask the bank for a loan.

One of the lads I'm playing with is called Mike Jeffries, he's a striker. His dad has one of those small local garages selling second-hand motors, so I tell him I need a car. Mike reckons his dad can get me a little Mini Metro for about three grand including the insurance – so long as I don't tell the insurance company what I do for a living. They don't like footballers apparently, they think we're all speed merchants and crap drivers.

The bank manager is a nice enough bloke who asks the obvious question. What do I want the money for? Bold as brass, I tell him I'm a professional footballer who needs to get from Liverpool to Bolton every day to get to work. I name drop Sammy Lee and Phil Neal, and he's impressed enough to give me the loan, but only if my nan will stand as guarantor. She does.

The word soon spreads that I have four wheels under my arse and it doesn't take long before I'm appointed the designated driver by the other wannabes in the reserve-team squad. As a result, the drive up the East Lancs Road from Liverpool to Bolton becomes a real chore. It takes hours every day to pick up Darren Oliver from Halewood then Andy Roscoe in Speke and, now and again, Neil Fisher in Warrington as well.

Even Alan Stubbs comes with us when he's not living the high life and hanging out with Phil Brown and my old chauffeur Sammy Lee in the first team.

The car's a little banger, not helped by the fact that I don't look after it properly as I drive the arse out of it up and down the motorway. Things come to a head the night we're off to a reserve-team game at Burnden Park. I warn Neil when I pick him up near Warrington that we might not even make the East Lancs Road, there's so much noise and smoke coming out of the engine.

That prospect is not even worth thinking about. Steve Carroll is a stickler for time-keeping. We can't be late and we can't even think about not making it to the match. Steve will go through us if we're even five minutes late. There'll be fines and we might even get suspended. There's only one thing for it as the car limps towards the ground. We're going to have to abandon ship, hail a taxi and sort the car out after the match, or I can come back for it with my dad in the morning.

One of the lads spots a big car park. It looks perfect. That'll do. We drive in, park up, grab our bags and make a run for the main road and the first taxi we can find. There's a cab there within seconds and we're on our way. We make the game and win it, but there's a surprise after the match when there's a copper waiting for me outside the dressing room.

He wants to know if I'm Jason McAteer and the owner of car registration number such and such. I tell him I am. 'Has it been robbed? Burned out? Crashed? What's happened to my little Mini Metro?'

He's not offering me any info. Instead he wants to know if I understand the seriousness of what I've done. I tell him I don't know what he's talking about.

'Tell me your movements tonight please, sir.'

I explain how the car was close to collapsing in a heap on the main road and how we had to get to Burnden Park in time for the game. I'd no choice but to abandon it in the car park and get a taxi.

He shakes his head as he gets the four of us together and asks one of the club officials if we have a room with a video recorder. The copper says we have to understand how serious this all is. We soon realise what he is talking about as he shows us CCTV footage of a car speeding into the car park and four guys jumping out and legging it out to the road and into a taxi – from the car park of a British Nuclear Fuels facility!

The security men come running out, sure they are about to become the victims of a terrorist car bomb as we speed away to Bolton.

They ring the cops and while we're playing the reserve game, the bomb squad are examining my clapped-out Mini Metro and deciding whether or not they want to blow it up.

We'd no idea. We hadn't even looked at the sign on the car park when we dumped the car. We were just scared shitless of being late for the match and scared shitless of Steve Carroll.

The police lighten up a bit when they hear what really happened. They're good enough to drop Neil home, then they drive me to the compound where they've impounded the car. Unfortunately, they give it back to me. They might have done me a favour and blown it up!

Abandoned cars aside, I'm loving it at Bolton. The reserve-team games draw decent crowds to Burnden Park and some big names to boot. We play Manchester United and Alex Ferguson is along to have a look. He comes back a few times, when they're not playing here as well.

Liverpool reserves arrive with my old mates Molby and Barnes in tow, and then we get to play them at Anfield. Now I know I've made it. Sitting in the away dressing room, running out the door and touching the 'This is Anfield' sign at the top of the stairs, getting out onto that pitch and playing against Stevie Mac and Robbie Fowler with my mum and dad sitting in the stands, almost in the very spot where I sat with my uncle Mack and cousin John and first saw Kenny Dalglish play in the flesh.

I've arrived and, as far as I am concerned, I'm here to stay. I can get a sniff of the first team. They're struggling a bit after the near highs of the 1990–91 season, when they reached the play-off final after missing out on automatic promotion to Grimsby on goal difference. They then lost that play-off to Tranmere of all people, and the expectation this season is that they have to get promoted. The fact they're mid-table and running out of games isn't sitting well with the locals. Phil is keeping a close eye on the reserves and says he'll give a few of us a run in the team at Easter, given that promotion is now all but beyond us.

He also says he's keen to extend my contract, but fate takes a hand and a hamstring injury means I don't get that first-team debut. But my troubles are nothing compared to Phil's, who gets the sack on 8 May.

Some of the older guys in the first-team dressing room take his dismissal on the chin. It's part and parcel of football.

They tell us to get used to it, but we're shitting it in the reserve squad. None of us have long-term contracts and who knows what the next manager will want to do with us. He won't know me like Phil Neal knows me. He might not keep Steve Carroll. The board don't help much when they tell us that no contracts will be awarded or extended until they appoint a new manager. We're in limbo.

At least we're not there for long. Bruce Rioch is quickly named as Phil's successor with the great Colin Todd as his number two. There are thirty pros now waiting to find out what the future holds, and the first thing Bruce does is tell everyone that we are all on a level footing. There is no first-team squad anymore as far as he is concerned. He says he'll meet us all individually with Colin, have a chat, look at us in pre-season training and the friendlies and then decide what he is going to do.

We'll get through the summer and pre-season and we won't know who is in the first team and who isn't until he names his squad for the opening game of the season in the newly named Second Division – the Premier League is the new name for the First Division, so we've been promoted, but in name only.

Bruce is prepared to give us all a chance and that's all I can ask for. At least I can start to relax. Alan Stubbs got one of the last contracts offered by Phil, and Stubbsy tells me not to worry. Steve Carroll, who's staying on and has to have some clout because he knows the players better than Bruce or Colin, is of the same mind.

The new management team make their minds up in July when a gang of us get one-year contracts, me and Darren Oliver, Andy Roscoe, Neil Fisher, Stuey Whittaker and

Nicky Spooner. I even get a pay rise, up to a hundred and fifty quid a week.

The one thing Bruce makes perfectly clear to me as we discuss the deal is that he is basing everything on my potential. He's liked what he has seen of me so far and while he's starting me in this new reserve-team squad, he wants me to push towards the first team and force him to pick me.

It's not all good news for the reserve-team dressing room, and I soon see the cruel side of football as Philliskirk, Kane and Felgate all leave. Reevesy hangs in there and Bruce brings in Keith Branagan as his goalkeeper and signs Andy Walker, John McGinlay and David Lee to strengthen his options up front.

Nothing else will change for those of us on the periphery of the first team. Steve Carroll remains in charge of the ressies but Bruce and Toddy are around us all the time. They're at all the games.

Toddy takes Alan Stubbs under his wing and seems to regard him as his pet project, maybe because he was such a good player in the same centre-back role for Derby and England.

Bruce sees me as a centre-midfield player, a position he filled so well for club and country for so many years, and he spends a lot of time with me working on my game and on my positional sense, making me a more complete footballer.

The hard work pays off in November. A year after I came home from America, I'm named on the bench for a first-team game at Chester. There's only a few minutes left when Bruce tells me to warm up and get ready to go on. I'm shitting it, but time runs out and the game is over before Bruce can get me into the action.

I'm almost relieved it doesn't happen for me, but I don't have long to think about it. We play Burnley in one of the local derbies the following Saturday and I get on for the last ten minutes. It's not long on the pitch, but it settles my nerves greatly.

Tony Kelly, one of the great characters of the game and a guy who should have been a superstar, is carrying a bit of a knock and there's a rumour flying around the training ground that I'll replace him in the team for the FA Cup second-round tie against Rochdale the following Sunday. Bruce takes me aside after training on the Friday. It's more than a rumour. I'll be starting in the centre of the park alongside Mark Patterson. He tells me to make sure I get tickets for my mum and dad and the rest of the family because I'll only ever make my full debut once.

They're sitting in the crowd when we run out to a fairly full Burnden Park. It seems like there's millions in the ground when I pop my head out of that tunnel. They go mad when I score. I'd go mad only I'm in shock. I've just scored in the FA Cup. I can't believe it. We win 4–1 and Bruce is happy with me – that's what he says in the dressing room straight after the game.

Then he drops me.

He leaves me out for a couple of games. I'm still in the first-team squad on match day, but I'm warming the bench for Bruce and playing most of my football for Steve in the ressies.

There's a great buzz ahead of the FA Cup third-round draw. Marine and their window-cleaner manager are still in there, but there's only one Merseyside club I want us to get.

My dream comes true when we land the champions Liverpool at Burnden Park in front of the television cameras on the first Sunday in January. It's bloody freezing and somebody at the club conveniently forgets to turn the undersoil heating on the night before the game. The referee comes and inspects the pitch early doors and passes it, but only just.

Bruce wants every advantage he can get, and a rock-hard pitch won't suit Liverpool's slick passing game. It's a day for cloggers and Brut, not fancy Dans and Hugo Boss. I make the squad but not the team. I'm happy just to see my name in the programme for a match against Liverpool. If I get on out there, great, but if I don't, I'll be rooting for the lads and ready for the call.

We lead Liverpool for a lot of the game. David Lee crosses for John McGinley to score the second goal and we're 2–1 up until late on when Ian Rush equalises. Graeme Souness is the Reds' boss and he's not happy. That much is obvious when I go into their dressing room after the game. Our young apprentices are trying to clean it up and someone's thrown cups of tea all around the place. It's in a right state. There's stuff all over the shop.

It doesn't get much better for Souey when we go to Anfield for the replay and John McGinlay and Andy Walker score. I don't get on from the bench but, again, I don't care. We've just dumped the mighty Liverpool, my boyhood idols, out of the greatest cup competition in the world.

It can't get much better than this and it doesn't. We beat Wolves 2–0 away in the fourth round but go out 3–1 to Derby in the fifth.

The bonus for me is that by the time the cup run comes to an end, I'm a regular in the team. It's like I'm Bruce's favourite child at this stage. He spends hours with me on the training ground, working my right foot, then my left, sharpening my passing and my awareness. He's got a real bugbear with the fact that I shake my head too much on the pitch, and orders me to stop it. He says it displays an attitude problem. And he's big on attitude. He makes that clear when there's an away fan giving me grief outside the dressing room after a game and I tell him out straight to fuck off. Bruce is livid.

The fan's been giving me dog's abuse and I'm not having it. I give him as good as I get before I escape into the changing room but Bruce is mad angry. As soon as I'm out of public view he pins me up against the dressing-room door. He grabs me by the throat and says if he ever hears me talking like that again to a fan – any fan of any team – he'll batter me. And he will. He is deadly serious.

I've also started to get a taste for the nightlife out in Bolton. After a few nights out word gets back to Bruce. He drags me into his office and tells me to cop on. He reminds me that I've waited too long and worked too hard to get where I am now to throw it all away on some night out in a dingy Lancashire nightclub.

He's right, of course.

I have to listen to him and I have to act on what he is telling me. He's becoming a father figure to me – another one – and if he says jump, all I can do is ask, 'How high?'

The gaffer is also happy to put his money where his mouth is with new contract offers. First I go from one hundred and fifty quid a week to five hundred. Then he promises to make it a grand a week in the summer, and two grand a week after that if I keep progressing. The chief executive Des McBain can't believe how many new contracts I'm getting. He's almost afraid to see me come near his office in case it's going to cost him more money.

Des and Bruce know what I am worth to the club, though. I'm showing a good return for their investment as my value goes up. Not bad for the bag of balls and five hundred quid for a new roof they gave to Marine.

It's still less than a year since I left Marine. Incredibly, I've graduated from the Bolton reserves to the first team. I've also learned that football is a greedy business and that you have to be selfish to succeed. The only number that matters, more so even than the one on your back, is number one.

It's not something that sits comfortably with me. I wasn't happy that I left my mates behind in the Marine reserves when I signed for Bolton. I miss them. It's the same with the lads in the Bolton reserves. It's not in me to forget about them and look after number one. That's not the way I was brought up.

I want Darren, Andy and Neil to succeed just as much as I want to make it in the first team myself. But it's not happening for them, and I struggle to cope with it, with the fact that not everyone's career is making as many big leaps as mine. It's breaking my heart to leave them behind.

Alan Stubbs and I are in the first-team squad now and those guys are waiting for a big break that might never come. That's football, as Bruce reminds me on a daily basis in an effort to keep me focused, but it doesn't mean it's fair.

The team is flying under Bruce and he's still in his first season with the club. After the injection of confidence fuelled by that cup run, we can smell promotion. A win in the derby fixture at Preston in the final game of the season will send us up.

We know what this means for the town, for the team, for us as players. It's the biggest game I've ever been involved in and I'm starting. He wants me running off the Preston midfield and taking advantage of the space and the passes that Andy Walker and John McGinlay can make for me with their first touch.

It's worked well for us of late but this game is hundred-mile-an-hour stuff from the start. The last team Preston want to help get promoted is Bolton, and that's made very apparent. Eventually we get a penalty in the second half. John McGinlay scores the penalty that sends us up. Pandemonium breaks out.

The fans are screaming for Bruce, screaming for the players. Not only has he beaten Preston, and that's a big one for them, he's got their team into the First Division as well – and all in a season that saw us dethrone the FA Cup champions Liverpool to boot.

We get a medal for going up. This is massive for me. It's going to sit on my bedside locker for months. That's how special a Second Division medal is.

Chapter Nine

Bolton are away at Palace tomorrow. We're in a hotel in London on the Friday night, having our dinner and wasting the time before bed. 'Pass the ketchup,' says Keith Branagan.
'Red or brown?' says I.

For professional footballers, the new season is like a new term at school. We report back for pre-season training full of giddiness. The sun's been on our backs for the summer, there's new faces to meet, new contracts to negotiate, new optimism to enjoy.

That's the first day.

As soon as the hard yards take their toll on the calf muscles, reality sets in. Pre-season is a pain in the hole. It's demanding, it's exhausting and it's endless hours spent, most days, with the smell of the Halls factory filling your nostrils. Glamour my arse.

The good news is that Bruce has another new contract for me, as promised. I'm twenty-two years old and, in the past year alone, it seems like I've signed ten contracts, each of them better than the previous one.

This one is for a thousand quid a week, basic. That's ten times more than the first contract I willingly signed for Phil Neal less than eighteen months ago. There's win bonuses, goal bonuses, appearance bonuses. There could even be a bonus for tying your laces. It seems that good.

Bruce says he wants to reward me for this fast-track progress at Bolton Wanderers. Fair dues to him. I want to reward myself as well. And I know exactly how I'm going to do it. I've known it for a month now, since we first reported back for pre-season training. There's a Lotus dealership on the road into Bolton. I drive past it every day. And every day this beautiful little Lotus Elan smiles at me. And it talks to me: 'Buy me, buy me, buy me.'

The Mini Metro is long gone. It barely survived the British Nuclear Fuels car park fiasco. It was ready to die on its feet at any minute. One of us had to go.

I'm in a Ford Fiesta now, the wheels of accountants and housewives everywhere. It's not what you expect to read your football hero is driving when you open *Shoot* magazine. I need a new car. I deserve a new car. I'm a professional footballer at the top of his game about to start a new season with a flash new contract. I need a flash new car to boot.

This Lotus Elan is perfect. It winks at me every morning when I drive past. It's like a woman with the come-on eyes in a nightclub. It just knows I'm going to stop and ask for a dance. Only the timing of the request is up for debate. This car is made for me, a sporty green with a black retractable roof. I want it and I'm going to have it. End of.

All I need is the money and a good excuse to buy it. Unknowingly, Bruce provides me with both when he signs that new grand-a-week contract in his office.

He hands new deals to Stubbsy and myself and he does what he always does – tells us to sign them. Like Alan Molden before him, he's a father figure to me now, and I do what I'm told.

To celebrate our new contracts, Stubbsy and myself hit the road where all the car dealers hang out in Bolton.

Alan is straight into the Vauxhall dealer and buys himself a brand new Astra. A poxy Astra. Comes with sports coat and elbow patches and slippers and a pipe. I swear. It's the car for an old-age pensioner.

I know where I'm going, the twenty-two-year-old professional footballer with the world at his feet. The Lotus dealer has had my car for a month now and I want it. It's the easiest sale the guy has ever made. I give him a big fat cheque and a clapped-out Ford Fiesta as loose change. He gives me the keys to my shiny green Lotus Elan.

We complete the paperwork and I'm out the door with my chest held high and my foot to the floor, down the East Lancs Road as fast as this dream machine can take me.

My mum likes the car but I'm not sure she's too impressed with the idea of paying all that money for a flashy motor, even though I've worked bloody hard to get to this point. She lets me get on with it and tells me to take it easy behind that leather steering wheel, particularly around the Mersey Tunnel.

The next morning I insist on picking Stubbsy up in my new wheels. There's no way I'm going into training in that new Astra of his, nice and all as it is. I'm going to show off now and he's going to have to come along for the ride.

The lads are going to stand back in awe at this marvel of a car when I pull in to the parking spaces in front of the main stand at Burnden Park. They'll treat me with respect when they see where I stand in the world. I'm the dog's bollocks and they will know it when they see this car. They'll just love it. And they do. I knew they would.

Before training all they want to talk about is my car. Where did I get it? How much did it cost? How fast will it go? It's a thoroughbred like its owner, and they know it. Even the gaffer is looking out the window of his office and admiring the car as we head off for the training ground in the minibus. I can tell he's impressed.

Alan Whittle is the old kitman who does everything for us around the club. He's Bolton's tea man and the agony aunt rolled into one, a real Mr Fixer. If your car has a puncture, he'll get it sorted while you train. If you need flowers for your wife or girlfriend – or both – on Valentine's Day, Alan is the go-to man.

There's nothing unusual about it when I see Alan's waiting for me as I get out of the dressing room at the end of the morning session, ready to head back down that East Lancs Road with Stubbsy in my green-and-black dream machine. He has a message. The gaffer wants to see me and he wants to see me now. I strike a bet with Stubbsy that Bruce wants to take my flashy new motor for a spin.

He wants to move it all right. He's sitting behind his desk with that stern face of his on – his father was a sergeant-major in the British army, which explains a lot – when he tells me to close the door and take a seat.

The conversation is short and not so sweet. 'Your car,' he says.

'It's lovely, isn't it?' I reply.

He says, 'Yeah, lovely.' Then he informs me that he has

phoned the bloke from the garage and they will give me all my money back. They'll return the Ford Fiesta I'd used as the trade-in since they haven't moved it on yet, and I might be able to drive it home tonight after they service it.

What?

'He's agreed to give you the full price of the car back and he will treat it like a test drive for the twenty-four hours you've had it,' says Bruce.

This has to be a joke. Someone has a camera on all of this It's going to appear on the latest version of candid camera.

Or is it?

'You can drop it back up to him now.'

What the fuck is he on about? I'm stuck to the seat. He's not laughing. There's not even a hint of a grin on that sergeant-major face. 'Just get into it now, drive it back up there and get all your money back,' orders Bruce. 'You'll get your old car back just as soon as they have it ready.'

This can't be happening.

He's on a roll now and it soon becomes clear what the problem is.

'If I ever see you in that fucking car again or in a car any bit as flash, then I will kick your fucking arse for you,' he adds as he kicks me and my arse out the door.

Where are the cameras? They have to be here somewhere. I'm being stitched up for *Football Focus*. I'm going to get to that garage and the salesman is going to start laughing and tell me it's all a big joke. Isn't he?

Stubbsy is waiting for me in the car park and he's not laughing either. He's doing a great job as the straight man in this set-up. He just tells me I should have bought an Astra.

I get to the dealership and the salesman has my cheque in his hand, ready for me when I go up to his desk. It's all very well-rehearsed. They've worked it well.

'Which camera will I look at?' I ask.

He shrugs his shoulders and shakes his head. 'Your boss didn't want you having that car, did he?' he asks. 'He made that perfectly clear when he rang me.'

'So this isn't a wind-up?'

'No,' he replies as he hands me the cheque and tells me they'll have the Ford Fiesta ready for me tomorrow. They'll throw the service and the valet in for free.

I walk back up to the ground and the gaffer is waiting for me. He tells Alan Whittle to drive Stubbsy and myself back to Liverpool in his car. Before we go, Bruce has one last warning for me.

'Go and buy yourself a proper car, the sort of car the supporters drive. Don't ever let me see you in a car that suggests you're better than our supporters. You think of them when you're looking for a proper car.'

This time I do exactly what I'm told. I buy a Vauxhall Corsa, the sporty one mind, from our local dealer in Birkenhead. Stubbsy is pissing himself laughing at me when I turn up at his house the next day. He offers me his pipe and slippers. But the gaffer is happy when I turn up for training in a souped-up hairdryer, and that's all that matters.

He'd rung my mum the night before and explained exactly where he was coming from. There was no way he was letting me drive a flashy car up and down the M62. He wasn't going to let me kill myself in that car. 'He's not a superstar and you keep telling him that,' he tells my mum. It's music to her ears. 'I'm not going to let him live a superstar life and you shouldn't either.'

She's happy to hear it and happy to see me learn a lesson.

It's not the only harsh lesson I'm learning right now. The relationship between my mum and dad has hit breaking point. His habit on a Saturday night is to hit the social club or The Sportsmans just after tea-time and not come home till closing.

One Saturday night, a gang of my mum's mates comes around. It's not unusual. My mum's not a smoker and she's not really a drinker, so the pub holds no real attraction for her. She's more into having her mates around and having a chat about this and that, as mums do. It's the most natural thing in the world to see all her mates round ours, even if, on this Saturday night, there does seem to be more of them than usual.

The reason soon becomes apparent. I've noticed in recent weeks that crockery and cutlery has been going missing. Maybe Beverly and Sam are more clumsy than usual and are breaking things because we are missing cups and saucers and plates, even knives and forks. There's no logical reason for it until that Saturday night, when my mum announces that her friends are here to help us move house – without my dad.

I don't get it. We don't have a house to move to as far as I know. Then my mum tells me everything. She's found a house beside my nan's, in the cul-de-sac beside the golf course in Bebington. For weeks she's been decorating it, moving little bits and pieces over, getting it ready for us. That's where all the cutlery and the crockery has gone. She's been moving house bit by bit without any of us even noticing.

She's been waiting for the day she has enough courage to walk out on my dad and into that new house. Today's the day.

Her mates are here to finish the move. It's bedlam, like an episode of *Challenge Anneka* on the telly as she tries to move her entire family and nearly all of our belongings out of the house before my dad gets home from his bevvy with the lads.

Everything goes – beds, sofas, chairs and tables. Everything bar the radiators attached to the walls.

We're crying our eyes out at this stage, us three kids. My mum offers me the choice to stay. As the oldest, she'll understand if I want to stand by my dad. She makes the same offer to Beverly and Sam, but we're with her on this one. I can't give up on my mum, I can't stay with my dad.

Beverly is taking it very hard. She thinks she is abandoning her father and it will take her a long time to get over that feeling. The whole move-in-a-night thing is sad but funny in a way – unless you're my dad that is.

I can't imagine how he will react when he climbs up the hill from the pub and turns the key on an empty house. He'll think he's in the wrong house or that we've been robbed by a bunch of scallies who took everything, even his wife and kids.

For weeks afterwards my dad has no idea where we've gone. Mum rings him and tells him what we're at and what's happening in our lives, but she won't tell him where we are living.

I am trying to keep what's happening at home separate from my football life but it's not easy. I can forget about it all on the training ground and on the pitch, but it is on my mind every other hour of the day.

The Anglo-Italian Cup offers some sort of distraction in the new season. The old-timers around the club tell me it originated in the early 1970s as a European outlet of sorts, even though even I can spot that it only involves English and Italian clubs. It makes a brief comeback in the 1993–94 season as a replacement for the Full Members Cup.

Teams from both countries play in a localised qualifying group before advancing to the knockout stages with home and away games in both countries. There's a bit of a buzz about me in Tranmere and Bolton when my hometown club and my current employers are drawn together, along with Sunderland, in Group 1.

There's a bit of history between Wanderers and the Rovers since the 1991 league play-offs when Phil Neal was still Bolton manager and they won promotion at Bolton's expense. The fact there was a bit of crowd trouble around that game just adds some more spice to the mix.

The Tranmere press, all two or three of them, want a piece of me before the game because I'm from Birkenhead, still live there with my family and even had a trial at Prenton Park and worked in the social club at the ground. The Bolton press, a bit bigger it has to be said, are keen to know my thoughts on going back to the club that let me down, none too gently, as a kid.

I've not been a pro for long, but I love talking to the press. There's nothing better than seeing your name on the back page, so this is too good an opportunity to miss. I'll talk to anyone who wants to listen from Bolton or Tranmere and I have a story to tell them as well.

The away game at Tranmere is first up on 7 September 1993 at Prenton Park. We don't play them in the league until October, so I'm getting plenty of stick about the cup match every time I put my head out the door at home. I don't help myself, to be fair. I've always been the type that if you knock me, I will do everything in my power to prove you wrong.

As far as I am concerned, there are plenty of people who have knocked me in Tranmere over the years. When I used to go back to The Sportsmans for a pint after I started doing well with Bolton, some of the locals would give me abuse and tell me to sign for Tranmere. They'd ask me who I thought I was signing for Bolton when there was a league team on my own doorstep. Some of my old customers, some of the lads I served behind the bar and listened to telling me their same old stories, would tell me I'd never make it with Bolton, I'd never be anything. So this is my chance to give a bit of stick back when the microphones, tape recorders and notebooks come out ahead of the Anglo-Italian cup tie.

The journos are happy to write it all down when I tell them I'm really up for this game. Tranmere had their chance to sign me when I was younger and they couldn't be bothered. They hadn't wanted me, so now I'm going to show them what they missed out on. I'm going to go back there with Bolton and I'm going to beat them, on my own if I have to. Revenge is an easy headline and even easier copy for the hacks.

I'm all over the papers in Bolton and Tranmere and I'm in bother. My mum doesn't know what to make of it when it's brought up every time she goes down the shop or sets foot outside her front door.

And Bruce is raging.

He's never afraid to give me a whack across the back of the head when he thinks I deserve it, and this time even I have to admit I deserve it. Those words have stirred up Tranmere and their fans, and I've let Bruce down. I know it, but I really wanted to get all that angst off my chest.

I play for the fans, but I also play for Bruce every time I pull that white Bolton shirt over my head, and this time I've gone too far. My words, out there in black and white, are a red rag to the Tranmere bull and he lets me know it. They'll have them splashed all over their dressing room – and we've got them twice in the league this season as well.

Only 2,786 fans turned up for the game in the end – I checked the attendance in the papers the next day – but most of them seem to be there to give me abuse. I'm public enemy number one, but I have the last laugh. We win 2–1 with goals from John McGinlay and a young striker down from Scotland called Owen Coyle, who's here to replace Andy Walker and who keeps telling me he's Irish. Good luck to him. We beat Sunderland 2–0 with two more goals from Owen, which qualifies us for the group stage against the Italians.

The first match is at home against Ancona and I score in the 5–0 win. The next three matches – at home to Brescia and away to both Pisa and Ascoli – are drawn, which leaves us fifth in the group-stage table and out of contention for the cup. In the end, it's Notts County who represent England against Brescia in the final, with the Italians winning 1–0.

Life in Division One is going well for us. I score my first goal of the season in a 4–0 win over Millwall and score again against West Brom and Watford.

When Gretna concede home advantage and lose 3–2 at Bolton in November in the first round of the FA Cup, we all start thinking about another cup run.

Lincoln City fall by the wayside in round two before the third round sends us back to Merseyside again. A year after dethroning Liverpool, we need a replay to knock Everton out of the cup. Mark Patterson scores in a 1–1 draw at home but lifelong Toffee Alan Stubbs, the red-hot McGinlay and Coyle score in a 3–2 victory at Goodison.

Cup fever grips the town again, and we're buzzing. Bruce is constantly giving it the old 'the league is our priority' in the dressing room and to the press, but he knows well what the cup means for the fans and for us players, even more so when we draw the mighty Arsenal at home in the fourth round at the end of January.

I'm like a kid in a sweet shop again. I've played on teams that have put Liverpool and Everton out of the FA Cup in the past year and now I'm going to be out there on the same pitch as Ian Wright, Tony Adams, Paul Merson and David Seaman. I can barely sleep the night before the game. The cameras are coming and this is another match that's as big as it gets.

Before the game, Stubbsy and I do what we always do – we check the VIP ticket list. We're always at it. We used to do it in the ressies to see who was coming to have a look. One night I discovered Kenny Dalglish was coming to the game, so before kick-off I snuck out of the dressing room in my kit, but without my boots on, and went looking for him in the players' lounge where I knew he'd be having a cup of tea.

Sure enough he was there, so I walked up to him bold as brass and said, 'I'm Jason McAteer, I'm playing tonight. Can I have your autograph, please?'

He looked at me as if I was mad, stood there before him in jersey, shorts and socks ready for action, but he signed it and I went back to the dressing room as happy as Scully, the kid in that TV drama who dreamed of playing for Liverpool.

When Scully eventually gets a trial, his hero King Kenny turns up. So instead of concentrating on playing football at the trial, all his focus is on his idol stood there on the sidelines. His fascination with Kenny Dalglish ruins his trial and his dream, it wrecks his chance of a lifetime.

That's the moral of the Scully story, but I'm not going to let anything ruin my big day against Arsenal – even if Alex Ferguson is down for a ticket with his chief scout Mick Brown, the same Mick Brown who spotted me for Bolton when he went to watch the Marine reserves with Phil Neal.

The skipper Phil Brown has heard a whisper that King Kenny is here again today, and gives my ego a little boost when he says the now-Blackburn manager can only be here to have another look at me – as if I'm not under enough pressure already! I also cop from the VIP list that Jack Charlton, the World Cup winner with England who's now in charge of Ireland, is down for a ticket as well.

Despite the lack of sleep, I'm like the kid who's eaten the full pack of Smarties in the dressing room beforehand. The papers are full of talk that George Graham fancies me as an Arsenal player. Bruce has been telling me I can be anything I want to be as a footballer. He's feeding my confidence and my ego and he's telling me I can do no wrong.

I'm invincible going onto that pitch. I don't care who Arsenal put on me when I play in behind John McGinlay and Owen Coyle. I'm ready for all of them.

I want the ball the minute that whistle sounds and I'm quickly into my stride. Martin Keown is following me around like a rash.

The ball's fed into McGin. I turn but he doesn't give it to me first time. Instead he looks up and plays it through Lee Dixon's legs. I'm in. There's only me and David Seaman left in the play now, so I nutmeg the England goalkeeper and slot the ball home. Burnden Park goes bananas. I go bananas. It's the biggest goal I've ever scored. It could be the biggest goal I ever will score.

The goal aggravates Arsenal. They get right back into it with a perfect response from Ian Wright. Owen Coyle gets us back in front, but Tony Adams nicks an equaliser at the death. We're gutted not to win the match, but they're more relieved to have got us back to their place for a replay. That's what we have to take from this game. Mad as we are for not winning it, we have to realise they are bloody happy they didn't lose it.

Wrighty is standing in front of me as we make our way off the pitch. I love him as a player and he strikes me as a top bloke. This is too good a chance to miss.

'Hey, Wrighty,' I say, as if I've known him all my life, 'if you're ever up in Liverpool for a night out and need somewhere to stay come round ours, you can stay at my mum's you know.' Bold as brass.

He just says, 'Oh thanks, like.'

I'm sure he's asking himself, *Who the fuck is this cocky kid with the big mouth who's just invited me to stay at his mum's house?*

He doesn't return the invite for the replay down in London, but he knows well who I am by the time we leave Highbury. It's my first time there and I love it, that whole sense of history when you walk through those doors and into the marbled hallway.

We've brought more fans than we normally get for a home game and they're buzzing. When we're warming up I can hear Bolton fans from every section of the ground. They want to win this one – they know we should have won on Saturday.

So do Arsenal. They batter us early on and take no prisoners. Alan Smith gives them the lead but somehow McGinlay grabs an equaliser. We hang on for extra-time and we start to grow in confidence and stature as a team.

Personally though I'm having a nightmare and I expect to get the hook any minute. Then Owen Coyle rattles the crossbar with a shot and the rebound lands at my feet. I rifle it through David Seaman and it rockets past Lee Dixon on the line. I've only bloody scored. I've just gone and scored against Arsenal at Highbury in extra-time in the fourth round of the FA Cup. Bloody hell, what have I done?

They're in shock. Andy Walker delivers the killer second late in extra-time, and Arsenal are out of the FA Cup. They can't believe it. Neither can we.

The next morning I'm all over the back pages and I cannot comprehend that it is me staring back at the lads from the papers over breakfast. This is big time. I'm a Bolton hero now. And I like it.

We get Aston Villa, Bruce's old club, in the fifth round. There's thousands of fans queuing for tickets and the gaffer sends Stubbsy and me out to them with big urns of tea. He tells us to have a brew with them, to sign anything they want signed, to make them feel that the cup run is as important to us as it is to them. He wants us to leave there knowing that we play for them, that they are our fans and are going to be just as important against Villa as us players.

This is big with Bruce Rioch and he's the same with all the players, first-team stars or reserve-team kids. When it's your birthday he makes you go across the road to the pie shop and buy pies for everyone working at the club. You buy about thirty and then everyone sits down in the canteen together after training and we all have them for our lunch. And that's everyone, from John McGinlay to the girls in the ticket office. Football is a family business for Bruce, and he's big on making sure we all know it.

The more excited the town gets about the FA Cup run, the more autographs we are signing, but Bruce loves it. I know from my own experience what it means for a player to sign something for a kid. We're lucky to do what we do, lucky to get paid to play football, so signing an autograph book is no hardship as far as I'm concerned.

The connection with the fans, fuelled by this FA Cup dream, is part of what I love about Bolton Wanderers. It's everything I was brought up to be rolled into one and I can't get enough of the place. We're real people, playing for real people with no airs or graces about the place, them or us. As players, we all pile into the minibus to go training at the Halls factory and then we all pile into the canteen at the ground for our lunch when we get back.

We're allowed two pounds and fifty pence worth of food and we have whatever everyone else is having. If the tea ladies are having chips and gravy or a pie, then we're having chips and gravy or a pie. If the mash dinner is good enough for the club secretary, then it's good enough for the rest of us. Some days we all head up to the snooker club for our grub. Phil Brown knows them up there and they look after us. Chicken and chips and a few frames. Bruce is trying to keep me away from Phil as much as he can, but he knows the score.

Phil is just a natural showman. He wants to entertain and he wants to be the centre of attention. He can sing as well, which helps with the karaoke and he's just loving all the attention that we are getting with this cup run. We all do, to be fair.

I've been on more back pages this week than I have time to read. And there's talk of international football for me as well. I knew Jack Charlton was at the Arsenal game but I didn't know he was there to look at me. I just assumed it was Owen Coyle he wanted with his Glasgow-Irish connections.

The papers say Northern Ireland are sniffing around as well. After the win at Highbury someone there got wind that my dad's family are from County Down, so I qualify to play for them, but also for the Republic because of an old passport ruling.

The headlines say the Liverpool boss Roy Evans has been having a look as well. Ron Yeats, his chief scout, is never away from Burnden Park. They fancy Stubbsy too, despite his Everton roots, and he's now taking as big an interest in the complimentary ticket list as I am. The only name he's looking out for though is Howard Kendall, the Everton manager, or Colin Harvey, his top scout. Stubbsy wants to be a Blue. I know he does – but he's not brave enough yet to go into the lounge and ask Howard Kendall for his autograph. He won't even let me do it for him.

I love autographs. George Best and Frank Worthington are in Bolton for a big dinner and some of our first-team squad goes along, Browny sorts it. We get invited for a bevvy and a game of pool afterwards and I end up on the table with the great George Best. I'm in awe of him, and he's dead nice, makes a big fuss of me, wishes me well in the cup and even signs the ticket to add to my bedside-locker collection.

I make sure to tell George I have Northern Ireland blood in me. He laughs when I tell him they've had a sniff and so has Jack Charlton. I tell him I have Welsh blood as well but they don't seem interested at all. George says I should jump at the chance to play international football if it comes along.

Bruce would love me to play for Scotland, but that's never going to happen. They're the only home country I don't qualify for but he is keen for me to listen to what's on offer from the North and the Republic.

Then Jimmy Armfield turns up for one of our league games before the FA Cup clash with Villa. He has his England scouting hat on, but he is well known at the club and a legend as a player and manager. He's been to loads of our games, and Bruce reckons Jimmy has tipped the FA off about myself and Stubbsy. The fact the papers are talking about Northern Ireland and the Republic looking at me is a factor for Jimmy and England to consider as well, according to Bruce.

It's no surprise then when I get back to the ground after training one Friday morning in February 1994 and find Jimmy Armfield looking to talk to me in Bruce's office. He wants me to play for the England B team in a game against Northern Ireland at Hillsborough at the end of the season.

This is mental. I only signed for Bolton two years ago instead of going to America. Now Jimmy Armfield wants me to play for England!

I'm not sure I want to play for England. It's not something I've ever really thought about or wanted, to be fair. I tell him yes straight away but only because he's asked and he's sitting there in front of me. Yeah, yeah, yeah. But at the back of my mind I'm not so sure.

Bruce was in the meeting too and straight away acts as the voice of reason, telling me not to rush into anything, to take my time and consider all my options before making a final decision.

'What's to think about?' I ask.

But Bruce knows what he's talking about, and says the England boss Graham Taylor has a list as long as my arm of players for B internationals, most of whom will never play a senior game for their country. He urges me to wait for any other offer that might come along – and as an English-born player who played for Scotland with pride for many years, Bruce clearly knows what he is on about.

He's talking sense. England want me to play for them, even if it's their B team, but I've never really wanted to play for England. I loved watching Ireland at the 1990 World Cup, like all of Liverpool, and that's the one that really interests me if truth be told, even though I have never got further than about a hundred feet across the Irish Sea.

The next morning I study the ticket list for the cup game against Aston Villa and I cop that Jack Charlton is back again. He has a few players at Villa, Paul McGrath is the best of them, so maybe he is here to keep an eye on them. Or maybe he wants another look at me?

We win 1–0 and this time it's Stubbsy who grabs the goal-scoring honour. I'm delighted for him.

The first person I see in the lounge afterwards is Jack. He's standing by the door with his son John, and John grabs me by the arm as I go by. He introduces me to his dad, but there's no need. Jack is one of those football faces you can never forget. Jack's as blunt as I've been told he is. He's quick and to the point. Ireland have qualified for the World Cup and they know my dad's family is Irish and I can get a passport. He also knows England have offered me a B cap before the season is over.

Jack says he's not interested in B caps, he wants me to declare for the Republic and he wants me to play in a friendly against Russia at Lansdowne Road in March. It's a full international and he will put me straight into the team that night if I will consider playing for Ireland.

I'm stunned.

I've just come to terms with Jimmy Armfield offering me a B cap for England, and now the great Jack Charlton is asking me to play on a team heading to the World Cup finals. He says to discuss it with my family and with Bruce, and get back to him when I am good and ready.

The only thing Jack does ask of me is not to declare for England without talking to him again. It's not much to ask and I agree to get back to him when I know what I am going to do.

My mum is in the lounge and even *she* knows who Jack Charlton is. She wants to know what our little chat was all about, and when I tell her, she says that she's aware my dad's family are Irish but she's not sure what part of Ireland they're from. She thinks they're from the North, as I do, though we're not certain.

This is all happening so fast. What am I going to do? It's an hour after the game but Bruce and Toddy are still in the gaffer's office when I go looking for them. They know Jack was at the match and he's already told them what he was going to say to me. Bruce was also in on the conversation with Jimmy Armfield when he offered the England B cap, so I ask him what to do.

A bit like Dave Ramsden at Marine, he tells me to buy myself some time and think about it for a week. That's what I do.

Liverpool are playing at home on the Wednesday night, and we've no game so I make arrangements to watch my other team in action. I even manage to blag a ticket for the players' lounge.

Ronnie Whelan comes in after the match and says hello to me as he walks by. He even calls me Jason, so he knows exactly who I am. I've played against Ronnie a couple of times but I've never met him before – but when has that ever stopped me talking to someone? I have to take this opportunity to speak to him about Ireland, so I go over and explain that Jack has just offered me the chance to play against Russia. I add that England have also offered me a B cap at the end of the current season.

Ronnie knows about my Irish connections. He says it's been all over the papers in Dublin that I could get a call-up on the back of my FA Cup performances with Bolton. I ask him what it's like to play for Ireland. 'What would it be like for me to play for Ireland the first time I ever set foot in the country? Would the players accept me? Would the fans accept me?'

Without even blinking an eye, Ronnie Whelan tells me that playing for Ireland will be the best thing I will ever do in my life. It will change my life and I will never, ever regret it.

That's it. Ronnie has spoken. There and then, I know I will play my international football with Ireland. I go home and tell my mum. She's made up for me and right behind my decision. I ring my dad and tell him that thanks to his Irish background, I'm going to play for Jack Charlton and Ireland. He's proud as punch.

The next day I go to see Bruce. He knows what I am going through after declaring for Scotland himself as a player, and he says the club will be right behind me. He rings Jimmy Armfield for me and lets him down gently.

I call John Charlton myself that afternoon and give him the good news. He says his dad will be delighted. Someone from the football association in Dublin will be in touch regarding my passport. They'll need to know my granddad's name and where in County Down he was born. They'll sort the passport and all the clearance needed for me to play against the Russians.

Jack comes to the next Bolton game and we have a great chat in the lounge afterwards. He will start me as promised against Russia but the World Cup is entirely down to me. If I do well enough between now and the end of the season with Bolton and with Ireland, then I will be going to USA '94, and group games against Italy, Mexico and Norway.

I can't believe this is happening to me. The last time I was in America it was to try to earn the scholarship that could save my dream of playing professional football. And that was only a little over two years ago.

I only played with Marine reserves that winter to keep fit while I waited for the academic year in Ohio to begin. I only got a move to Bolton because I played for Marine against their second team. I'm only going to play for Ireland because I got a chance with Bolton. And I will only go to the World Cup finals with Jack Charlton and his Republic of Ireland if I prove myself for club and country in the next three months.

It's down to me now – and that's all I have ever asked of football.

Chapter Ten

I'm getting the lads to sign some Ireland shirts for charity. I pass one to Roy Keane. 'What's it for?' he asks.

'Charity,' I reply.

'How do I know?' says Roy.

'Well don't fucking sign it then if you don't believe me,' I snap.

Ireland.

Okay, so let's face facts here – I have never been to Ireland and I have never felt Irish. I did shout for them at the World Cup in Italy four years ago and I really fell in love with Jack Charlton's team that summer. I actually *did* want to be Irish that June, and part of me is, thanks to my granddad from County Down.

That's not unusual round these parts, mind. Everyone in Liverpool has an Irish granny and it's the most natural thing in the world to back them. We all celebrated when David O'Leary's penalty went in against Romania.

My dad reckons half the city here is Irish and the other half wants to be.

Liverpool, my boyhood club, has been well served by Irishmen. Ronnie Whelan's a proud Irishman. John Aldridge and Ray Houghton, and if it's good enough for Aldo, then it's good enough for me. I'm in good company now, Jack's company.

There's something about Jack Charlton that makes me want to play for him. He could be the manager of Swaziland and I'd have jumped at the chance to play for him that night we spoke at Burnden Park. The man is infectious.

He's been on the phone to make sure I know what I am doing. He's about to announce his squad for that Russia game and my name is going to be on the list. He wants me to be aware of the attention that is going to come my way. He knows England will make another attempt to get me, and Northern Ireland might finally move when it's confirmed that my dad's family came over from Down. And, sure enough, England tell Jimmy Armfield to let me know that they will name me in their squad for the B match against Northern Ireland, of all sides, later in the year.

Name away, lads. I'll go along to support Stubbsy who's also going to be in that squad, but I'm not going to play in the game. I've no interest in playing for England. Even when I was at those trials for Lilleshall with them, it was a professional contract I wanted, not an England cap. Playing for Liverpool always meant more to me than playing for England. International football never even entered my head until a few weeks ago. And now I'm going to be Irish. And that's it. Done.

Bruce makes sure that Jimmy Armfield knows exactly where I stand. The England B game isn't until the end of the season. By then I could be on my way to America for the World Cup finals with Ireland.

The Bolton lads start to take the Mick, no pun intended, at training. They're calling me Paddy now and they're loving it. I start wearing the brightest green tracksuits I can find just to wind them up. We've a big FA Cup match at Oldham coming up and the banter is great.

Bruce tries to calm things down, and he goes through Mark Patterson when he cuts me in two in a practice game. Bruce brings himself on as a sub and, within seconds, he's done Mark, six studs into his chest. He's done one of his own players in cold blood for having a go at me. And it works. Mark never comes near me again.

Big Jack rings again and says he'll see me in the car park before the Oldham game on Saturday. His son John is going to drive him to the match and he'll be waiting for me.

Jack's standing at the bottom of the steps when I get off the bus. My Irish passport's in the post and I've to book a flight to Dublin for Sunday afternoon. The game's on the Wednesday, but the lads like to get in on a Sunday and have a night out together. Some place called Gibney's in a village called Malahide, and then they head into a club. John says I'll love the Sunday night out. His dad just shakes his head and smiles.

Jack says to make sure and get my family over for the match. I'll be starting, just as he promised, and I'll want them there. We shake hands on it. The minute I get into the dressing room, the lads start calling me Paddy again. McGin even wants to know if I can get him tickets for the game against Mexico in Orlando if he's out there on holiday with the family.

The conversation with Jack is as good as it gets that day. On the pitch we just never get going. Oldham are struggling in the top flight but a mistake puts us out of the cup. My training-ground mate Mark Patterson hits a poor back pass and Darren Beckford scores. We're out of the FA Cup, just three games away from Wembley. Typical.

The day before I fly to Ireland, we play Nottingham Forest at home in a big league match. The cup is gone and we have to start pushing for promotion. Stan Collymore has it in for me. He must be able to read the papers because he spends the afternoon calling me 'plastic Paddy'. It's priceless coming from a player Jack has been looking at as well.

I start giving him the stick back, so when he scores, he laughs in my face. Phil Brown isn't having it and has a right go at Stan the next time he gets near him. Stan elbows Phil in front of the referee and gets sent off. All for calling me a plastic Paddy. Serves him right.

I'm sitting in the departures lounge at Manchester airport the next day when I clap eyes on Phil Babb for the first time. He's a defender with Coventry City and he's already played for Ireland and for Jack. He was on the bench when they qualified for the World Cup in Belfast last November thanks to a late goal from Alan McLoughlin.

Babb looks like an international footballer. He has that swagger.

I have to talk to him, ask him what it's going to be like. Jack must be brainwashing them because Phil tells me exactly what Ronnie did that night in the players' lounge at Anfield – it is the best decision I will ever make in my life. I know he's right, but I can't stop myself saying, 'I hope so.'

We land in Dublin and there's a bloke from the FAI called Mick Byrne waiting for us. He's the Irish team physio, wearing a green tracksuit with a big smile on his face, standing there with this big shock of grey hair. We've never met before, but he throws his arms around me and greets me like his long-lost son. He gives me the biggest hug ever and says, 'Welcome to Ireland.' I've arrived.

Mick brings us down to the Trust House Forte hotel at the entrance to the airport. Jack is waiting with the royal welcome, made up I'm finally here. There's no going back now.

Jack brings me into the dining room and introduces me to the lads. These are all familiar faces. They're the guys I've seen on *Match of the Day*, the guys I've played against for Bolton, the guys I followed on the telly when they were playing in the World Cup in Italy just four years ago.

They're all well known to me, but I'm petrified. I'm in awe of them. It's the most natural thing in the world for them to be in this situation, but I've a brick in my stomach. I'm so nervous, I'm almost shaking. They make me feel at home and they introduce me to the Irish way of doing things. There's no training on a Sunday, it's against their religion. And Babbsy is under strict instructions to bring me down to Gibney's, the pub John Charlton was talking about, with the security man Tony Hickey.

The lads buy me pints of Guinness, even Ronnie, and settle me in. It's just like Bolton, one big happy family, we're all in this together. I'm barely in the door and they're treating me like I've been here all my life. The fans are the

same. A few come over in Gibney's and welcome me to
their team. They're delighted to see me and wish me well
for the game on Wednesday.

We head in to town to this club called Rumours. It's
owned by a big football fan called Krish Naidoo, a mate
of Chris Hughton's and a Spurs nut. Before we head in,
Babbsy and I have to wait for Gary Kelly. Kells is from
Drogheda and has gone home to see his family. He's in
his early twenties, like me and Babbsy, and we're Jack's
'youth policy'. That's what the old fellas like Kevin Moran
tell me in the pub. I'm pretty sure Kevin's laughing as he
says it.

It's a Sunday night but Rumours is chocker. Tony
Hickey says it's always like this when the boys are back in
town. He seems to know everyone. He's introducing me to
the guy on the door who's about to shake hands with me
when he says, 'Excuse me,' then punches a bloke who's in
the middle of a mêlée. The bouncer adjusts his tie, shakes
my hand and welcomes me to Dublin. He turns out to be
the nicest bloke in the world.

I've not slept a night in the country yet, never mind
kicked a ball for it, and already I feel at home. It's like
everyone here wants me to play for their team. They're all
in this adventure together, the team, the public and Jack. I
can identify with that. It's a family and I'm big on family.

We train the next morning at the AUL complex across
the road from the hotel. It's part training ground, part
flight path for the main runway at Dublin airport. Every
time Jack opens his mouth to tell us something, a big jet
flies overhead. It's like the control tower are in sync with
his voice. He's a big man is Jack but even he has to stop

talking when a plane comes in. Planes or no planes, I could listen to him all day.

People say Jack's ways are simple and his style of football is predictable, but it's also very, very effective. He drums it into me that my job as a midfielder is a basic one – get the ball to the front men as quickly as possible, then follow it up the field as fast as my legs will carry me. It's the same job that the other ten players, even Packie Bonner, has – hit the front man.

Jack makes it clear I'm not here to prance around – 'fanny around' he calls it – or look clever on the ball. That's not what got us to the World Cup and Jack's not going to change his ways just because I've landed in from Bolton with any fancy ideas. He makes it clear that his way of playing the game is why we're going to be playing against Italy, Norway and Mexico in the States and it's his game we'll play over there, nobody else's. I'm already calling us 'we' and I've only been in Dublin a wet Monday!

Jack pulls me after training for a chat and it's as direct as his style of play. He can bring twenty-four players to the World Cup and I have a chance, but only a chance. I've got to show him against Russia that I can play his way. I've got to show him with Bolton that I can play at all. Form and fitness will be everything when he sends those twenty-four names to FIFA. And he'll be watching me for the next two months. Like a hawk.

This is a big carrot to dangle in front of me. If I can get into Jack's head that I can play the game his way, I could have twelve to fifteen years in the Ireland team. There'll be more World Cups and European Championships to look forward to. I can be his man for the future, I can be the cornerstone of his team for years to come. And I want that. I've seen enough of him and of Ireland to want to stick around here for a long time to come.

Monday night is cinema night and everyone has to go along to watch the movie, even Charlie, the kit-man.

We train at Lansdowne Road on the Tuesday morning. It's one of the oldest rugby grounds in the world, and it looks it. There's two little houses in two of the corners. It's like Craven Cottage. There's an old stand like the one at Burnden Park and a big ugly concrete one on the other side of the pitch. There's two terraces and the lads say the atmosphere is something else when there's a big match on. Away teams take one look at the place and hate it, it's not for fancy Dans. That'll do me nicely.

Tuesday afternoon we go into town and go shopping, another ritual. We walk up and down Grafton Street, a big, posh street full of big, posh shops. The lads buy clothes and coffee and say hello to the public. It's all very civilised and it's all very friendly.

I can hardly sleep on Tuesday night. Jack's named the team and I'm in. My mum's on the first flight over in the morning and we agreed she will see me in the lounge after the match.

I'm desperately trying to spot her in the crowd when we line up for the national anthem. It's in Irish and some of the lads know the words. I haven't got a clue. I can't even pretend to hum along. I've been told by Mick Byrne that the old Arsenal and QPR defender Terry Mancini thought it was the other team's anthem when he first heard it and went on about the length of it. I won't be making *that* mistake.

The game kicks off and I settle into an early rhythm. I know what Jack wants and I know to do what I am told. Hit the strikers early and get onto the second ball. It's simple and it works.

Chelsea's keeper Kharine is playing for Russia and I test him early on with a shot from a knockdown. He makes a great save and denies me the fairy-tale debut, but I'm happy with how I play. So is Jack. And the press are raving about the new blood coming through in time for the World Cup as Kells and Babbsy draw praise from all quarters as well.

I get good marks in the papers the next morning, but Jack snatches them out of my hand and tells me there's only one person I need to impress if I want to go to the World Cup – him. Then he smiles at me. Now I really want to go to the World Cup. Before the Russia match I was thinking long-term with Ireland. The World Cup would be a bonus. Now I've had a taste of it, all those other World Cups and European Championships and my fifteen-year Ireland career can wait. I want the World Cup and I want it now.

There are a few more Ireland games lined up before the World Cup but, really, everything depends on what happens with Bolton. The first morning back at training after Dublin, I am clapped on to the pitch by the first-team squad and the coaches. Bruce tells me he is delighted for me; he knows things went well with Jack.

We've still a dozen games left in the First Division, but we are only mid-table. Promotion is a non-runner but we need to push up from our current position before the last game of the season, at Barnsley on 8 May. I owe that much to Bruce. And if I can help improve the Wanderers' lot, then it can't do me any harm with Jack either.

Stubbsy is playing for the England B team towards the end of the season. I go along to support him, but part of me wants to have a look as well, just in case! I take my seat in the stand, pick up the match programme and know within minutes that playing for Ireland is the right thing for me. There's an article in the programme highlighting the players who have played B games for England over the years. There's hundreds of them. And most of them never went on to win a senior cap. Some of them are household names who never got a full England cap. I'm sticking with Jack on this one!

I'm playing well enough as the league season comes to a close, but I just can't score. I'm not the only one. We finish fourteenth in the table with fifty-nine points, just fifteen wins from forty-six games, with fourteen costly draws.

John McGinlay is top scorer for the season with a very creditable thirty-three goals but Owen Coyle is next with seventeen. Alan Thompson has just eight and I'm fourth best with only six goals. Just six goals. It's a poor return from an attacking midfield player on his way to the World Cup – if I get to the World Cup.

Ireland's next game is at the end of April, when we're going to play Holland in Tilburg. Then we've three matches in two weeks. First up is Bolivia in Dublin, and by the time we play Germany in Hanover and the Czech Republic in Dublin at the start of June, Jack will have named his World Cup squad.

I get called up for Tilburg and the game against Holland in April. So does Owen Coyle, whose Glasgow family has a direct line to Donegal. We both get on as second-half substitutes, but I have a feeling Owen has a job on his hands to make America. Jack needs options up front because Niall Quinn is out with a cruciate knee injury but it looks to me like Aldo, Tommy Coyne, David Kelly and Tony Cascarino are ahead of Owen in the pecking order.

The fact that Tommy scores the only goal of the game in Tilburg should be enough to book his ticket. The win against the Netherlands seems to take a lot of people by surprise, particularly the Dutch, but not Jack. He's adamant that his system works and will work in the heat of America and he says this result proves it.

We do get a night out in Tilburg, but it's far from one of the world's great entertainment hotspots. The Bury goalkeeper Gary Kelly is on the trip and, not for the first time, Jack brings him along as cover but never actually plays him.

Tilburg is clearly making an impression on the cigar-smoking Gary, who falls asleep at a bar in the town's main square. It's too good an opportunity to turn down, so we do what all footballers would do and throw his shoes into the street. The look of confusion on his face when he wakes up is priceless.

I really am living in a mad world right now. As the World Cup draws nearer, every day seems like a day out at Alton Towers. I'm on the roller-coaster I always dreamed of, but I have to be careful not to fall off it, intentionally or otherwise. My mates back on the Wirral are out in Liverpool every weekend living the life. I can't do that if I want to live the dream.

Germany are next up in Hanover. The game was arranged before both teams qualified for the World Cup, and Jack is happy to go along with it. It's a final World Cup trial as far as he is concerned and he throws me in at the deep end against one of the favourites for the tournament and in their own back yard.

Three years after playing park football in front of Jan Molby on a Sunday afternoon, here I am playing against Lothar Matthäus in a World Cup trial on a sunny Sunday afternoon in Hanover.

So what can be so different from that game on the Wirral, temperature aside? Part of me wants to be nervous, but another part of me knows I can't afford to be afraid or show any fear if I want to be on that plane to Florida. No fear is the order of the day as I set up a goal for Big Cas. Kells scores as well. We win and the three 'kids' – Messrs Kelly, Babb and McAteer, or more like Messers Kelly, Babb and McAteer – get rave reviews.

Jack admits after the game that he's seen enough in Hanover to give us our boarding cards for the World Cup. It's not public knowledge yet though, and we're to keep our mouths shut. Asking me to keep my mouth shut is like asking the Pope to deny there's a God. I tell my mum and that's it – it's killing me to keep quiet, but I manage it.

Bolton are on an end-of-season jolly in Majorca when the news breaks on Sky Sports. Bruce and the lads throw me a party. He's genuinely delighted for me. I want to cry when he throws his arms around me.

In no time at all I'm on the plane to Dublin and Mick Byrne is hugging me again. The whole country has gone World Cup mad. There's bunting all over the airport and there's hundreds of kids waiting to see us at a training camp at the Nuremore Hotel, in the County Monaghan town of Carrickmacross.

I get there on a Sunday morning. Charlie O'Leary hands me some training kit and, next thing, Mick Byrne has me running up and down the Nuremore's golf course while the other lads have their lunch. Jack knows I've been in Majorca and wants the arse run off me. No better man than Mick, who picks every hill on that golf course. There are guys out for their Sunday morning fourball and they're not amused. They're dodging me and I'm dodging golf balls. I doubt Romario is running around a golf course in Brazil.

We're back in Dublin for the farewell friendly against the Czech Republic and some off-field work that just has to be done. My new mate Louis Copeland has the World Cup suits ready, and a fine job he does. Then we're into Windmill Lane Studios to record our World Cup song with Christy Dignam and the lads from Aslan. The recording is done in the same studios U2 used for much of their work, but the real reason we're using it is because it's next door to the Dockers pub. If only someone had taped *that* night out!

We're invited to see Take That in concert on one of the nights before the game and Jack decides it's a good idea for the whole squad to go. Some don't make it past the VIP lounge – Alan McLoughlin even remarks that it 'sounds like a Take That record' when the band are actually live on stage around the corner. That's like something I'd say.

The Young Guns – Kells, Babbsy and myself – are big into it. We meet the band backstage beforehand and then we're ushered up to the balcony at the Point Depot venue. Take That come on and the crowd go mental. Then some of the young ones – and their mammies – spot us up on the balcony and the whole crowd starts to turn and stare at us.

Next thing they're singing 'Olé Olé, Olé' and pointing up at us. Take That are forgotten about, and they're not happy. All the girls want to see are these young Irish footballers – and Kevin Moran – maybe. The band ain't happy, and their security chief asks Tony Hickey, politely, to get us out of the place. We have to leave, even Kevin, and the show goes on.

That's how mental it is getting around town. The journalists have started to call Kells, Babbsy and me the Three Amigos, and there's a bit of a buzz building around us. We didn't plan it this way. We didn't dream of playing at the World Cup just so we could grab all the attention from Take That. We didn't even imagine that the three of us would become the best of friends that night we first met in Malahide.

It's just happened, partly I suspect because we have halved the average age of the Ireland squad in one fell swoop. All the attention and interest in the build-up to the World Cup has become a story in its own right, and Jack is happy with that. He's quite content for us to take the attention away from him and the rest of the team. So long as it doesn't interfere with our football – that's the secret.

I do wonder what makes it all so special for the three of us. The age thing has to be a part of it. Gary and Phil are roughly the same age as me, and we are the new kids in an ageing Ireland squad. The difference with Gary is that he came through the ranks with Ireland, starting off as a striker, and a bloody good one, with various underage teams before becoming a full-back, first with Leeds and now with Ireland. Phil had a tough upbringing in the London borough of Lambeth and, by his own admission, could be in jail but for football. He'll tell you that himself.

We've a lot in common, and it's like we are filling some sort of a pin-up void in Ireland, if that's the right way to put it. The kids, and the girls especially, are crying out for heroes, and thanks to the World Cup fanfare we fit the bill perfectly, even if it is starting to get out of hand at times.

The traditional Tuesday afternoon stroll down Grafton Street on the day before a game has become almost impossible. We were in the Alias Tom clothes shop and had to leave via the back door because teenage girls were screaming and shouting out the front.

Babbsy and I are signing some World Cup things in the Artane Castle Shopping Centre one day when it all gets completely out of hand. We're sitting at a table with a queue a mile long in front of us and there are young ones coming up with bras and knickers and everything to be signed. I'm even asked to sign a baby's forehead! There are kids fainting and it's getting dangerous.

Next thing, there's a big push and a surge of people coming at us. Tony Hickey decides it's time to go, we've got to get out. He gets us into another shop and asks the girl if we can leave through their back door in two minutes when he pulls the car around. He leaves us with the shop's security man but, by the time we get to the back door, there are dozens of girls running up the lane towards us.

Babbsy and I decide to run the other way and leg it out of the shopping centre. We get as far as this roundabout in the car park, and then bang on this car with a man, his wife and his daughter inside.

He takes a second look and I persuade him to open the window. We beg him to take us down the road to safety, far enough away from the centre that we can draw our breath.

He agrees, we jump in and he speeds away with all these young ones chasing him out of the centre's car park. We're not a hundred yards down the road when he's on his mobile phone to his brother or someone telling him that he's never going to believe who's in his car. He gets us to a garage and we manage to ring Tony Hickey, who comes to rescue us from the madness. It's bedlam and there are times when it is twenty-four-seven bedlam, but I wouldn't swap it for the world. There's even girls turning up at the airport hotel looking for an autograph, a chat and even a kiss.

The only other youngster in the squad is the Manchester United midfielder Roy Keane, but he's not one of us. He made it clear from day one that this isn't his scene. He wouldn't be caught dead near a Take That concert – he likes Neil Diamond apparently – and he has absolutely no interest in becoming the Fourth Amigo. He makes sure we know exactly where we stand with him, and good luck to him. I decide early on that I wouldn't want to cross him.

The other lads on the team seem fine with it. I think they're quite happy to bring us out with them for the night and let us take all the attention while they enjoy their pints. They can have a good laugh about it.

When I get back home to Liverpool I try to tell my mates what it is like in Ireland but they can't comprehend it. The Bolton lads don't even believe me. They think I'm trying to be the Irish Ryan Giggs or something. They don't realise that in Ireland, we've become superstars!

The World Cup is on everyone's agenda now and we're a big part of it. People want a piece of us and that's something to be enjoyed as a twenty-two-year-old footballer. It's as big an adventure for us as it is for the fans.

One day we're out in RTÉ recording with Dustin the Turkey on *The Den* and we bump into Billy Connolly. Another night we're living the high life in Lillie's Bordello with Valerie Roe, who ran the place so well, and the models Vivienne Connolly and Amanda Byram, and we're calling the shots. Tequila shots, if truth be told.

This is now our normality, and there's no edge to it, no big-time Charlie stuff. The minute we lose sight of ourselves we're in trouble. Jack Charlton will slap us down. Andy Townsend and John Aldridge will slap us down. My mum will clip me round the ear and bring me back to earth with a bang.

I'm off to the World Cup and I'm going to make the most of it. Disney World here I come. Literally.

Chapter Eleven

Jack's given us the day off and we're in a diner in Orlando, two weeks out from the start of the World Cup finals. The waitress is a bit of a looker, but she's tetchy with the Three Amigos. Time to calm the waters. 'Where are you from?' I ask.

'Pennsylvania,' she replies.

I stick my teeth out and do my best Dracula impersonation. She's still looking at me, puzzled.

Our kit-man Charlie O'Leary is standing at the Aer Lingus check-in desk at Dublin airport with about a hundred bags and skips and all sorts in front of him. We can barely see him – he's not the tallest – as we saunter by, but I can hear him.

'Can you send that bag to Chicago please, that one to New York and that one to Amsterdam?'

'But you're flying to Orlando via New York,' says the girl in the Aer Lingus uniform.

'I know,' says Charlie. 'But that's where you sent them last time we went to America!'

The banter is up and running.

We're off on a six-week adventure in America, and I'm living the dream. I'm at the airport, checking in for a transatlantic flight with the likes of Ronnie Whelan, Paul McGrath and John Aldridge. I'm with my new heroes in life. It's like I've won the biggest holiday competition in the history of holiday competitions, and I'm off to America to play footie with my mates Babbsy and Kells at the World Cup finals! I can't wait to get up to the lounge, say goodbye to the dignitaries and get on that plane.

This is the adventure of a lifetime, and there's no pressure on me at all. I don't expect to play any games – I want to, but I can't expect it because I didn't get us here. I'm going as a squad player. If I get a chance then great, I will take it and give it the old 110 per cent. But it will be a bonus.

Right now the adrenalin is flowing. They've sent our bags ahead of us with Charlie. The next time we see them will be in an American hotel room. President Mary Robinson came around the hotel last night to wish us well and the cameras are out at the airport. They send us through our own security channel. No queuing for us! We're sitting in this posh Aer Lingus lounge upstairs and we want out.

The Three Amigos want to go down to the shops in the duty free and get some magazines for the plane. Tony Hickey's not keen on the idea, but he has no choice. We breeze through the shops, get what we want and then we're on the plane, down the back like regular punters but feeling like a million dollars. We're Ireland. We don't need business class.

Jack's easy with us on the flight over. We can have a bevvy if we're sensible, so we have a few. And we have a laugh, like we always do. We're all in this together, and that makes us special. This flight typifies that spirit. It's like the Jolly Boys' day out on *Only Fools and Horses*. We're having a laugh and we're having it together. No airs and no graces. No cliques and no egos. Look like you're getting too big for your boots and Andy Townsend will bring you back down to earth before Jack or Mick Byrne get a chance to.

As we get closer to JFK for our connecting flight, one of the air hostesses comes down to Kells and me. The captain wants to know if we'd like to land the plane. The lads are falling around themselves at the idea of me landing a jumbo jet!

I'm not so sure what she means, so I ask her exactly what 'landing' the plane involves. She says we're welcome to go up into the cockpit for the landing, and the captain might let us land the plane. Aldo is cracking up and one or two of the lads are starting to look a little nervous when me and Gary head for the cockpit.

The next thing we are landing the plane! Well, not really. The captain shows us all these buttons and explains how the plane basically lands itself via computer. We just sit there and pretend to be in charge of it all.

'Captain McAteer would like to welcome you to America and thanks you for flying with Aer Lingus today. We look forward to welcoming you onto one of our planes again in the very near future.'

When we get off the plane in Orlando there's an official World Cup bus waiting for us. We're royalty now, whisked through immigration and straight to the hotel. We have our own rooms, a break with the Irish team's tradition of sharing.

Not only am I in a room on my own, but it's bloody huge, one of those big American bedrooms with *two* king-size beds and enough room to play a game of five-a-side. But I don't really like it. I'm bored on my own. Jack's room is close to mine as well, which doesn't help. He'll be able to keep an eye on me, and I don't fancy that.

I last one night in that room before asking Kells if I can move in with him. Like the big brother he's always been to me, he agrees and I get away from Jack's clutches.

Jack seems to be keeping a close eye on us, even the senior players. Aldo and Kevin Moran have been called in to see him most evenings since we got here. I've seen Packie and Ronnie head in there late at night as well. This World Cup is serious business. I think they're having meetings without the 'kids'. Maybe they're only for the players who will be playing.

Then the truth outs. Guinness have installed a keg and a tap for Jack in his room. That's why he has the most popular room in the hotel. The older lads have been sneaking in for a pint with Jack. Every night. The one night I do get in there, Jack has closed the bar. I knew they were strict on the age limit for serving alcohol in the States but it's like you have to be fifty like Kevin Moran to get a pint in there.

The heat is stifling here. Jack's going to have to work us hard to get us acclimatised. He can't understand why they want us to play games in this heat. It's going to be over a hundred degrees Fahrenheit when we play Mexico in the Citrus Bowl. Jack tells the press that FIFA are playing with our lives. He warns that someone could die trying to play a World Cup match in these conditions if they don't let us take water on the pitch.

Our money is on Stan Staunton to collapse first. His skin is so pale in this sunshine he's now known as Casper. He gets sunburned when he goes home to Dundalk, so this is going to kill him. Everywhere he goes, Stan has the baseball cap and the factor fifty on. Even at night!

I don't mind the heat. It does take a lot out of me, but nothing compared to some of the other players. Jack keeps telling us to rehydrate and get fluids into us. That's never been a problem in my short time with the Ireland team!

The training camp at a local college is a hard grind. Boredom sets in easily. Then Jack heads down to Miami for a day with his mate Frank Gillespie to see Mexico in action against Bryan Hamilton's Northern Ireland in a friendly. He leaves his number two Maurice Setters in charge and the power goes straight to Maurice's head.

He runs the bollocks off us for the morning. We're going box to box then across the field in the midday sun and the sweltering heat. It's ridiculous. The lads get pissed off very quickly and let him know about it.

Terry Phelan cracks and gives Maurice an earful. Then Cas has a go at him. Finally, it all comes to a head when Roy Keane tells Maurice that his training stinks. It blows up between them. Roy has a point, but he also has this habit of getting himself into trouble when he tries to get his point across. He's far too aggressive. He's always right and everyone else is wrong. At one point it looks like his row with Maurice is going to come to blows. Maurice is fuming and gives as good as he gets.

Jack's already in a bad mood when he gets back from Miami after his plane was thrown all over the place in a thunderstorm. He explodes when he hears what happened on the training ground and gives Roy a right bollocking.

Somehow the story makes one of the papers back home. It's not the first story to make that particular paper from this trip. They've also claimed that a serial killer was stalking the Irish hotel – a serial killer who had murdered people in a part of Florida about 500 miles from where we're staying. And they blew up a story about a skin infection Andy Townsend had. By the time they were finished with it, he was living through a 'flesh-eating disease nightmare'. We pissed ourselves laughing at that one.

Roy's row with Maurice isn't funny. Jack goes through Roy for a shortcut and threatens to send him home from the World Cup for disrespecting Maurice. The next morning there's the press conference. Roy makes a statement to the media that the row never happened and says that he has no problem with Maurice and no issue with his training methods. The message to the players comes out loud and clear – don't mess with Jack and his staff.

The story is manna from heaven for the media. The regular football press are out from Ireland with us and there's a huge contingent from England as well, mainly because England didn't qualify for this World Cup.

There are daily press conferences and we have a rota system for attending them drawn up by John Givens and Trevor O'Rourke, who are here working for the team sponsors Opel. Even the press are getting bored. It's hard to give them something new every day. 'I saw Paul McGrath going to dinner' doesn't count as a story, apparently.

The attention the Maurice row gets highlights how stuck the press are for a story, and we need something to deflect them from the dirt-digging. John and Trevor think it would be a good idea to hit the press conference tomorrow with something different. They ask Phil, Gary and myself if we'll go in together and give them a bit of colour and a bit of life.

It's time for the Three Amigos to hit the stage. And if truth be told, I need a bit of a lift as well. Football-wise I need a boost. I'm not training well and I know it. I can tell from the work on the pitch that I am well down the pecking order for the opening game against the Italians and definitely won't start.

I came here happy just to be part of the squad, but now we're getting closer to the start of the tournament, my desire to play is growing. But I know it's just not going to happen for me against Italy. Kells is getting the same vibe.

Babbsy has a chance. The beers on the plane over didn't sit well with Alan Kernaghan's diabetes and Jack didn't take kindly to that. Alan's under pressure with Jack, and Babbsy has a real shout for the Italian game. We're made up for Babbsy, but there's a selfish nature to this game and I'd love to be the one in the frame for Giants Stadium.

I am in the frame as chief messer on the trip and I need to be careful with Jack. We all do. One night we sneaked into the swimming pool at the hotel after it had closed and we jumped in. The security guard catches us on the camera and when he comes down to throw us out, Kells throws him into the swimming pool instead. He can't swim. He's there, paddling around doggy-style to stay afloat and trying his best not to drown. We're breaking our arses laughing at him before we realise it isn't funny. The guy seriously can't swim. We drag him out and he loses it with us.

He starts screaming at us and threatens to call the cops. Then he does call the cops. We scarper back to our rooms, shitting ourselves. The cops are going to call Jack and drag us into custody. Jack is going to go mad and send us home, and we'll never play for Ireland again.

There's only one man to sort this out – Mick Byrne, our guardian angel. As usual, Mick makes a mountain out of a molehill and makes it sound ten times worse than it actually is. All he is short of doing is saying a novena before he orders us to stay in our rooms and goes out to find out what's really going on.

We're there for an eternity. Mick calms the guard down, the cops never arrive, we never get arrested and Jack never knows a thing about it.

Do we learn our lesson? Do we hell. We're as hyper as ever. Another night, Des Lynam is in the hotel for the BBC and we grill him at the bar for hours. He sounds awfully British does Des, but he was actually born in County Clare. He's brilliant company. He even laughs when I tell him my nan back in Bebington would love him – and might even fancy him!

The Irish comedian Brendan O'Carroll is also hanging around the place with his business partner Gerry Browne and his young son Danny. Brendan's here for RTÉ and he's a scream a minute. You can't miss him with this big baldy head and a ponytail that runs down the length of his back. His comedy is catching. He has them in stitches at the accreditation centre when he discovers that the guy handling his accreditation is called Roy Rogers. The whole room is eating out of Brendan's hand for the next half hour as he cracks gag after gag about Tonto and Hi Ho Silver and Trigger the horse.

He even tells them that we have our own Trigger with the Irish camp – me! The lads have started calling me that after Trigger from *Only Fools and Horses* and the name is sticking.

Brendan winds us up all the time and a competition soon develops between the Three Amigos and himself to see who can push things the farthest.

He's in the bar at the hotel with some of the Irish journalists, chatting away to us one night when we decide it's time to rid the world – and Brendan – of that ridiculous ponytail that he seems to regard as some sort of trademark. Kells has been saying for days now that he's going to cut that ponytail off before we leave Orlando, and this is the perfect opportunity when Brendan's relaxed in the bar, surrounded by family and friends and with a real feel-good factor about the place.

There's only one small problem with our cunning plan to become hairdressers for the night – we don't have a pair of scissors. But that doesn't stop Kells. When he gets a plan into his head it becomes a military-style operation until he gets it executed. Operation Ponytail is no different.

He's looking everywhere for some scissors. Reception don't have any, or they don't have any they will give him. The barman can't help either but then Kells spots a knife behind the bar for slicing the lemons. This is manna from heaven.

Now he has his plan and his weapon of choice. Babbsy and I are ordered to hold Brendan down and he'll remove the ponytail with the lemon cutter.

It works a treat. Before he knows where he is, Brendan is pinned down on the bar by me and Babbsy. Within seconds Gary has the knife out and the ponytail is cut. We release Brendan and race to the lifts and our escape route. He's spitting blood, though not literally. The bar is in fits of laughter as we leg it. The last thing I hear as the lift door closes is Brendan threatening revenge. I'm still waiting.

Jack smiles when he hears the story, but he's onto us now. He knows we're the troublemakers in the camp and he knows we're bored to death. We've been here an eternity, or so it seems, and the Italian game is still a week away. We need things to keep us occupied, and that's when the problems start.

Tony Hickey is despatched to man-mark us. We can't move without him. We go to a water park and he's like the armbands your mother puts on you when you first start to swim. We go to Disney World and he's in every photo with Mickey Mouse. Every single one of them.

That's why the request from John Givens to do the press conference together is music to our ears. Jack has just given us a licence to have a bit of fun, a chance to break the monotony for all concerned. Media and players alike.

We start to hatch a plan and decide to dress up for the occasion – we'll put on a show and give them all something to talk about. We drag Tony down to the nearest mall at Altamonte Springs to go shopping for props. We get wigs, hats, toy cigarettes, all sorts. We're made for mischief now.

The other players sneak into the back of the conference room to have a look as we take the piss out of each other, out of the squad and out of the World Cup. Babbsy is dressed like a Rasta man. Kells has a hat as big as the smile on his face. I'm not Jason anymore, I'm 100 per cent Trigger. The press guys love it.

The photos hit the front page of every paper in Ireland. It's all over the telly and the radio, in Britain as well. The Three Amigos have arrived. The camp is a laugh a minute again, and Jack approves. We've lightened the mood days out from the Italy game and that's good as far as he is concerned.

Jack's the one man we don't wind up. He has this look, it's a sort of a wink, and that means don't mess with me. There's a few others to stay away from as well, most notably Roy Keane – you just never know how he is going to react.

The rest are open house. We tie Aldo up with socks in his hotel room one night. Another day I buy a load of Immac in the mall and replace all the shampoo in Aldo's room with it in the hope that it will be 'wash and go' but it never works. He keeps coming down to dinner with a head full of hair and we can't figure out why.

We get into Ronnie's room and empty all his drawers. He gives us a bollocking, so next time we move all the furniture around in his room. We hide his boots. We cut the laces out of Aldo's shoes, cut the pockets out of his tracksuit. It's all silly and it's all juvenile but it helps to pass the time.

When you're a messer, though, you have to be alert and on the lookout for revenge. You can't leave the door to your room open for fear of reprisal. And there's not a day goes by that one of us doesn't get dunked in the pool. That's the one area the other players can get at us.

Poor Tony Hickey bears the brunt of the messing. We're the bane of his life at this stage. When we can't find anyone else to annoy, we just annoy Tony even though he's the one looking out for us. We give him a dog's life. We're regularly in his room. We use his toothbrush to wipe a certain part of our anatomy then stick it back where we found it. We've done the same thing with Aldo's toothbrush. And they've never let on that they found out. It all keeps us amused. And that's a good enough reason for now.

Game time is different. Footballers know when it is time to stop the messing and play. We've trained for weeks now in Orlando. We've sweated our bollocks off in the heat. Stan has been burned to a crisp. We've laughed and joked and thrown security guards into the swimming pool. But now it's time to stop. Time to get serious.

It's three days to the Italy game, our opening match of the 1994 World Cup finals. No more messing. We won't turn Paul McGrath's bed upside down because Paul is marking Baggio on Saturday in Giants Stadium. The jokes are out the window, the lemon cutter is put away. Aldo's toothbrush is safe again. It's showtime.

It's time to switch back on. We do everything we are told, as we are told. Jack says to jump and we jump. Jack says to take the ball in here and hit the channel. We hit the channel. No more questions, no more throwing your eyes up to heaven.

The team for the Italy game is picked. I'm only listening for one name. I don't hear it. All I can hear in midfield is Houghton, Keane, Townsend and Staunton. No McAteer. I'm gutted. Ray Houghton is in there ahead of me. He scored against England at Euro '88. He played all the way to the quarter-finals of the 1990 World Cup in Italy. He's a Liverpool hero. There's no shame in finishing second to Ray Houghton in this pecking order.

I have to do what is right for the team now. I have to tell him I'm delighted for him, proud of him. I tell him to have the game of his life. He's playing for me now, playing for Jack, playing for Ireland.

Kells is in the same boat as me, but Babbsy is in the team ahead of Alan Kernaghan. He needs this. He's had some bad news from home. We've been keeping an eye on him and this is just what he needs. He's ready for it, ready to play.

We fly up to New Jersey on the Friday night and get a police escort to the hotel. There's an edge to the atmosphere now. Jack is cold and clinical, and we know not to go near him. Mick Byrne is doing his best to keep the banter going, but nobody wants to know, not even us. Not tonight, Mick, thanks. There's a nervous tension. We all know there is serious business ahead of us tomorrow afternoon, and nobody, not even me, wants to be the one cracking the jokes and leading the laughter.

We're up for breakfast early and out for a walk as normal. The team talk is back in the hotel. Maurice goes through the set pieces and tells us who's to be picked up, what to watch out for on their free kicks and corners. Jack is nodding his head and throwing in his tuppence worth. They make sure everyone knows exactly what is expected of them. That nervousness is still hanging around the room.

The buzz kicks in on the drive to the ground. Mick Byrne sticks on the rebel songs and the bus is singing along. It's always like this on the way to a game. Sean South moves from Garryowen to the Meadowlands of New Jersey.

The crowds are building on the approach to the ground. There's green, white and gold everywhere. The Irish in New York and the Irish from home seem to outnumber the Italians two to one. It's the battle of the immigrants.

There's a swagger about the Italians, even about their fans. We've had Italian football on Channel 4 on a Sunday for years now. We know all about them – Baggio and Maldini, Baresi and Signori. I admire their football. They are aristocrats and they'll regard us as navvies. Let them.

We arrive at the ground two hours before kick-off and the bus drives deep into the bowels of the stadium, right to the door of the dressing room. Jack get us into the air conditioning asap and tells us to stay there as long as we can, away from the heat. Mick Byrne is busy strapping ankles. I'm looking for a match programme. I desperately want to see my name in a World Cup programme.

We go out for the warm-up, and nothing can prepare us for the sight that awaits us. I look up into the stands and all I can see is Irish green. Everywhere. Every seat, every row is jammed with Irish fans. I've never seen anything like it. There are thousands of Irish fans, with little pockets of Italian supporters thrown in here and there. It's like we're playing Italy at Lansdowne Road only with twice as many fans behind us.

I'm still taking it all in when this roar goes up. The Italians are coming out of the tunnel. They look a million dollars and about ten feet tall. They are immaculately groomed and look like they're straight out of the hairdresser. It's sweltering and they have their tracksuit tops on, not a thread out of place.

These are the guys I watch on television every Saturday morning and Sunday afternoon. My jaw is open. If one of them looks at me, they'll think I'm a crazy Irish fan who has jumped the fence and got onto the pitch. I'm in a daze. I can't believe they're on the pitch beside me.

Jack lets out a shout at me and I snap out of it. We finish the warm-up and get back to the refrigerator that is our dressing room. Stan is looking for a baseball cap to protect the back of his neck from the sun when we go back out there. He's red raw again. I'll bet the Italians don't have transparent County Louth skin.

The hooter goes for us to get onto the pitch. Stan stays in the dressing room for as long as he can and misses some of the team photos. The anthems are breathtaking. Theirs takes forever. Ours takes the roof off, there's so many Irish fans singing 'The Soldier's Song'.

The game starts and I'm off the bench, on my feet shouting and cheering and kicking every ball. I'm still a football fan at heart, always will be. I'm hitting every tackle with Babbsy, applauding every ice-cool touch from Big Paul. He's on fire today. I've never seen him this good and that's making it easy for Phil beside him.

Ronnie and I get the nod from Big Jack to go down behind the goal and warm up. We're there, half-doing our stretches and half-watching the game, when Ray Houghton lets one fly from the edge of the box and beats the keeper. The place erupts. I'm jumping up and down behind the goal. I want to jump into that crowd and hug every Irish fan I can find.

We calm down, settle down. Jack has us throwing water and encouragement onto the pitch. Big Paul has Baggio in his back pocket. He's flicking balls away, heading them away, he's even back-heeling them away. The pitch is perfect and the game is living up to the World Cup stage. So is Paul McGrath. And Babbsy can't put a foot wrong beside him.

The first half is over in an instant. We're still a goal to the good. The Italians are trying everything they can, but they just can't get past the colossus that is Paul McGrath. We're back in the fridge and Jack is telling the lads to carry on as they are, frustrate the Italians and hit them on the break. We've got them rattled and the more desperate they become, the more we have to stay calm and collected. He's warning the lads about the heat too, telling them he will have to make changes in the second half for their own sake.

My ears prick up.

Midway through the half I can hear him talking to Maurice and Mo Price, one of the coaches, about 'Jason'. I'm ready for this. Get me on, quick. He sends me to warm up. It's a hundred degrees, I couldn't get any warmer. Then he calls me back to the bench. I'm going in there and goal-scorer Houghton is coming off.

Ray gets hauled ashore and he's fuming. He's so gutted he forgets to shake my hand as I go on. I don't have time to think about it. The first ball I get onto is hit into the corner and I chase it. Maldini comes across and I smash him, hit him as hard as I can. Meet the fighting McAteers, Paolo.

He's one of my heroes but this is war, World Cup war. I don't care that I idolise him. This is my chance and my game now, and he's exactly the same as a full-back from Southport or Scunthorpe. He's there to be hit.

The game is flying by me. Kells gets on and the Three Amigos are on the pitch together. I get on a few balls, put in a few crosses. I even miss a chance to shoot in front of goal. In the final minute, I nutmeg Baggio. It's just me and Roberto Baggio and I put the ball through his legs with Ireland 1–0 up against Italy in the World Cup finals. I've just died and gone to heaven.

The referee blows the final whistle. I look up at the giant scoreboard – Italy 0 Republic of Ireland 1. It is true. We have just beaten the Italians. I try to shake hands with all the Italians and swap shirts with Casiraghi. I wanted Maldini's but one of the other lads has him in a headlock.

My mum's up there somewhere in the crowd, her and Beverly and Sam. The scarves and the flags are raining down on us as I try to find them in that sea of emotion. I want to wave to them. I want to share this moment with them. I want them to be part of this incredible experience. We've just beaten Italy and I got to play.

Back in the dressing room, it's mental. There's beer flying all over the place, the rebel songs are hitting the roof. High fives and Mick Byrne hugs are the norm. We stop in the mixed zone and I talk to any reporter who wants to listen. How good was that? It was so good that Franco Baresi was walking through the Irish players looking to swap shirts with Paul McGrath and only Paul McGrath. That's how good Paul was – so good that the other best defender in the world wants his shirt, my team-mate's shirt.

Paul's the hero. He's my hero. He's Ireland's hero. And how good was Phil Babb? Almost as good as Paul. That's the highest compliment I can pay him.

He was magnificent. The Italians are out of their dressing room and the Adonis look is back as they stride off in their immaculate suits alongside their designer girlfriends. We don't care. They can look as good as they want, we won the match. We're back on the bus and we're screaming, 'Who put the ball in the Italian net? Houghton, Houghton.' I could sing it all night.

Dinner is on the table back in the hotel when one of the lads announces that Jack says we can have the night off. We can go into New York as long as we're back in time for breakfast. We have a game to play after all! Then Mick Byrne has news for us. Larry Mullen, the drummer with U2, wants us to have a pint with him and his dad in his bar in Manhattan. He wants to say thank you for one of the best days of his life and he's going to send some limos to pick us up. Wow.

We're dressed and ready for action by the time two stretch limos arrive at the front door to bring anyone who wants to go to Larry's bar, just off Lexington Avenue. One of the coolest rock stars in the world is buying me a pint in his New York bar and I'm talking through my twenty-six minutes with his dad. They're happy to relive the game all night long. We kick every ball, salute every Paul McGrath tackle, replay that Ray Houghton shot. It's all too good to be true.

Next up on the agenda is a club that's been recommended to us called The Limelight. The Cockney guy who runs it is a big Chelsea fan. When we walk in and see two girls kissing the face off each other in the hallway, and two guys at the bar about to start, we know this isn't the club we want to be in a few hours after beating Italy.

Stringfellows is after that, a New York nightclub with the same name as the London venue but more of a nightclub feel. This is more like it, and the night happily grows old.

By the time we leave, the dawn chorus has clocked in for work and I'm hungry. We're all hungry. We ask the limo driver where we can get food and he drives us to McDonald's in Times Square. It's the perfect end to the perfect day.

The Italians are probably asleep in their five-star luxury right now and here I am, sitting on the bonnet of Larry Mullen's limo and eating chicken nuggets with Kells and Babbsy.

New York is walking by us and nobody cares. We're just three more World Cup tourists, coming to terms with our new reality in the city that never sleeps. Can it get any better than this? Do I want it to get any better than this? I doubt it.

Fighting with my uncle Les' boxing gloves in my Liverpool jersey.

The Liverpool kit my mum made.

My first day at Rock Ferry High School, standing on Town Road outside my house on that hill.

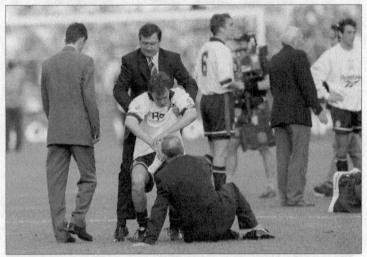

Bolton manager Bruce Rioch helping me up after our defeat in the Coca-Cola Cup final. My first defeat at Wembley.
Coca-Cola Cup final, Bolton Wanderers v Liverpool, 2 April 1995

Signing for Liverpool, a dream come true.
6 September 1995

**The infamous white suits we wore to the 1996 FA Cup final
– we still talk about them today.**
FA Cup final, Liverpool v Manchester United, 11 May 1996

**Roy Evans giving me a hug at the end of the 1996 cup final.
He knew that losing hurt me really badly.**
FA Cup final, Liverpool v Manchester United, 11 May 1996

**Scoring any goal in front of the Kop was amazing,
scoring two in one match was unbelievable.**
Premier League, Liverpool v West Ham, 2 May 1998

With Brian Kidd when I signed for Blackburn.
28 January 1999

Keeping up with Marc Overmars was always a challenge.
Premier League, Blackburn v Arsenal, 6 April 1999

All I did was give as good as I got from Roy.
Premier League, Sunderland v Manchester United, 31 August 2002

Managing Tranmere with John Barnes.
15 June 2009

I love working in the media.
I have made some great friends and met some great people.

My family made me very proud when Lucy and I got married, especially my nan.

My stunning wife, Lucy.

My boys.

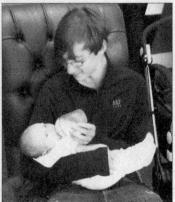

With my mum.

I love where I am in
my life right now.

Chapter Twelve

I'm in RTÉ with Babbsy to go on live television with Zig and Zag. We're in the make-up room when Meatloaf walks in.

'How you doing? I'm Jason,' I say as I offer my hand. 'Do I call you Meat or Mr Loaf?'

'Meat is fine,' he says.

Not everyone will agree!

The nuggets are history now. So is the win over Italy. We're on a plane on the way back to Orlando and Ray Houghton is still spitting blood. He's mad with Jack over being taken off, but I'm not getting involved. I was the winner when that decision was made and I'm probably the last person he wants to talk to, Jack excluded.

Reality has to wait a while to bite when we arrive back at the team hotel to find it's been taken over by a *Star Trek* convention. There's men with funny ears all over the shop. Cas looks right at home.

Jack's not saying much today. I did what I was told against Italy, got in at Maldini, hit that long diagonal ball behind the defenders that Jack is infatuated with. That's what Jack wanted, pressure on Maldini.

He knew the Italian would crack if I could get on top of him in the end third of the pitch, hassle him when he was on the ball, make him turn back to it when we were chasing it. Jack wanted to force Maldini to make decisions closer to his endline than he ever has to make in Italian football. He wanted to make him uncomfortable, and that was my job for the final twenty minutes as we looked to close the game out.

And it worked. After the game, Jack gave me that wink of his and said, 'Well done.' That's as close to a compliment as you are ever going to get from the big man. He will let you know when you're in the bad books but the wink, and only the wink, means you're doing okay.

I feel better than okay as Captain Kirk wishes me a good day. I feel invincible now and the fairy tale shows no sign of ending. After beating Italy, the whole of Ireland seems to think we've become world-beaters. That's the word filtering out to the camp and Jack doesn't like it.

He's worried about the heat. It's going to be over a hundred degrees on the pitch when we kick off against Mexico on Thursday. Some idiot in FIFA has fixed the kick-off time for 12.30 in the afternoon to suit the European television audience. They're going to see an international footballer fried to death live on their screens. Stan's still the favourite to land that part.

I don't care. I'm young enough and fit enough to think the heat won't affect me – and I don't have Dundalk skin. Get me out there and let me do my stuff.

Jack and Ray have mended their relationship and

Ray starts again for this game. It doesn't begin well. The Mexicans think this is a winter's day, and they're quickly into their stride and a two-goal lead. They take their chances and we don't. Simple as that.

They've clearly studied the Italian video and they know how to stifle this new Irish system with just one striker up front. We're all over the shop. There's no cohesion, no fluency, no confidence. Jack tells Aldo and myself to warm up, quite a command considering it is now 110 degrees Fahrenheit on the pitch, according to the sideline thermometer.

After a few stretches, we're on. At least I am. I'm bursting to get out there, ready to bust a gut. So as soon as the linesman gives me the okay, I'm across that line. What I don't know is that Aldo has been told by the fourth official to wait, it's one sub at a time and he's to 'stay there till we tell you that you can go on'.

Aldo's livid. The lads shout to Jack to get him on. It's the first time I realise he's not out here. I look to the sideline and Aldo's giving the FIFA official a right bollocking. Jack and Maurice are out of the dugout. All hell is breaking loose.

We're running out of time. The official seems to think that you have to have two minutes between substitutions. Nobody told Jack. Nobody can hear anything other than Aldo telling the fourth official to feck off. He has a point. Even when he finally gets onto the pitch, Aldo turns around and has another go at the official, then sprints up the pitch screaming and shouting.

Just a few minutes later, John Sheridan hits a perfect pass in behind the full-back. I work my nuts off to get to the ball. The left-back has been on from the start and must be knackered at this stage. I get there ahead of him and dink the ball in. It's a great cross, I know that the minute it leaves my boot. Aldo rises majestically and directs the ball straight into the net with that beautiful head of his. It's 2–1 and we're back in the game – just.

There's no time for celebrations. Time is running out. Stan is on his arse. The lads are knackered. The heat has killed them. We just can't get at them to get that second goal. The ref blows the final whistle and we're beaten. The euphoria of Italy is gone in an instant. The only feeling is one of emptiness, a vast emptiness.

The doc can't do anything about the result but he has a lot of work to do dealing with the dehydration. He's seriously worried about some of the lads. We leave that Orange Bowl with heavy hearts and heavy legs scattered all over the team bus.

There's no party tonight. Larry Mullen and his limos have gone to ground. Nobody wants to go out. Not even Brendan O'Carroll can cheer us up. We've the serious faces on and they're here to stay.

Niall Quinn does raise a smile the next morning when he pops into the hotel with the RTÉ camera crew. He tells us how he was out with his wife at a country-and-western club when he was approached by an Ireland fan wearing a shirt bearing the name Houghton and the number eight. '"Do us a favour, Niall," says your man. "If I introduce you to that American bird I'm dancing with, will you let on I'm Ray Houghton? She thinks I'm the bloke who scored the goal against Italy. Don't disappoint her,"' Niall tells us. He didn't.

There's talk of a change on the team sheet for the Norway

game, which is only three days away. The press are calling for me and Kells to start when we return to Giants Stadium. Not that Jack has ever listened to the press. I'm with them, by the way. I feel I've made a real impact as a sub in the two games to date and I agree that we need fresh legs and fresh ideas against a Norway side that are bound to be stubborn if their manager insists on wearing Wellington boots on the sidelines even in this heat.

We train in Orlando the day before the match and Jack tells me I'm in before we leave for the airport and the flight to Newark. I shit myself. Yeah, I want this, but now that it's real I've a mind full of ideas and thoughts and maybe even the odd doubt.

In New Jersey I'm rooming with Kells again, and neither of us sleep well. He's also got the nod and we have a bit of a restless night, one of those 'are you awake?' conversations is a regular occurrence as we wait for dawn to break. We're in this together, the Three Amigos will be on the same pitch, and our emotions are off the Richter scale.

I meet my family outside the ground to give them their tickets, and I tell them I'm in. They can sense my anxiety but my mum says to treat it like just another game. 'You'll be fine,' she says.

Aldo's my tunnel buddy today. I always like someone I know with me going out onto the pitch. He's in front of me and Roy Keane is right behind me.

We keep that order for the national anthems. I can see a whisper coming down the line, starting with the captain Andy Townsend. It must be some sort of last-minute instruction. Maybe it's a ritual. The captain passing on some words of wisdom before a big match, something Jack told him on the way out perhaps.

This is the biggest game of my life, I've got to concentrate. We need at least a draw. If Andy has something to say, I have to listen. I have to take this seriously.

Aldo gets the nod. He leans over to me. I'm ready for this.

'Row F, bird with the Viking hat.'

'Yeah,' I go, with a look of puzzlement.

'Look at the size of her fucking tits. Pass it on.'

I want to burst my hole laughing, but the cameras are on me. And I have to pass it on – to Roy Keane. I'm shitting myself again.

There's no way I'm passing that on to Roy Keane seconds before the biggest game of our lives. So I just go, 'Roy, manager says to keep it tight for the first twenty minutes, pass it on.'

Kells gets the message next as I'm laughing. He must be wondering why I'm cracking a smile at such a mundane command.

At least the bird with the Viking hat and the big fucking tits has relaxed me. Not that it matters much. It's a shocking game. I get one decent cross in to the far post and Ned Kelly knocks it back for Roy, but Roy balloons it over the bar. Shez – John Sheridan – gets onto another one and hits the bar with Erik Thorstvedt beaten all ends up.

They hit the bar as well, but the game ends scoreless. We shake hands and I swap shirts with a bloke I've never heard of called Strand. But there's not much cause for celebration, even if the draw is good enough to get us out of the Group of Death and back down to Orlando for the last sixteen, maybe against the Belgians or the Dutch.

Jack is off on a nightmare journey to check out the Belgians just in case, while we are on the way back to the hotel in Orlando, happy with the outcome but not with the result, or the performance.

Tommy Coyne is the random selection for the drug test after the game, and he's struggling. He's been playing up front on his own all tournament and it's killing him with the heat and the humidity. When you get selected for doping control, you can drink as much as you want after the game so long as you give a sample. The tester is following him all around the room as Tommy drinks loads of fluids. But no matter how hard he tries, he can't pass any fluid.

We can't leave without Tommy. We have a charter flight booked out of Newark for Orlando and the captain is on the phone to Eddie Corcoran from the FAI giving out yards. Eddie manages to get the departure time put back, and Tommy is eventually able to pee after downing gallons of water.

He's still not in a good way though as we board the plane. As soon as we get to high altitude, Tommy collapses in a heap. He's got so dehydrated during the game and then taken so much fluid on board that the altitude has a really bad effect on him.

The medics reckon his brain has started swelling with the pressure inside the cabin. They get the pilot to bring the plane down to a low altitude to ease the pressure on his brain, and he comes around. We land, and Tommy is taken straight to the hospital. There's real concern for him and we're a subdued lot arriving back at the hotel.

Jack's trip to see Belgium play turns out to be a waste of time because we draw Holland in the last sixteen. His mood isn't helped by a flight cancellation that forces him to spend the night on a bench at Denver airport. As usual, Jack has no money and only for a British tourist spotting him, he wouldn't have got a cup of tea or a fag.

He's not a happy camper when we get back on the training ground in Orlando, and I suspect that, for some reason, I'm a part of the problem. You always get that sense from the manager. There's a coldness, an aloofness, there's a game being played and you're not really part of it. Footballers know.

A mate in the press confirms as much back in the hotel. Jack is thinking of changes for the Holland game. He wants to be a bit defensive and stop the supply of ball to their young striker, Bergkamp. It's me that's under pressure to stay in the team, not Kells. That's the vibe the press guys are getting and I have to admit I'm getting it myself. But what can I do?

I did well as a sub against Italy and he left me on for the full match against Norway, so he can't be unhappy with me. I'm too young and too nervous to say anything to Jack. I'd be afraid, even though I can see from the way he is shaping the play in training that I'm going to be back on bench duty against the Dutch.

Sure enough, he calls us together the day before the game and names the team. No McAteer. He could have told me before announcing it publicly, but that's Jack. You live with his way of doing things or you don't stay around for long.

He's going with experience. That's what he says when he finally pulls me aside the night before the game. He wants my legs fresh for the final thirty minutes. I could suggest it'll be over by then, but he'd give me a clip across the ear for being cheeky, so I don't. I'm not going to start picking arguments with Jack Charlton a few months into my Ireland career.

We've another ridiculous FIFA-o'clock kick-off, twelve noon with the sun right up there above us. It's boiling on the bench, never mind on the pitch.

We start brightly this time. The game's only five minutes old when Terry Phelan gets a great cross in, but Tommy Coyne slides and misses it. You don't get many opportunities like that against the Dutch, and they will always punish you if you don't take your chances. That's what happens a few minutes later. I can see it in slow motion in front of me from the bench – it's like watching a car crash. Terry hits a back pass and we all know it's going to be short. Bergkamp is on to it in a flash and gets there ahead of Packie, rounds him and the ball is in the net. For the second time at this World Cup we're a goal down early on. There's only eleven minutes on the clock and we're rattled.

We never get back into the match. Wim Jonk makes it 2–0 with a shot through Packie's hands just before half-time and our World Cup is dying as fast as the day itself. Jack throws me in for Stan in the sixty-third minute. I get at Frank de Boer a couple of times and throw a few decent crosses in, but there's no end product. It's not our day and we know it. We've known it from the minute Tommy failed to score off that Terry Phelan cross.

When the final whistle goes we start to think of our summer holidays. A World Cup that began with a bang against the Italians ends with a whimper against the Dutch.

Packie is distraught back in the dressing room. We have a big team dinner in the hotel that night and he is bawling his eyes out. I've never seen anything like it. I want to cry for him. He's taken it all to heart. He's blaming himself for the two goals, blaming himself for the end of the World Cup adventure. It's horrible to watch. The lads repeatedly tell him that we're all in it together, but he is taking it personally and nothing we say can change that.

He knows this is his last tournament for Ireland. It wasn't meant to end like this. Four years ago he brought the country to a standstill. Tonight he is on his knees emotionally. He's done too much for Ireland to go out like this.

I want to tell him it will get better, but I don't have the words. I want to tell him that the game has kicked me in the teeth so many times but football always finds a way to make it better. I don't want him to go.

I look around this room at the faces I have only known for four months, and I don't want any of it to end. There's talk of Jack quitting. There's talk of senior players retiring. There's loads of speculation and I don't want to hear any of it. I want it all to stay as it is – me and this new football family I've joined, together forever.

I've a pain in my arse in this dining room and a pain in my face as well. There's a bloody big insect bite on my cheek. It's been here for days now and it won't go away. It would have saved me, though, if the players had gone through with Andy Townsend's suggestion of copying the Romanians and dyeing our hair blond for the tournament. I wasn't doing that – I've enough blond moments, thanks.

There's one last team meeting. The FAI wants us to go home for a big civic reception and a party with the fans.

The lads aren't sure. Some of them have their families here and have holidays planned in the States. Others want to get as far away from football as they can.

The government are putting pressure on Jack and the FAI. They've sorted a big reception in the Phoenix Park. The lads agree to go when the FAI sort out flights back to America for those who have holidays booked.

It's only when we get to Dublin that we realise how much the whole country has been partying for the past three weeks. They fly us by helicopter from the airport to the park and it's incredible. There are hundreds of thousands of people there.

They even sing 'Happy Birthday' for me, because it was my twenty-third birthday on the day of the Italian game. The pain of that Holland result is still raw but this welcome lifts my spirits.

My mum is waiting for me back at the airport hotel. We get a quiet corner, eventually, and I'm nearly crying as I tell her it's been the best six weeks of my life. It's been an amazing journey. I want to do it again at the next World Cup and then the one after that and the one after that. I've just played football at the highest level imaginable against some of the best players in the world, played with the best team-mates possible on the best pitches, stayed in the best hotels, lived the dream.

I want more of the same with club and country now. But, I tell her, if it all ends tomorrow I won't complain.

Chapter Thirteen

I've locked my keys in my car and I'm late for training. Bruce is going to go mad. And he'll fine me. I call the police. An officer arrives, looks at the car and tells me to go inside the house and get him a coat hanger. He breaks out laughing when I hand him a wooden coat hanger. 'I thought you wanted to break the window,' I explain.

The World Cup hero is back in town. Bolton are in for pre-season training, and the lads will want to know all about how I nutmegged Baggio and what I did with Casiraghi's shirt. 'What about that Larry Mullen fellow, is he sound?'

They'll have read the papers as well. George Graham was spotted at the Mexico and Norway games – and he knows I can score a goal at Highbury – and the *Echo* is saying that Liverpool took note of the way Phil Babb and myself took to the World Cup stage. I'm a big noise now. Bruce Rioch will be thrilled to have me back, his very own World Cup wonder. He's bringing us to Scotland for a low-key pre-season tour – from Giants Stadium to the Highland League outposts.

There's no fanfare from Bruce when I report back, it seems I'm just the same as the lads who spent their summer in Magaluf. We're here to work and to play.

I'm in and out of the games in Scotland. No big deal. Bruce wants to rest me after my World Cup exertions. I can understand that. Then he leaves me out of his team for the first game of the new season. There's not even as much as a chat about it. The team gets pinned up on the dressing-room door an hour before the game, same as usual, and I'm nowhere to be seen. This goes on for weeks.

Just weeks after telling Casiraghi that if he ever fancies a bevvie in Liverpool to call me, my football career consists of games against the reserves at Hartlepool, Scunthorpe and Bradford. No disrespect to them – I've been that player – but I've just come home from the World Cup finals with a spring in my step.

This is not what I expected, not what I wanted. And that's not my ego speaking. Phil Brown wouldn't let me get carried away with any of it. It's just ambition, pure and naked ambition.

I'm left out for the first seven games of the season. It's a real kick in the nuts. The silent treatment from the gaffer makes it even worse. I knock on his door to ask him why and he just tells me to 'get out'. He'll see me and he'll talk to me when he wants to see me and talk to me, and not a day sooner.

Eventually I'm called into his office. He demands to know what I want. *What I want!* All I want is an explanation.

'Why am I not in the team? Why are you leaving me out of the first-team squad? What did I do to you?'

He won't answer me. He says he'll tell me when the time is right.

'I want to play and you won't play me. Why?'

'I don't have to tell you. Now get out of here.'

Why is he treating me like this? He's more like a dad to me than a manager.

I'm more confused, more annoyed than I was going into the meeting. I can't figure this out. It's killing me. I'm training with the first team, eating with the first team, mixing with the first team, but I haven't played with them yet this season.

Eventually he puts me back into the team. And he calls me into his office and tells me why. He wants me fresh and fit for the promotion push at the end of the season. The Premier League is all that matters now. The World Cup is history.

He wants me rested after the summer and ready to do my best, and only my best, for Bolton as we look to get out of Division One. That's why he left me out. Ignoring me was his way of making sure the World Cup didn't go to my head.

He could have told me! I think I can see the logic of his thinking. And now I'm back, I'm ready to bust a gut for him.

We're down in London for a game, and Bruce suggests Stubbsy and I sit down for a coffee with his brothers, Ian and Neil. They're football agents and they could do a job for us. Neil was a player at Villa in his day and Ian is a financial whizz kid. He's not forcing them on us or being pushy about it, but he thinks they could help us with contracts and the like.

I trust Bruce more than anyone in football, so if he says it's right, I'll do it. The meeting goes well. It seems a natural fit, so we sign with them. It's the first time I've had an agent. When Phil Neal signed me for Bolton, I was happy to get any contract and ended up with the same money I was getting playing for Marine and picking up the glasses in The Sportsmans Arms. Phil offered a chance to play league football, and that's what I really wanted at the time.

Since Bruce became manager he has been straight up with me. If I do well for him, he will do well for me, and he's been true to his word. No matter what contract I've been on, he has improved it when I deserved it. Each of my contracts has been better than the last. I'm on two grand a week now, not bad for a lad who signed for a hundred quid!

Ian brings some sense to my financial life. He sits down with my mum and he goes through investment opportunities whenever I get a bonus or a signing-on fee. I'm happy to let them get on with it. All I want to do is kick a football.

The best investment he makes for me is a house on the Wirral. It was time to move out of home when I got back from America – my mum will need the room for Casiraghi and Ian Wright! Her and my dad have divorced, and my sister and brother are teenagers, and there's just too much noise in the house. I need them around the corner, not downstairs. I've a girlfriend as well, and I don't want to bring her home to my mum's every night.

I know exactly where I want to live, so I start driving up and down the roads looking for the perfect house. I find it, go up to the front door and tell the bloke who answers that I want to buy his house. I write my number down for him and tell him to ring me if he ever wants to sell. The look on his face says he's more likely to ring me to tell me to do one.

Ian comes up a few times and we drive around the area again. We get into this cul-de-sac and it's there, right in front of me. My dream house.

It's in the corner and it's made for me. For some weird reason I am infatuated with corners. In the dressing room I will always change in the corner. In a hotel I always want the bed up against the wall. This house is nice and secluded and it's in the corner of the cul-de-sac. It's perfect.

I get Ian to do the digging this time. It turns out that the house is owned by the company that makes Fairy Liquid. They have a factory nearby and they use the house for their executives.

Ian must be good. Within the space of a few phone calls they agree to sell it. They'll even sell below market value if I can sort a quick sale for them. Can I what? Within weeks I'm moving in, around the corner from my mum and family.

I'm made up now, my self-confidence is supersonic. I understand what power really means.

Up to this point I've just been grateful for everything that's come my way, for all the things that seemed like second chances. Bolton was a second chance after so many rejections. The World Cup with Ireland came out of the blue. The contracts of two grand a week have been beyond my wildest dreams.

But now, with this house under my arse, I realise I am the one who got me here. It is my hard work and my skill that is making all this happen. I've earned all of this. I'm still grateful, don't get me wrong, but I'm aware of my own ability and power, and that is enlightening.

I can demand respect in the game now. I don't have to be saying thank you at every second turn anymore. At twenty-three years of age I'm finally self-aware and self-assured. I can start calling the shots.

It takes time for that awareness to transfer itself onto the pitch – sitting on a wooden bench at Caledonian Thistle and Heart of Midlothian after starring at a World Cup finals would knock the cockiness out of you fairly quickly.

I know I can be the best player on the pitch for Bruce and for Bolton, but that Scotland experience told me that I can only be the best player if he puts me on the pitch.

He's taught me a lesson and I can see now where he is coming from. He always wants to push me, to make me realise how good I can be. Stubbsy, whom I love, and Alan Thompson, are the two other players on the up at Bolton. Bruce knows we can do more for the team, and if that means leaving me out in Scotland and making me sweat every Saturday before he names his side, then that's exactly what he's going to do.

The expectations at Bolton this season are massive. Our recent FA Cup runs have given us a sniff of Wembley, but this time it's the League Cup – known at the moment as the Coca-Cola Cup – and not the FA Cup that offers us a glance at some silverware.

In January 1995 Portsmouth thump us 3–1 in the third round of the FA Cup at Burnden Park on a day when

Richard Sneekes got our only goal, but the League Cup is a different experience altogether.

Back at the start of the season, we'd beaten Ipswich 4–0 on aggregate – 3–0 away, when I scored one of the goals, and then 1–0 at home. The third round was straight knockout, and that's exactly what we did to Sheffield United, 2–1 at Bramall Lane. We'd beaten West Ham, 3–1 away in the fourth round, and Norwich, 1–0 at home in the quarter-finals.

By February 1995 we found ourselves in the two-legged semis, and facing Swindon. We lose 2–1 in the city with all the roundabouts. Alan Stubbs gives us an early lead, but Peter Thorne scores either side of half-time and Swindon defender Mark Robinson gets sent off for a late tussle with John McGinlay.

The second leg gets delayed by bad weather but on 8 March it's game time at Burnden, and we're 3–1 down on aggregate after Jan Age Fjortoft scores for Swindon in the fifty-seventh minute.

It's time to get the finger out if we want to go to Wembley. And we do. I pull one back in the sixty-fourth minute and Mixu Paataleinen gets us level seven minutes later, before McGinlay breaks Swindon's hearts with an eighty-eighth-minute winner. We win 4–3 on aggregate and we're off to the Twin Towers.

There's a Brucie Bonus for me as we celebrate in front of those loyal fans. Liverpool have beaten Crystal Palace and we'll be playing them in the greatest football stadium of all on 2 April. Brilliant.

The build-up to the final is incredible. They're red-hot favourites – they are the Premier League side, after all –

and there's huge interest in me because of my Merseyside background and my lifelong dedication to the Reds.

The story about my mum making me a Liverpool kit on her sewing machine makes the local papers in Bolton. They love the fact that I've been out socially in Liverpool with the likes of Jamie Redknapp and Steve McManaman. And my best mate these days is Phil Babb, who's moved to Anfield from Coventry since his World Cup heroics as one of the Three Amigos.

The papers are talking about the final being my trial game for Liverpool as well. Kenny Dalglish had been to see me play for Bolton when he was in charge. The new manager Roy Evans is supposed to be keen on me as well. Their chief scout Ron Yeats and his assistant Tom Saunders seem to spend half their lives at our place.

The fact that I'm still living on Merseyside, which is an advantage most of the time, is now only adding to the pressure and the hype going into the game.

The League Cup is also a distraction from our main aim for the season – promotion to the Premier League, which is what really matters to Bruce and the club. At least when you are through to an FA Cup final it's the last game of the season and you have nothing else to think about. This is different, it's only April. We will be back in the thick of the First Division as soon as Liverpool are out of the way.

But I intend to enjoy this final. Wembley can't be any more daunting than the World Cup against Italy, so I'll give it my best shot and see where that takes me.

I've sorted the tickets for my family. We've about two minibuses going down with everyone from my nan to my aunts and uncles, brother and sister and the mates who helped me along the way.

We're staying in St Alban's, Bruce's hometown, and he's keeping everything as normal as he possibly can. There's no special cup final suits, it's trackies as normal for an away match. The pre-match meetings and the team talks are exactly the same as for any other away game. The thing is, we all know this is no ordinary game. It's an occasion, a day out in London for the family and friends, and it is going to be something special.

I want to take it all in, the journey from the hotel, the drive up Wembley Way, the fans shouting and screaming at the bus as we go into the tunnel. It all happens so quickly. Before I know it I am in the Wembley dressing room. All I want to do is get out there for the warm-up, wave to my mum and family in the stands and play football against Liverpool.

We're the underdogs, but that's fine with me. It's the situation Irish teams have always thrived in. Jack has been on and told me to enjoy the game and the occasion and to do my best. This is my team we're up against – one of my heroes, Ian Rush, is their captain.

They have class all over the park. Jamie Redknapp and Steve McManaman in midfield, Razor Ruddock and Babbsy at the back. They are household names, well used to 75,000 people in the crowd and big matches.

We have a big-name striker at Wembley as well – but Nat Lofthouse is up in the stands with his old mates Stanley Matthews and Tom Finney.

We could do with some Nat Lofthouse magic on the day. We pay them a little too much respect early on and they can sense it, like all good teams do. Stevie Mac is on fire. He scores two great goals, the first in the thirty-seventh minute and the second twenty-three minutes into the second half. He goes by me on his way to scoring that one – and I thought we were pals!

We're on the ropes now, just like we were in the semi-final against Swindon, but we're fighters. Alan Thompson has a lot to thank Bruce for. Bruce gave him a second chance after he broke his neck in a car crash when he was an apprentice at Newcastle, and today is Alan's day to show his gratitude.

He's already missed a great chance, set up by yours truly, just after the break, but with twenty minutes to go he gets onto the ball and lets fly with a screamer that almost breaks the net.

We're 2–1 down, but we're not out yet. We run ourselves into the ground but we run out of time as well. We should have got more out of this match, but it's Ian Rush who goes up there to collect the cup as the tears flow down my cheeks. I'm so upset I can't even swap shirts.

Jamie and Babbsy bring the cup over to me and I get my hands on it, which is something, I suppose. I even try to lift it in front of the Liverpool fans, but it's no consolation. I've got my hands on the League Cup but it's going home to Liverpool.

After the ceremonies and the post-mortems in the dressing room I go to see my family in the car park. I just couldn't get enough lounge tickets for them all. My mum and dad are dead upset – they'd had their faces painted, and the paint is running down their cheeks with all the crying when we kiss and hug outside Wembley.

We do get a hero's welcome back in Bolton, but there's no time to mope about the result. We've a month or so of league action left, and Bruce is the man with the plan to get us into the Premiership.

Wembley is quickly forgotten when Tommo scores the winners away from home to both Swindon and West Brom. A scoreless draw at home to Luton, however, and then a defeat at Tranmere – of all places – bring us back down to earth.

John McGinlay steadies our nerves with the only goal at home to Sunderland, but we then go and lose away to both Reading and Oldham. A 1–1 draw with Stoke just keeps us in the play-off places, and it all comes down to the final game of the season, Bolton against Burnley in front of 17,000 fans at Burnden Park.

A Mixu Paataleinen goal is enough, not just for the 1–1 draw but to get us into the play-offs. We're third in a league table topped by Bryan Robson's Middlesbrough. A decision to reduce the Premier League from twenty-two teams to twenty for the 1995–96 season means that only one other club will join Middlesbrough via the play-offs.

Second-place-holders Reading are up against Tranmere, and we face a Wolves side managed by the former England boss Graham Taylor and led from the front by the great Steve Bull. Peter Shilton, who signed as cover late in the season, starts in goals for Wolves in the first leg at Molineux when Bull gives the home team the lead in the forty-fourth minute.

We come out with all guns blazing at the start of the second half, and I score the equaliser almost straight from the kick-off, before Mark Venus grabs a winner for Wolves five minutes later.

The second leg, on 17 May in front of 20,000 fans at Burnden Park, is a tense affair. John McGinlay levels the tie a minute before the break, but nobody can get a winner and the game drifts into extra time. After 109 minutes McGin scores the greatest goal of his life, or so it seems at the time, to send us back to Wembley and a play-off final date with Reading.

That League Cup final defeat to Liverpool is going to really stand to us now. There's nothing a day like this can throw at us to surprise us. We know the hotel. We know the drive down the M1 through Watford to the ground. We know what it's like to drive up Wembley Way on match day with fans everywhere.

We might just have been in awe of Liverpool and the occasion in the early stages of that League Cup final, but we won't be caught out twice. Bruce is quick to remind us that this is just another league game in a stadium we know well against a team we know inside out – we've beaten them 1–0 at home and lost 2–1 away already this season.

That's the plan at least, but when does football ever go to plan? The blue and white balloons are still floating around the pitch when Lee Nogan puts Reading ahead in the fourth minute. We've barely recovered from that shock when Adrian Williams makes it 2–0 in the twelfth minute. The game should be over when Reading get a penalty after half an hour, but Stuart Lovell misses. Their regular penalty taker is the Northern Ireland international Jimmy Quinn, but he's also their player-manager and he's left himself on the bench for this one.

Bruce is fuming when he gets us in the dressing room at half-time. We've taken ages to get going in big games all season, and it doesn't help that this is the final game of the season. The penalty miss means the Premier League is still there if we really want it. Do we want it?

The game is seventy-five minutes old before we prove we do, when Owen Coyle gets us back into it with a goal. Substitute Fabian de Freitas leaves it until four minutes from time before getting the equaliser for us that forces the match into extra time.

Mixu puts us in front for the first time in the game just before the half-time whistle in extra-time. Then Fabian makes it 4–2, before Jimmy Quinn finally gets his name on the scoresheet in the 119th minute to make it 4–3.

After his goal I suffer the most nervous sixty seconds of my life, waiting for that final whistle. The game has been up and down like a yo-yo, and they could still snatch an equaliser and deny us the Premier League.

The ball is hopping around. I just want to kick it into touch and high into the stands. The ref finally blows that whistle. It's over. We've won. We're in the Premier League.

Now I can get my hands on a trophy for real. But first there's something I have to do. I have to give Bruce Rioch the biggest hug ever. I owe him that much. He has turned Bolton Wanderers Football Club around. He has turned my life around. Nine months ago he taught me a harsh lesson on a wooden bench in Inverness; now he has transformed me into a Wembley winner.

Before the match the papers told me that Manchester United, Everton, Blackburn and Liverpool would all be looking at me at Wembley. But right now I don't care.

We're going to stick together, this Bolton team. We've achieved something as a unit, we've put Bolton back on the football map and we are going to march forward together. We are going to tackle the Premier League as one. Anyone who leaves now is stupid or selfish or both.

As we hit the town in London, the enormity of it all hits me. This means more than winning the League Cup a month ago could possibly have meant. I realise that now.

A cup is the reward for a few games. Promotion is the reward for a season's-worth of hard work. That's why getting Bolton into the Premier League means so much to us as we finally get to celebrate it all.

The lads will all be back in Bolton tomorrow for an open-top bus tour of the town, but I'll be on a flight to Dublin. We have two qualifiers for the 1996 European Championships coming up, against Liechtenstein and the big one against Austria, and Jack wants me in the camp. So while the lads are parading around Bolton, I'll be running up and down the golf course at the Nuremore Hotel with Mick Byrne snapping at my heels. Now that's a promotion party with a difference!

Chapter Fourteen

*We're on the training ground at Liverpool, and Barnesy asks me
if I'm religious.*

　'Yeah,' I say. 'Church of England, just like Jesus.'

　He goes, 'What?'

　I reply again, 'Church of England, just like Jesus.'

　He just goes, 'Shut up.'

It's the big move you've always wanted. Arsenal. Top
of the Premier League. The marbled halls of Highbury,
big club, great crowd, huge fan base. It's a chance to
compete with Liverpool, United, Leeds and the champions
Blackburn for the big trophies. You're going from the top of
the world after the First Division play-off final at Wembley
to the top of the league with the Gunners.

　So, well done, Bruce Rioch. And give me a call whenever
you want me to join you at our new club. We are an item,
you know that. You're my dad in everything bar name.
You're the man who keeps me on the straight and narrow.
So why didn't you tell me about these Arsenal stories that

are on the back page of every paper I pick up? Why did you come into training this morning and tell us you're leaving for Arsenal? Why are you abandoning me for life in the big smoke after everything we did together? I need to know. You're breaking my heart.

I'm not the only one you're leaving behind. Colin Todd is on his tod, so to speak. The board want him to take over as joint manager with Roy McFarland, his old centre-back partner at Derby County.

I'm not sure about this McFarland fellow – the feeling's mutual – and I think he senses my disappointment. I don't understand why Bruce hasn't asked Colin to join him at Arsenal. Maybe he did and Colin said no. Maybe Colin wants to be a boss in his own right.

That's why appointing Roy McFarland to work alongside him as joint manager makes no sense to me. If the board believe Colin can only do half the job, then they mustn't have much faith in him to do the whole job. This Roy guy seems to be standing in his way, if you ask me.

Roy is a nice enough bloke, but he's not my man. My man has gone to London. His assistant is still here but there's another bloke getting in his way. So I'm not going to like this other bloke. I don't care what he does or how good a coach he is. He's taken Bruce's place and he's taken Colin's job. He can think again if he thinks I'm going to make his life easy for him.

Yep. There's a bit of paranoia creeping into my life. So much has happened in the past eighteen months and so much of that was down to Bruce Rioch and Jack

Charlton. Jack's still the Irish manager, despite all the speculation after the USA '94 exit, but Bruce has gone.

Maybe the dream will all come crashing down around me just as quickly as it became reality. There's a real uncertainty about Bolton now, and I don't like it. I'm starting to buy into it, I'm starting to think it's about time I look after number one for a change and look to move on as well. I don't owe this Roy McFarland anything. Some of the papers are linking me with Liverpool again. Others are speculating that Bruce will bide his time then make an offer to take me to Arsenal.

Colin and Roy soon sense I'm out of sorts. I do what I always do when I'm uncertain – I throw the toys out of the pram. I'm acting like a real prima donna on the training ground. Bruce would've clipped me around the ear, but they give me a bit of space until the day they have to take action.

I'm called into their office. I'm told to accept the fact that Bruce has gone and that I'm going nowhere. They're not going to sell me. The board has assured them that I won't be sold. I'm stuck at Bolton whether I like it or not, and I have two choices – play like a pro in the first team or sulk like a spoiled child in the ressies.

It soon becomes an easy choice to make. We're in the Premier League now, the big time, and the trappings soon follow. As soon as we won promotion, the club bought a new site in Euxton to develop a proper training ground, on the site of the old Royal Ordnance Survey headquarters. We're also swimming in Lucozade energy drinks from the day we report back for pre-season training. No more throat lozenges for us.

Reebok have supplied us with a smashing new kit. The training bibs are brand-spanking new, there's no holes in them and everyone has a number. We're real footballers now and it's time to enjoy it. The toys are back in the pram.

Stubbsy and I talk about the future a lot on the way to and from training. He's getting loads of media attention as well and, like me, he reckons it will soon be time to take another step up the ladder. We both know the best way to do that is to play our way to a move. Get in to the Premier League and take it by storm. Make the big boys sit up and take notice.

It's all going to plan when the phone rings. It's Bruce. He does want me after all. He's given the Arsenal board a list of names, the three players he wants to turn his squad into title contenders. There's the Dutch striker Dennis Bergkamp, Brazilian left-back Roberto Carlos – and me! Wow.

He's got Bergkamp, and now he's got the green light from the Highbury board to go after me. He says he won't give up on me, but to keep it under wraps.

That's all well and good until Saturday night's *Match of the Day*, when the BBC interviews Alan and myself at the end of the game. The reporter asks if anything has happened about the two of us leaving the club. Stubbsy looks straight at the camera and says, 'Watch this space.' Oh shit. That's not going to go down well with the fans. Colin and Roy won't be too happy about it either. The cat is out of the bag and well amongst the pigeons now.

I'm getting anxious again. Mark Seagraves keeps telling me to relax, it will happen when it's meant to happen. I'm worried. We're six games into the season and there's still no sign of an official approach from Arsenal. I keep pestering Bruce's brother, Ian. He's supposed to be making this happen for me. Why isn't he doing his job?

Then, just as Mark had predicted, it all happens in an instant. Alan and I are driving up to the training ground one Monday morning as normal when Ian Rioch rings on the mobile and says that we're to go straight to the ground and meet Colin Todd. He has news for us. Both of us. I'm sorry I don't have that Lotus Elan anymore.

Colin comes straight out with it. Bolton have had an approach from the Blackburn manager Kenny Dalglish and have agreed a fee of nine and a half million pounds for the two of us. That's nine million for me and five hundred grand for Stubbsy. Joke! We're free to meet Kenny and talk terms with the league champions. The deal is done as far as Bolton are concerned, and we're to get over to Blackburn and get working on the contracts straight away.

King Kenny wants to sign me. And Stubbsy as well.

'Can I go out to the training ground and tell the lads?'

'No. You and Alan have to get to a meeting with Blackburn as soon as Ian arrives up from London.'

We follow Ian to the Haydock Thistle Hotel on the Old Lancs Road. Kenny and his assistant Ray Harford have hired a boardroom. This is surreal. It's not Alan going to Rovers, it's not me – it's both of us. I give my mum a quick call. She's delighted that it's Kenny who wants to sign us, and she tells me to make sure to say she was asking after him, but she knows I'll be star-struck when I meet him. She warns me not to sign anything without thinking it through.

Fat chance. Two years after asking Kenny to sign my Bolton programme, he wants my autograph on a contract! Just show me where to sign, Kenny.

It doesn't work like that, does it? Kenny wants to talk to us separately. I'm first in, with Ian leading the way. I almost want to ask Kenny for his autograph again. I have to stop myself!

There's small talk to begin with. 'You're a great player … You can fit into our team … You're part of the future.' Talk, talk, talk. Kenny wants to strengthen the team that won the title. I will fit into his midfield. This is how he wants me to play. It's all making sense, but it's just not sinking in. That's Kenny Dalglish, sitting in front of me. And he wants me to play football for him. Any day, Kenny, any day.

A phone rings and brings me back to reality. Ian says he has to take this call and leaves the room. There's Kenny, Ray Harford and me, and there's this big awkward silence from one side of the boardroom table to the other. I don't know what to do.

Should I tell him my mum was asking after him? Ask him about the team? Does he miss Liverpool? Maybe I should talk wages and signing-on fees and bonuses. Maybe it's too early for all of that. Maybe Ian has done that deal already. I've no idea what wages they're offering me. I'm not bothered. If they're going to pay Bolton nine and a half million quid for the two of us, I'm sure the pay will be OK.

Ian's comes back into the room. He drops another bombshell. Bolton have just accepted a four-and-a-half million pound bid from Liverpool for me. Just me. No Stubbsy. He looks Kenny in the eye and tells him he has to talk to Liverpool on my behalf. He doesn't even ask me. He says he has to suspend these talks and he'll get back to Kenny when he knows what Liverpool are offering. He'll happily bring Alan into the room and discuss his move, but he can't talk about mine until he's spoken to Roy Evans and Liverpool.

Jesus. What's happening here?

I'm just staring at Ian, wide-eyed and feckless. I barely notice as Kenny starts to fume. Without blinking an eye, he tells Ian that the deal is off if he talks to Liverpool. There will be no transfers. No move, not just for me but for Alan as well.

This is not a debate. It is clearly a statement of fact.

Ian argues with the King. Surely as a former player himself he knows we have to talk to Liverpool. He tells Kenny he'd do the same thing if he were in my shoes. Kenny relents just enough to give us five minutes outside to talk about it – and break the news to Alan. But he is not budging on his offer and the terms. If we talk to Liverpool, any Blackburn deal is dead in the water.

We retreat out to the reception area, and I have to give Alan the news while Ian makes a call. 'Liverpool want me but Kenny will only sign both of us. It's all or nothing. If I go to Liverpool, you have to go back to Bolton. He won't sign you without me.'

I know this is killing him, but it's Liverpool. Alan doesn't even think about it. He tells me I have to walk away from Kenny Dalglish and talk to Liverpool. I remind him that if I do that it will kill his Blackburn move. To his eternal credit, he is not for turning. He tells me that he knows better than I do what Liverpool means to me. If Everton came in for him, he'd do exactly the same thing, and I'd be just as supportive. He insists I have to be selfish. He'll be fine either way. He won't stand between me and Liverpool. It's an incredible gesture and tells you everything about Alan.

I don't want to let him down but I have to. If a club like, say, Southampton had made the offer under the same circumstances I wouldn't even have considered it – but this is Liverpool FC. This is my dream.

I have to walk back into that suite and tell Kenny Dalglish that he's not good enough for me. I get the words out as quickly as I can. 'Thanks for the offer, but I have to talk to Roy and Liverpool. If it doesn't work out at Anfield, then I'd gladly consider Blackburn again.'

The Scottish accent is getting thicker by the minute as Kenny's blood boils. The offer from Blackburn is withdrawn. The deal is gone no matter what happens with Liverpool. I've never seen this Kenny Dalglish on *Match of the Day*, but I know where he's coming from.

Alan just shakes my hand when I come out of the room. He's gone from a footballer in the middle of talks on a nine-and-a-half-million-pound joint deal, to a worker going home for his tea without even opening his mouth. Bolton are trying to sell him on his own but Kenny won't have any of it. I've ruined that one for Alan. I'm both gutted and embarrassed.

Kenny can't understand how Liverpool got wind of his interest, and I'm not going to tell him, but it's mostly my fault – and Sammy Lee's.

We stayed close since he used to drive me to training at Bolton, and he's working for Liverpool now. When I told him about Bruce's call and his promise that he would try and get me to Arsenal, Sammy asked me to keep Liverpool in the loop if anything ever developed. He's kept in touch, always checking to see if anything is happening with Arsenal, so that Monday morning I just had to let him know about the joint bid from Blackburn.

That's how Liverpool found out. It just took me by surprise how quickly they reacted. I thought I was just passing on a bit of news to Sammy, I didn't think it would trigger a bid from Liverpool! All I wanted to do was let him know that Bolton were finally prepared to sell me, even if the initial bid they accepted was a joint one.

We leave the hotel and Ian arranges to meet Liverpool. They're happy to have the talks at Anfield as soon as we can get there. There's no need for secrecy as far as they are concerned, it's all out in the open, and the press already caught wind of it.

It's about 6.30 on Monday evening when we pull in to the car park. My feet have hardly touched the ground all day and my head is swimming. I thought I was going training when I left home this morning. Instead I've told my idol and his football club to wait for a call and I'm about to sit down with Roy Evans in one of the lounges at Anfield to discuss a move to Liverpool.

This feels right from the minute I get out of the car. It's pitch black outside but they've turned the floodlights on, just in case I need any reminder about what a special place this is. They're pushing the boat out to make an impression. I laugh. I've been coming here for years, and I know the place inside out. This won't be a hard sell, Roy!

I look out at the floodlit pitch and I tell Ian they're running the leccy bill up just for me. We're laughing. The anxiety that had been in the boardroom with Kenny has gone. We all know this is going to happen.

Roy and Peter Robinson bring us to the home dressing

room, then down the tunnel and past the 'This is Anfield' sign. I want to reach out and touch it, but I tell myself I'll wait until I'm a Liverpool player and do it properly.

We talk business in a suite up in the Centenary Stand. Roy asks how the talks went with Kenny, how keen I am on Blackburn and how interested I am in signing for Liverpool. It's all I can do to stop myself grinning like a cat from down the road in Cheshire.

Roy sells a good story, not that he has to. He has worked hard to bring new blood into the team. He's already got Rob Jones, Jamie Redknapp and Stevie McManaman. He's happy with my Ireland mate Phil Babb too. He's looking to mix that youth in with Ian Rush and John Barnes and he wants to strengthen the squad. He's looking to play me wide right in front of Rob Jones. He sees me as Jamie's long-term partner in the centre of midfield when Barnesy loses his pace.

This is all so positive. He's worked out my future. He wants me outside Barnes and Redknapp to begin with, then in there alongside Jamie after Barnesy retires. I'll sign now, Roy. Where's the pen? I don't care what's on offer.

Ian's not like that of course. He's sat through hundreds of these sales pitches. He wants to talk hard cash. Roy warns me there's no bonus culture at Anfield. The club ethic is that you shouldn't need a bonus to play for Liverpool FC. Dead right. I'll be on the same money as other players my age starting off, over twelve grand a week. Christ! I'm well paid at Bolton and this is nearly four times as much.

Twelve and a half grand! A week! I wouldn't have earned that in a year not so long ago. I don't care what Liverpool are offering me. I just want to sign.

I ask to be excused from the meeting while Ian sorts out the details of the contract. That's his job. As long as he tells me I'm a Liverpool player when he calls me back in, I don't care what he does. He can sort a pay cut for all I care. Nothing is going to stop me signing that contract, whatever it says.

I leave the suite and go for a walk. As my future is decided, all I want to do is walk down the corridors and look at the photos of all the Liverpool greats down the years, players and managers. I want to join them. Get my mug on that wall in a red shirt. There's Bill Shankly and Ian St John, Emlyn Hughes and Stevie Heighway. There's Keegan and Kennedy, McDermott and Clemence – even Kenny Dalglish ...

These are my heroes. These are my people. I want my photo up there, framed with the legends. Don't screw it up, Ian. Tell them I'll sign anything.

They call me back into the room and tell me I'm going to be a Liverpool player for at least the next four years. Where do I sign? I'm told I have to do a medical tomorrow. I want to do it there and then. Roy says the medical will be a formality, but he does advise me to do the decent thing and ring Kenny Dalglish personally. 'He'll understand,' says Roy. Yeah, right. You weren't in that suite at the Haydock Thistle Hotel, Roy. I'm not so sure.

I'll get round to Kenny later. First I have to ring my mum and Alan Stubbs. They need to know. They're made up for me, both of them. They know it's the move I was born to make.

Kenny isn't so supportive.

Ian collects me the next morning and takes me to get my car at Alan's house. I ring Kenny on our way there. He's not happy at all. He's quite angry on the phone. He says I can look forward to playing my football at Haig Avenue.

'Who plays at Haig Avenue?' I ask Ian.

'Southport and Liverpool ressies,' he replies.

I'm gutted. My hero's basically telling me to do one because I've chosen the team he played for over the team he manages.

When I hang up I'm a bit distraught, to be honest. I never expected my idol to talk to me like that, so I keep telling myself that it's all his fault anyway. I only ever wanted to play for Liverpool because Kenny Dalglish played for Liverpool. All my life, all I ever wanted to be was Kenny Dalglish in a red shirt. Now the only person who isn't happy that my dream is coming true is Kenny Dalglish.

I loved his skills, his eye for goal, his ability to turn a game on its head. What I never realised until now is that Kenny has a ruthless streak. I saw it in that hotel room and I've just heard it on the phone. It surprises me, and it disappoints me, but maybe I need to develop a ruthless streak as well if I really want to be Kenny Dalglish.

He's certainly ruthless with Alan Stubbs and stays true to his word – it's both of us or neither of us, and Alan is left back training with Bolton and playing for a team whose fans now know he was within minutes of leaving them for one of their nearest and oldest rivals.

I'll be okay with the Bolton fans. Unlike Kenny Dalglish, they'll understand why I had to sign for Liverpool, and my transfer fee won't do Bolton any harm either. Not a bad return on the five hundred quid they gave Marine to repair the roof of their social club and the bag of balls they threw in for good measure!

The medical is at Liverpool University Hospital, MRI scans, brain tests and all. I'm like a racehorse, there's not an ounce of fat on me. Turns out I do have a brain and a pair of healthy lungs, and I sail through it. The story's out now and I'm floating on cloud nine. Just pass that contract and a pen and I'll sign on the dotted line. I'm a Liverpool player at last.

There's no chance to get back to Bolton. I don't even have time to collect my boots or clear out my locker. That'll have to wait. Instead I send flowers to all the girls at the club, in the office and in the canteen, and anyone who helped me. I want to send something as a thank you to Alan Whittel, the old fella who looked after us, but I don't think he'll fancy flowers. I'll get back soon for a proper goodbye.

I'm sad to go. I tell Browny and some of the other lads that on the phone, but they understand. This is football and this is my future. I'd been going on at them for so long about Liverpool that I think they're partly relieved to see the back of me. They might get some peace and quiet now.

I throw a party in the Nag's Head pub for family and friends. Alan Molden is there and I'm delighted to see him. He's one of the people who's got me this far.

Liverpool are away on European duty and not due back in until Friday morning. I'll be there for them. I've a press conference to do while they're gone, and time to think about it – never a good thing for me. The first thing I have to do is go into town and get some decent clobber. I want to be accepted by the lads. I want them to think I'm as cool as they are. I have to hit the ground running. I'm not turning up in a tracksuit to announce my arrival at Liverpool to the world.

New clothes are needed – nothing too pretentious, just a grandfather shirt and a waistcoat and a nice pair of matching trousers to complete the modern footballer look. The lads will see the photos from the conference in the papers and they'll think I'm as trendy as they are.

That's the plan. They might also see me on TV. Rob Palmer has been on from Sky Sports. He wants to film my first day as a Liverpool player, but he wants to do a bit on the story of a Liverpool fan growing up to play for his boyhood club. We're getting a bit theatrical here, but I've nothing else to do until the lads get back from Europe, so why not?

Rob has the storyline sorted. Sky will come to the house and film me sleeping in this massive Liverpool shirt – Neil Ruddock's of course – and dreaming of playing for Liverpool. That's the easy bit, by the way. My boot sponsors, Adidas, had sent me a huge Liverpool shirt with Razor's name on it after the League Cup final and I have been sleeping in it most nights since then anyway!

It's too good to be true for them. Rob and the cameraman come to the house and film me getting out of bed in Razor's shirt. Then Rob knocks on the door and tells me my car is waiting to bring me to sign for Liverpool FC – with me in the full Liverpool kit, ready to play for my heroes. He interviews me in the car – I've the waistcoat gear on at this stage – before we move on to the ground for the press conference.

There's even a fan waiting for me as we drive into the car park at Anfield. He knocks on the window. I'm sure he's looking for an autograph, so I wind the window down.

All he wants to know is where the club shop is! I tell him I'm about to sign for Liverpool, for his club. I don't know where the shop is. He just shrugs his shoulders, says 'fair enough' and moves on. It's the greatest day of my life and this Liverpool fan doesn't even know who I am. Welcome back to reality, Jason.

The press conference is a doddle. I can't stop smiling from start to finish. It's the easiest story the press will ever get to write. Boyhood Liverpool fan signs for hometown club. Even I could write it!

Sammy Lee calls me in to train with the reserves while the first team are away. The fact he's an old friend and a familiar face is a big help. Cocky and all as I am in front of the cameras, I'm still nervous old Jason behind closed doors. Liverpool have just paid over eight million quid for my plastic-Paddy mate Stan Collymore, and I'm their next biggest signing on four and a half million. That's a hell of a lot of money.

Roy Evans has sorted the number four shirt for me and I'm made up with that. It's the number Steve Nicol wore when Liverpool were winning everything in England and Europe and now it's mine. Forever more if I have my way.

There's an expectancy about my move, and I get a sense of that the first morning at Melwood – when I find the place. I'd never been there with Bolton or Marine because Liverpool play their reserve and junior games in Southport, as Kenny Dalglish kindly pointed out, so I have to ring a mate for directions.

Breakfast is the first order of the day when I arrive. Ann and Paula – two loveable Scousers – are in charge of the kitchen and we hit it off like a house on fire. It's obvious from that first cup of tea that they're going to mother me through my time with the club. They're everything from counsellor to nutritionist. I've to watch what I eat, they tell me – there's a nutritionist for that job as well – but a good breakfast is vital at the start of the day. Nothing is too much trouble for Ann and Paula. Do I want scrambled egg or toast with my bacon or maybe just a sausage sarnie with a big mug of tea? Breakfast at Melwood is sacrosanct, and rightly so.

Ian Rush and Jan Molby train with us the first day. They're coming back from injuries and, once again, I have to stop myself from asking for an autograph, bowled over to be in the same dressing room. Sammy keeps the session simple. It's the Liverpool way, he explains to me.

It's low-key for the first couple of days, but that all changes on the Friday when the first team return. It's like someone has hit a switch, and the whole place goes into overdrive.

The first thing that hits me is the huge media presence outside the entrance at Melwood. It soon becomes apparent they're not here to see me, as I meet my heroes on my first official day at work. The press is here every Friday when there's a big story brewing. And there's a big story brewing.

Rumour has it that Robbie Fowler cut up Neil Ruddock's shoes as they sat in the plane waiting to take off on the way home from the European game. Razor went mental and punched Robbie in the face while the plane was still on the tarmac. That's why all the cameras and all the reporters are outside the gates this morning. They can sniff a scandal. It's like the attention we got with Ireland when we played Italy in the World Cup. Ann and Paula tell me to get used to it – I'll have to fight my way through the press scrum regularly. Just don't be the reason they're here, they warn me. As if I would.

I'm still coming to terms with the fact that I'm training alongside Rushie and Jan Molby when the first team arrive and I'm changing beside Nigel Clough, Paul Stewart, Razor, Dominic Matteo, Robbie Fowler, Steve McManaman and Jamie Redknapp. I'm trying to get used to the idea that these are my work colleagues now, my mates even. I still feel like I should be outside the gates looking for autographs as they pass by in their Range Rovers, BMWs and Mercs. They're big names and I'm now the small fish in the big pond, a big change from Bolton.

Even the coaches here are famous, the likes of Ronnie Moran and Tom Saunders and Stevie Heighway, who works with the kids. Ronnie's always running around with a pencil in his hand, making up another list. He seems to have a list for everything.

The four corners of the dressing room at Melwood are taken. As the new kid in town I don't get a choice about where I sit. I'll just have to make do with this space, with Jamie Redknapp one side of me and Neil Ruddock the other. Babbsy is close by and Steve McManaman is directly opposite me.

My first game for Liverpool is a Cilla Black special – surprise, surprise. It's against Bolton! I'm only named on the bench and I'm relatively anxious, but I'm dead proud as well. I sneak a look at myself in the mirror in the bathroom to make sure it's all real, me in the famous red shirt with the Liver bird crest. That's my name and my new number four on the back.

The lads don't see me sneaking off. They have their own pre-match rituals. Watching the new bloke admire himself in his kit isn't one of them. Macca just sits there and reads the programme, every word of it, right until the bell goes to get onto the pitch. Barnesy is always in the bath. Robbie Fowler gets a rub down. Rushie's a giggler. Razor's loud enough to be heard in the away dressing room. He'll give me grief for sure if he spots me looking myself up and down in the mirror on the bathroom door.

The Kop welcomes me with open arms, shouting mouths and a big handclap. Nice touch. The Bolton fans greet me like one of their own as well. I made sure to clap them when I went out for the warm-up, and they clap me back. It's a mutual-appreciation society out here today.

We win 5–2 but I don't get on. Unused sub. Kenny Dalglish will no doubt have a good giggle at that when we're on *Match of the Day* later.

My debut comes on Wednesday night, Sunderland at home in the League Cup with all the family up in the main stand. Paul Bracewell smashes me early on, but no damage is done. Soon enough I rattle the post and Rushie misses the rebound. Then I cushion the ball down for Mickey Thomas who whips it into the top corner to complete a 2–0 win.

It's only when we beat Manchester United 2–0 at Anfield a few months into my time at the club that I feel like I really belong. I've had to snap out of the boyhood-dream stuff, and quickly. I won't survive otherwise. If you want to play for Liverpool, the first thing you have to do, stupid as it sounds, is accept that you are good enough to play for Liverpool. You have to realise where you stand at the club.

Me acting like a fan around Ian Rush and John Barnes is going to get me nowhere other than Southport with the reserves.

I've got to snap out of the I-could-cross-the-ball-for-Robbie-Fowler-and-he-could-score mind-set, and just cross the ball for Robbie to score.

Roy pulls me in training one day and asks if I'll play wing-back for him, the position we discussed at our first meeting. We've got a few injuries at the back and he wants to play Mickey Thomas and Jamie together in the centre of the field with Macca in a free role behind Robbie and Stan. Mark Wright, John Scales and Babbsy will play as three centre-backs, so he wants me to play in front of them, wide on the right. Roy reckons my energy will make me a natural for the role and he's right on that front. I've not been here long, and I don't feel tired at all.

It's not that we train hard. There's actually very little running involved on the training ground. It's all about football – lots of football. It's all about ball work and technical work and loads of five-a-sides with Doug Livermore and Ronnie Moran calling the shots. There's not much running or physical stuff. Ronnie Moran takes pride in telling me that it's a leftover from the boot-room days. It suits me fine because I'm always full of energy and adrenalin.

The system works to perfection the day we beat United. Robbie scores in each half, the first from a free kick and the second when he dinks one over Schmeichel. Beating United is always special for Liverpool fans and it's the day the Kop seems to really take to me. At last I feel like I belong here, but more importantly, I've come to terms with what's expected of me.

Roy's on cloud nine after the win. He's a decent bloke and he deserves this. I reckon he's got a bit of a soft spot for me because I'm local, but he loves us all, he wants to like everybody. If he could, he'd pick twenty players to start every game. That's the sort of bloke he is. Dougie is the eyes and ears of the operation. He watches everything that goes on. And Ronnie's the hard man. If you're going to get a bollocking, it's going to come from Ronnie and definitely not from Roy.

The philosophy at Liverpool is certainly different to anything I experienced at Bolton. There we all had to work bloody hard to make something of ourselves, and everyone from the manager down bought into that philosophy. Here there is an acceptance that if you are good enough to play for Liverpool, you are able to comprehend what is expected of you. It will come easy to you.

They take it for granted that you will understand things quickly. We don't work on technique or passing or control because you are expected to have all those qualities in abundance if you are good enough to sign as a Liverpool player in the first place.

A lot of our work is about buying into the Liverpool philosophy, playing as a team, getting used to each other and knowing what the guy on the ball is going to do with it. Macca and Barnesy are the decision-makers on the pitch, our version of a quarterback in American football. They will come and take the ball from you or they will look for the ball from you. We might all be characters in our own right, but we have to know how we should play and what is wanted of us as Liverpool players.

It's the Shankly way and it's the right way. We pass the

ball and we keep the ball. That's the cardinal rule. You keep the ball as best you can. Always.

You can hear Ronnie Moran on the sideline constantly telling you when to pass it and when to hold it. Training match or Premier League match, he's giving the commentary and talking you through the Liverpool way of playing – where the pass is, where the opponent is, what to do next. 'Get it.' 'Go back.' 'Go back.' 'Go down the line.' 'Go inside.' His voice is in my head, twenty-four-seven. In training he has this whistle as well, just to make sure we are paying attention. The ball is everything when you play for Liverpool. You are so conscious of it that you lose sight of everything else that's around you.

The night they switched on the lights for me when I arrived to discuss my move from Bolton, I was worried about playing in front of the Kop, anxious that it would be too emotional for me. The truth is that when the game kicks off I don't really notice if the Kop is in front of me or behind me for those first few games. I'm concentrating so hard on keeping the ball, on making the pass, listening to what Ronnie Moran is telling me to do, that I become oblivious to everything else, the surroundings and the noise of the crowd. It's only when the ball goes out of play or there's someone down getting treatment that you can take a break and stop, look and listen. Then the whistle goes and you are back in the zone again.

The first game when I really notice the Kop is the FA Cup clash with Rochdale when I score my first goal for the club. It's one of many in an easy enough win for us, but for me it's the most important goal in the history of football. Mickey Thomas puts me through and I smash it into the corner of the net, right in front of the Kop. My family are all over on the right and I swear I can see them celebrating with me as I turn away after the goal. The Kop start chanting my name and it's special. They just chant Jason McAteer and I'm the proudest man in the world. This is never going to end. I'm here forever. Liverpool for life.

Liverpool have never won the new Premier League and Roy Evans knows that has to change. He's building a side to challenge for the 1995–96 title, and my first season at the club is all geared up to achieving that goal.

The games are coming thick and fast from the start of the season – and they're all big. In October Eric Cantona's return after his kung-fu suspension is against Liverpool at Old Trafford, and this time his stray boot catches me full on in the face and costs me a tooth and a cap on another one. All accidental of course.

There's nothing accidental about his touch that day. The game has only just started when he hits a brilliant pass for a Nicky Butt goal. Then he takes the mickey out of Razor Ruddock by patting him on his stomach in front of the Stretford End. They love that. There's history between the pair. At Anfield last season Neil flattened Cantona's collar down, so this time Eric pats him on the tummy and shakes his head in disapproval. Even I get a laugh out of that one.

Robbie Fowler soon softens United's cough with goals either side of half-time to put us 2–1 up before the inevitable moment arrives: Jamie fouls Giggs and Cantona scores from the penalty spot to end the scoring at 2–2.

I needed that laugh courtesy of Razor that day following my first skirmish with the tabloid news press. At the time I was going out with a girl who'd split from her husband, but somehow the papers got wind of it and were camped outside my house in the cul-de-sac. They managed to get a photo of her leaving the house and rang to say they were going to publish it on the morning after the match, amid all the hype about United and Liverpool and Cantona's return.

I get the call on the day before the game when we're already booked into a hotel in Manchester. Do I want to comment for their story? No. This ain't going to please the girl or Roy Evans, and it certainly ain't going to please the Liverpool board if it appears around the game.

I need help and the only man I can think of is a friend called Dave Lockwood. He's my mate. He's sorted things for me before, nothing as serious as this mind, but I just can't get hold of him. I spend the morning of the game ringing him, but I can't get an answer. Hours later I get a call from a woman I don't know, Dave had had a brain haemorrhage the night before and is critical but okay. He was so bad at one stage that they gave him the last rites. And I thought I had problems. The story appears without any comment from me but with a photo of the girl leaving my house. And we all survive.

The October draw at Old Trafford heightens the belief in the Liverpool dressing room that we can compete with them for the Premiership, but November is a bad month and we don't win a game.

December includes the win over United at Anfield, and another Robbie wonder-goal, and we're back as contenders again. Problem is, we can't see off the smaller teams. We've no issue competing against United and Arsenal and their likes. It's the teams fighting for survival at the other end of the table that kill us.

April 1996 proves it. We beat Newcastle – the side managed by the great Kevin Keegan who were nine points clear at Christmas – 4–3 at Anfield in a game that's voted one of the best of the twentieth century. The game has a bit of everything, including two goals each from Robbie and Stan Collymore, and gives Man United a three-point lead at the top of the table.

We're in third, five points behind United but we're on a roll. Or so we think. Coventry, Babbsy's old club, are in the relegation places when we go to Highfield Road three days after the Newcastle match. We lose 1–0 to a Noel Whelan penalty. That really knocks the stuffing out of us. We take just nine points from the last five games of the season, as United leave Newcastle and ourselves in their wake.

It's a real let-down. I just can't get why we can beat the likes of United then lose to a side like Coventry. We seem to click in the really big games and play some incredible football, but then we switch off in others – and it's those lapses in concentration that cost us dearly. We went a goal down at Coventry after eighteen minutes and couldn't get back into the game. It was the same throughout the season. We conceded a goal seven minutes into the match at Sheffield Wednesday and had to wait until the eighty-second minute for an equaliser from Rushie. Teams come to Anfield and shut up shop, and we can't seem to break them down.

Consistency is the real issue for this Liverpool team, which is why the cup competitions still offer the best chance of success, when it's all about one-off games. We can turn it on for ninety minutes in a cup match and not have to follow it with another win three days later. That seems to suit this team.

We only get as far as the second round of the UEFA Cup – losing 1–0 to Brøndby of Denmark at Anfield – and the fourth round of the League Cup – again going out 0–1 at Anfield, this time to Newcastle – but the FA Cup is a different story altogether. We started in January with that 7–0 win over Rochdale, and my first goal for the club, in a game that saw Ian Rush set a new record for FA Cup goals scored.

Shrewsbury Town and Charlton fall next before we advance to the quarter-finals, and there's a 3–0 replay win against Leeds at Anfield.

Aston Villa are then overpowered 3–0 in the semi-final at Old Trafford. Robbie is man of the match. He has two goals in the bag before I pop up from wing-back with about five minutes to go and score with my left foot after a brilliant and typically mazy run from Macca.

We're off to Wembley for an FA Cup final date with Manchester United, the side in search of an historic second league and cup double. It's going to be something special.

The week before the United match, we play Manchester City in our final league game of the season, and they're in a bit of bother and facing relegation. We're not, mind; we can't win the league but we can finish third behind United and Newcastle, and at least guarantee UEFA Cup football again next season.

Oasis is playing Maine Road for a big outdoor gig before the match and I'm at the party backstage afterwards when Liam Gallagher jokingly offers me his Rolex to throw the game against City and ensure they stay in the Premier

League – at least I think it's a joke. We're talking football with the Gallaghers and how City could go down if we beat them and, next thing, Liam takes off this massive watch and offers it to me. His great plan doesn't work.

Because it's the last game before the cup final, there's no way we're going to get injured. Caution is the word, for us and for them. The City players are shitting it. You can tell from their warm-up, never mind the game. I put Rushie through for the first goal and we're 2–0 up before City burst into life. They get it back to 2–2 and then they go all cautious again, afraid of conceding a third. Steve Lomas gets a ball late on and goes into the corner with it – instead of looking for the winner that could keep them up.

We know they have to win the game with the way results are going elsewhere, but he clearly doesn't. The crowd starts to get on their backs but City can't score, and it finishes 2–2. They're relegated, and I can never look an Oasis CD in the eye again.

A week later it's the cup final and it's going to be special, even more so because it will mark Ian Rush's last game for the club. Roy's giving him a free at the end of the season and we want to send him out on the high he deserves, with a last FA Cup medal in his pocket.

We also want to teach United a lesson. They've a few kids coming through, the likes of Beckham, the Nevilles and Scholes, and they really fancy themselves as the next big thing in English football because they've won the league. We have our eye on that claim too with Jamie, Macca and Robbie in the ranks, so this is going to be a bit spicy.

Everything about this build-up is much more intense than it was at Bolton for the League Cup or the play-offs. There's a cup final song, which we record in Partridge Studios a few weeks before the game – but it's not very good, not a patch on 'Put 'Em Under Pressure', which was Ireland's song for the 1990 World Cup. The video is fun though, with me and Robbie clowning around in these black curly wigs and false moustaches like stereotypical Scousers. We have them on when we pull up alongside a taxi outside the studio – and the driver looks the spitting image of me with the wig and the 'tache. We're cracking up just looking at him.

David James is organising the cup final suits for us, something nice and smart and trendy. He's been doing some modelling and advertising work with Armani, and they're going to sort us as they see us as the perfect fit for their brand: young and handsome! We'll let Razor and Barnesy wear them as well.

We got measured up soon after the semi-final and don't give the suits a second thought until the lads from Armani arrive at Melwood for the fitting – the suits are white! More cream than white, claims David, but he expected them to be brown in the first place. The rep says they didn't have enough material in the brown – that's probably Razor's fault – so they had to make them in cream – or white, if you're standing where I'm standing. We'll get on with it. The colour of our suit isn't going to define our cup final and we have some nice shades to wear anyway to protect our eyes from the dazzle!

If we get a bit of attention from the press, so be it. It's a suit to wear to the match and onto the pitch. We won't be wearing it when we're beating United.

Roy and his backroom team opt out of the white suits. It's a bit too bright for them, he says, and they'd rather go out there in their tracksuits. Fair enough. They're not young and hip like we are. United have their own young players, they're dating models and singers as well, and Beckham's always in the papers, so they're bound to have a trendy suit themselves, meaning we'll hardly stick out.

We have other things to occupy us in the lead-in to the game. Roy announces the team when we get to the hotel in Hertfordshire on Thursday, and Razor Ruddock isn't in. Roy's going with Scales, Wright and Babb at the back. Razor is gutted and reacts by trashing his hotel room. We can hear it and we feel for him. The hype has been all about his rematch with Cantona, and now he's not playing.

It just adds to the tension. The morning of the game, there's a story going around amongst the lads in the breakfast room that Stan Collymore had real trouble sleeping and was down at reception at four in the morning, walking the floors. It's that sort of build-up.

The drive up Wembley Way is as special as ever though. We've plenty of tickets each for the game, so all my family and friends are here. I'm straining my neck out the window trying to see them.

The game itself, however, is something to forget.

We're no great shakes and United aren't much better. Jamie puts one half-chance over the bar but nothing really happens for either team, until five minutes from time when the ball goes out for a corner and David James only half-punches Beckham's cross to the edge of the box. Who's waiting there? Only bloody Cantona, and he hits it on the half-volley into the net, despite Rushie's best efforts to keep it out. We have six or so minutes to salvage the game but we barely get close to creating a chance.

It's all going to end in tears, and it does. The ref blows his whistle. I slump to the turf, take my boots off and cry my eyes out. There's around 90,000 people inside Wembley Stadium but, as I look up to the sky, I am the loneliest man in the world. Mark Wright and Roy Evans come over to hug me and console me, but it's no good.

I get up in time to congratulate the United players and collect my loser's medal but none of this means anything. It's such a devastating end to a season that promised so much but delivers nothing. Wembley is not a place to lose. It's a very lonely place.

At least I'm a Liverpool player now, and there will be dozens more big days like this to look forward to – and I do get to see Kate Moss in the players' lounge afterwards.

My date for the final is the TV presenter Donna Air, the girl who once famously asked the Irish family group The Corrs how they met, live on air. We finish soon after the final. Maybe she didn't take defeat well. Maybe she didn't like the white suits. Problem is, they are now infamous. Richard Tanner in the *Mirror* has branded us the Spice Boys on the back of the white suits and our friendship with the Spice Girls, particularly Sporty Spice who's become a good mate of mine.

The Spice Boys tag sticks. I've a feeling I'm going to be hearing that one for quite some time.

Chapter Fifteen

We're off the train from Dublin and settling into the Castletroy Park Hotel in Limerick for a week-long training camp. It's a down day, so we're continuing the session in the hotel bar. I'm first down from my room.

'Do you serve Guinness?' I ask the barman.

'This is Ireland, what do you think?' he replies with a big grin on his face.

It's hard for me to forget the Liverpool way when I travel with Ireland, and Jack's not best pleased, despite the fact that he was one of the first people to ring and congratulate me when the deal went through.

Right now he's calling me a 'fanny merchant' as he pins me to the wall in the Dublin Airport Hotel and lets me know exactly what he thinks of the Liverpool way just hours after a game at Lansdowne Road.

He's none too pleased that I passed the ball inside to Andy Townsend and John Sheridan when I should have hit it into the corner and chased it like he's had me doing for the past two years.

After the game he told me to come and see him back at the hotel, and that's never a good thing. Jack doesn't ask to see you like that unless you're in trouble, and the minute I go into his room I can smell the danger. The lads had warned me he wouldn't like me passing the ball inside like that.

I'm getting brave now though. So I tell them. I'm not backing down. I'm going to stand up for myself here. I'm a Liverpool player and this is how we play at Liverpool. I feel like I'm getting pulled from pillar to post. Ronnie Moran gives me a bollocking at Liverpool if I hit it long and Jack's giving me a bollocking with Ireland for hitting it short. It's all too much for my brain to take in.

It's not like I'm giving the ball to players who can't play. Andy and Shez are great players, they have great feet and they have an eye for a killer pass. Why can't I give it to them?

Jack's fuming. If I want to play that way I can stay in Liverpool next time he names a squad. This is Ireland and we play his way. If I don't like it, then basically I know where to go. He's only saying this to me because he rates me, because he wants me to be part of his system, but I have to play it his way.

It's time to back down, and quickly. He's bigger than me – and I owe him. Since we're going well in the European Championships – we've beaten the great Portugal in Dublin already – I'll take Jack's way. Next time I'll ignore Andy, hit it into the corner and chase it. Sorry, Jack.

The bizarre thing with Jack is that he never gets my name wrong, even when he's angry. The lads in the squad have been calling me Trigger for the past eighteen months or so, after the character in *Only Fools and Horses*. And the Liverpool players call me Dave from the same show, but only because they already have a Trigger in Rob Jones, who makes me look like a candidate for *Mastermind*.

Jack is constantly getting names wrong, but not with me. He's even shown us a video of a team and started talking about them when it was obvious to us that we were watching their under-21s and he's been scouting the wrong video! He's got a reputation for getting things wrong, and at times it seems to me that he likes to play on it. But he's never got my name wrong. I was Jason McAteer the first day we met at Bolton and I'm still Jason McAteer, even when he's bollocking me about trying to pass the ball like a Liverpool player.

There was talk of Jack leaving Ireland after the 1994 World Cup. Some even suggested that Irish football needed him to move on for the national team to progress. I'm not around long enough to know about the politics of the FAI and I've no interest in what the TV pundits are saying, I just want to play for Jack. So if I have to hoof it from here on in, then I will.

Truth is, Jack knows better than anyone else that it won't last forever. The best place he can bow out is the European Championship finals in his native England, the very land he helped to World Cup glory back in 1966. There's still money to be made for him, but the big earners are coming to an end and he has to make the most of it over this European Championship campaign.

The World Cup earned us top-seed status for the qualifiers, and we're in with Portugal, Northern Ireland,

Austria, Latvia and Liechtenstein, a mountain somewhere near the Alps, from the forty-six other countries in the draw.

The campaign opens with wins away to Latvia and at home to Liechtenstein before a tricky visit to Windsor Park, venue of our final World Cup qualifier in 1993, when Alan McLoughlin scored the goal that sent us to America.

It was nasty around Windsor Park that night, but by now the peace talks are in progress and the atmosphere is much more relaxed. Some of the lads still don't want to sit by the window as the bus takes us from the Nuremore to our hotel outside Belfast, but I'm not bothered. I soon discover Windsor is a very different place when you come here with an Irish team. I'm a Fenian bastard apparently when I warm up off the bench, which is quite amusing – I must find out what a Fenian bastard is.

Our talking is done on the pitch as early goals from Aldo and Roy Keane set us up for a comfortable 4–0 win to keep the pressure on Portugal at the top of the group.

By the time Northern Ireland come to Dublin the following March and do a number on us with an Iain Dowie goal in reply to a Quinny effort en route to a 1–1 draw, I've become a Liverpool player.

It's a big thrill when I sit in the Lansdowne Road dressing room reading the programme and seeing Liverpool against my name for the first time – but I don't want anything to change with Ireland. I love Big Paul and Packie, Aldo and Andy, Ray Houghton and Stan, have done since the day I got here.

The Portugal game is one of the special nights of my Irish career as we dump the likes of Figo, Rui Costa and

João Pinto on their arses, even if Aldo's goal was more of a Vítor Baía own goal.

By the time we go to Liechtenstein in June 1995, Jack and I have mended our relationship. A year after facing the aristocrats of Italy, we're up against the side of a mountain, as one hack put it, a classic collection of butchers, bakers and candlestick makers. We're red-hot favourites. Sure what can go wrong? Lots, as it happens.

In the first half we batter them and do everything bar score – I hit the crossbar. Jack tells us at half-time that there's no more he can do for us, we're on our own. He can't put the ball into the back of the net – neither can we, it seems. Or Liechtenstein. Their one and only shot comes to nothing when Alan Kelly shouts at the striker with a volume that can be heard all around the mountain. The striker's nerve melts like the snow and he hits it straight at Alan.

It's funny, but there's nothing else to laugh about. Jack goes ballistic as we head for home and a week-long training camp in Limerick before the match against Austria that will bring the curtain down on the 1994–95 season.

Moving base to Limerick for the week is a recipe for disaster from the word go. We're used to staying at the Dublin Airport Hotel and training at the nearby AUL Complex in Clonshaugh. The only distraction is the next Aer Lingus plane landing just as Jack is about to tell us something really important.

Limerick is new to all of us. Anything can happen with the FAI and we're used to that, but sending us to Limerick for a week? Come on.

We get the train down on the Sunday, the day after the Liechtenstein debacle. Jack has calmed down enough to let us have a drink or two. This sets the tone for the next four nights.

Somehow we make training the next morning, but we're a sorry sight. Then Jack calls a meeting on the Monday night. He's heading to Belfast to see Northern Ireland play Latvia, and he's leaving Maurice Setters in charge. That went well in Orlando, you might remember. John Charlton will be keeping an eye on us as well. We're allowed out for a couple of nights, but we're to be sensible about it. 'Don't take the piss.' As if we would!

Jack has given permission for one final blast of Limerick hospitality. It's party time on the Wednesday night, our final night out before the serious training begins for the Austria game. Babbsy is rooming with Paul McGrath, and I call in to get him ahead of our night out. Paul is lying on the bed, having been put under house arrest by Jack. There's a knock on the door and a kid from room service arrives with a load of bottles of Coke for Paul. Tony Hickey and Mick Byrne are straight in behind the waiter.

The conversation starts to get heated between Paul and Mick, something I haven't seen before from Mick. It's an eye-opener. I don't really have a relationship with Paul. I love him to bits as a player and have nothing but respect for him as a footballer. He's world class, at a level I will never reach, but this is sad. I thought he was the perfect footballer with the perfect life but it soon dawns on me that things are not quite right with Paul.

John's given us a midnight curfew, but that's only a challenge as far as we're concerned. We've found a new HQ at a place called Doc's, and anything goes – including our new game, which is to see who can get home the latest and break the curfew by the longest time.

It's well after two when Babbsy, Kells and me arrive back to the hotel. We know Mick Byrne is going to be waiting for us at reception, probably behind the big curtain that runs the whole length of the wall opposite the main desk.

Sure enough, we can see Mick's feet sticking out from under the curtain and nothing will do Gary but to run behind the curtains, grab Mick and lock him in a massive bear hug.

Mick's none too pleased but Jack goes ballistic when he gets back in time for training at the university grounds the following morning. There's still drink on a few of us, if I'm honest, and some of us are doing our best not to be sick. We can't do what Jack is asking, so he stops training, calls us into a circle and gives us a full-on bollocking. The night before is still alive, and one or two are trying very hard not to start giggling. It's not good, just three days before a big game back at Lansdowne Road.

Things are back to normal by Friday when Jack informs us that we'll be getting the coach up to Dublin on Saturday and stopping for a meal at the Harry Ramsden's fish restaurant that he has a stake in on the Naas Road just outside the city. It's the first outlet the English chain has opened in the Republic, and Jack, the best-known fisherman in Ireland, is the face of their business.

What better publicity stunt than to have his World Cup heroes stop at his restaurant on their way to a big European qualifier against Austria? We'll be stopping for an hour or so before moving on to Lansdowne Road for our normal pre-match training session. It's actually the second stop of the day for us, because first we meet some kids in a sports hall on a council estate. We're training at five, so Harry Ramsden's will actually be our pre-match meal.

There's media guys all over the shop when we arrive, but they only want to talk to Jack. We're left to our own devices when the waiter brings some water and the menus and tells us we can order anything we want. Me and Kells are only on the bench tomorrow, so we can afford to go a bit mad, or so we think, as we spot this thing on the menu called Harry's Challenge. Basically you get this massive piece of battered cod, about eight foot in length, 3 million chips and a huge portion of mushy peas, all washed down with tea, bread and butter. If you complete the challenge the meal is free, and that's a good enough challenge for us, even though the meal is already free, thanks to Jack!

We try to coax as many players as we can to accept the Gary and Jason Challenge to take on Harry's Challenge, even if something should be telling us that eating a big mound of fish and chips before a training session might not be the brightest idea in the world.

There's not a dissenting voice in the room. Not one of the players says stop. Nobody voiced a word of complaint when we were on the lash in Limerick and nobody's saying no now we're on the fish and chips in Dublin. Tuck in lads, and pass the salt and vinegar.

As it happens, Kells and me can't finish Harry's Challenge. We do pay for it though when we get on to that pitch at Lansdowne Road and the fish starts to roll around my stomach before I deposit a good-sized catch onto the side of the pitch. Not a pretty sight.

The Austria game is stomach-churning as well. We start well enough but it takes us sixty-five minutes to get the lead goal through Ray Houghton. Then the great Toni Polster equalises four minutes later and we collapse. The trip to Limerick and the fish and chips in Jack's restaurant were maybe taking their toll. A quarter of an hour after Ray's goal, Austria are 3–1 up as Polster and Ogris score. We fall apart.

The defeat is a big blow to our European hopes and the stories start to get out about the active social life in Limerick, and the fish and chips in Dublin the day before the game. The usual suspects, mostly those who had called for his head after the World Cup, start to ask questions of Jack. They doubt he has control over the squad and they suggest a conflict of interest over our visit to his fish-and-chip shop. We go off on our summer holidays with Portugal top of the group and Austria pushing us hard for second place.

When the qualifiers start again in late summer, Latvia and Northern Ireland help to get us out of the hole. Latvia score an eighty-eighth-minute winner in a 3–2 victory over Austria in Riga, and Michael Hughes grabs an equaliser for Northern Ireland in a 1–1 draw with Portugal at the Estádio da Luz in Lisbon.

We're set up nicely for the trip to Austria on 6 September when Jack hands Mark Kennedy his debut, but it's soon time to say goodnight Vienna as Paul McGrath scores in another 3–1 defeat. We seem to be the only ones the Austrians can put away. We beat Latvia 2–1 in Dublin the following month, and Portugal draw 1–1 with Austria at the Ernst Happel Stadium.

Then Michael O'Neill scores twice as Northern Ireland do us a favour with a 5–3 win over Austria at Windsor Park on the same night that our very depleted squad loses 3–0 to Portugal in Lisbon – a night it rains so heavily that there is a real chance the game will be abandoned.

That win is enough to send Portugal to England as group winners, and we have to make do with a newfangled play-off between the two teams with the worst records of all the runners-up across the groups. The idea is that the play-off game, to be held in England, will add to the interest of the competition and it certainly does just that when we are up against Holland, our World Cup nemesis, at Anfield two weeks before Christmas.

I'm buzzing for it. Having the match at Anfield is a huge bonus. I know every blade of grass on the pitch, every inch of the stadium. The game is made for me to do an Aldridge and an Alan McLoughlin on it and score the goal that gets us to another major tournament. It's just a pity nobody told Jack of my cunning plan.

There's huge hype about the game. There's thousands of Irish fans making the short hop to Merseyside by any means they can. Irish Ferries revive the Dublin–Liverpool route for one night only. The Dutch are bringing their Orange Order to the northwest of England. It's going to be a special night, and it is just that. The Kop is full of green, white and gold, bouncing to a soundtrack that features the Pete-St-John-penned 'Fields of Athenry' for the first time.

It may be my city and my ground, but it's not my night. Jack's left his happy face back in Newcastle as we prepare for the game near Chester. He's worried about Holland's new young striker, Patrick Kluivert. Jack knows the Dutch did a number on Ireland and his style of play in Orlando. His methods have been found out at this level and he doesn't like it.

The team he goes with is packed with defenders, but I'm not in it. He wants to curtail the Dutch, worry about their threat, instead of working on winning the game. Gary Kelly and Denis Irwin get picked at full-back, outside Paul and Babbsy. In front of them he goes for Jeff Kenna and Terry Phelan, two full-backs he is asking to play farther up the pitch to keep the Dutch hemmed in as he tries to protect our defence.

Andy Townsend captains the team with John Sheridan beside him. Aldo and Cas are up front. It's Jack's team for the Dutch, but it's the wrong team. Jeff has won the league with Blackburn and he's a great full-back, but he's not an attacking option. I'm the man to play wing-back for Ireland at Anfield, exactly the job I do for Liverpool and Roy Evans on the very same pitch week in, week out. Everyone feels Jack's gone with the wrong option.

I'm fuming, but who am I to tell him he's made a mistake? I'm not going to argue with him; he could throw his World Cup medal at me. I've learned my lesson.

As the game takes shape, it turns out I'm right. The only thing we win is the singsong up in the stands. My gut instinct is that we've gone too heavy with defenders. At one point we have about eight full-backs on the pitch, and Holland have too much threat up front. Jack's fears are founded when Kluivert scores in the thirtieth minute and then finishes us off with another in the eighty-ninth minute. We have nothing to offer going forward and not enough pace to stop Kluivert when he breaks. He's the real deal.

I do get on the pitch when Andy gets injured in the fifty-first minute, but our night is best summed up when Aldo is substituted in the seventy-second minute and Jack sends on Alan Kernaghan, another defender, with the score at 1–0.

It's all over with the final whistle and Jack knows it. He goes back out to say goodbye to the fans after the game – and they're still there, an hour after our European Championship hopes have bit the dust.

Jack doesn't mention retirement in the dressing room afterwards, and he tells the press he wants to carry on, but deep down he has to know the Ireland squad needs new players, new ideas and a new voice. It's over in that cruel manner that football specialises in.

He's been the greatest thing for Irish football, for Ireland and for me, but all good things must come to an end. The FAI call him over to Dublin a week later and on 21 December it all ends – amicably according to the reports.

Chapter Sixteen

We're on the Liverpool team bus with a long drive to London ahead of us. I've a credit card application form to fill in. Name? Jason McAteer. Employer? Liverpool Football Club. Position held in company? 'Babbsy, do I put down right-back or midfield here?'

The Trigger persona gets me into trouble in Liverpool one night, not long after I've signed from Bolton. The usual crew of Babbsy, John Scales, Jamie and me go out for a meal and then move on to some clubs – the Continental, or the Conti as Scousers call it, not far from the nightclub Cream.

We're well known and well looked after in Liverpool's clubs and, this night, we're upstairs in the VIP room and I'm giving it the full Trigger treatment as I tell one of my stories about something and nothing. There's this girl who keeps tapping me on the shoulder, so I tell her to give me a minute to finish my story. Next thing, she goes off on one and abuses me from a height. Who do I think I am? What the hell am I doing in the VIP area? It's all the usual guff Liverpool players get on such occasions, more often than not, and usually from jealous Everton fans! So I ask her to leave me alone, not that politely it has to be said, and she gets a bit upset and walks off.

I think no more of it until the Monday when I arrive for training at Melwood and Mark Kennedy – Sparky – asks me if I'd had an argument with some woman in a club on Saturday night.

I said I hadn't, we were out having a laugh and a joke as we do every Saturday night, but he tells me I've verbally abused some girl. Now, he knows I don't abuse girls but he says he's got a call from one of his mates to tell him that I've only gone and upset some gangster's missus. Sparky's mate, a lad into martial arts, has got wind of the story from the gangster's camp, and rang him to warn me that the bloke is none too pleased and is threatening to take action against me – more physical than legal, apparently.

The first thing I'm told to do is to ring the bloke, so I do – and Sparky's mate is right. The heavy isn't pleased with me at all. His girlfriend has told him I made a show of her, which I didn't, and he wants to see me. I'm panicking a bit now, so I tell him I'm too busy to meet up. I kind of dismiss him, but it's not the end of it.

A few weeks later I'm in a clothes shop in town run by a friend of mine when I meet up with another mate who owns a bar nearby. He knows the heavy simply because the heavy runs his door staff for him, and he says the bloke's *still* not best pleased. He wants to talk, so my mate rings up the heavy and puts him on the phone to me: I had no idea just how bad things were.

The bloke is threatening me. He says he knows my uncle Neil is a copper but he doesn't care. He wants ten grand in cash left in an envelope with my mate who owns the bar. I'm shitting it now. He starts telling me that the money is the only way to 'appease the situation', I'm saying, 'Yeah, okay, no problem', just to get him off my back.

I get off the phone, and my face is as white as a sheet. My mate the bar owner starts to apologise. He had no idea the heavy was this serious about it all and his only advice is to pay the money and not even think about the consequences if I don't.

My uncle Neil is the first person I ring when I get away from the shop and his response is simple – 'Don't give this bloke the steam off your piss.' He says he'll sort it and I trust him.

So the cops start stopping the heavy in his car, search him every chance they get, make life really difficult for him. It gets hot for him, but it all dies down for me. I reckon it's as good as over when I venture out in Liverpool again with Babbsy, about three weeks after the phone call demanding the cash.

Mind you, I've nothing to tell me it's all over. The bloke hasn't been on to say anything else, he's been too busy with all the police attention, though the cops haven't been able to arrest him or anything. I just relax on the basis that no news is good news. But then Stevie Mac invites Babbsy and myself on a night out in another club in the city, and we're on the way there when he rings to warn me that the heavy is out on the town and has told him that he's looking for me.

He's bowled into the club and he's given Stevie Mac a hard time about me, grilled him about where I am and what I'm doing, asking if I'm coming in. Stevie Mac's advice is to stay away, so I do – I don't go out in Liverpool for months and months and months.

Then one afternoon I'm with my mates in the clothes shop when four lads walk in behind me and lock the door. They ask my mate if the security cameras are working and he says they are. They tell him to switch them off, which he can't do. Then one of them comes over to me and says the heavy wants ten tickets for the European game with Celtic at Anfield. I tell him I can't get him ten tickets, so he goes over to my mate and starts shouting at him to turn the cameras off. Again my mate tells him it can't be done, and warns him that he won't be doing anything to me in his shop, if he wants to do something he'd better do it outside. They back off but hang around outside the shop for about an hour before my mate gets a car and smuggles me out a back door and down a side alley.

I know it's serious now. I ring my uncle again, and again he tells me he'll sort it – but I am still bricking it.

There's a lad in Liverpool called Tony Kelly who I used to play with at Bolton, and in the end he comes to the rescue. I used to drive Tony into training, and more times than not on a Monday morning I'd have to go and rescue him from a pub where he'd fallen asleep on the Sunday night. Tony is matey with a fella called John Smith, a big Everton fan as it goes, who, for some reason, takes a shine to me every time I meet him with Tony. Thankfully, I see Tony in town one afternoon and John Smith is with him.

He's obviously heard of my problem on the grapevine, and he asks me if I am still having bother with the heavy. I explain that it's getting heavier and heavier, that he's looking for cash and tickets and that the four blokes had followed me into a shop.

John tells me not to give him money on any account, not to talk to him and to leave it with him.

I take John at his word and start to live my life again, until one Saturday night when I'm out with Babbsy and we walk into a club and there he is, the heavy. Babbsy wants to know what I'm going to do, so I tell him we'll just play it calm and hope nothing happens.

Next thing I know, Babbsy is only going over to the bloke and I have to follow him. I'm kacking it when the heavy stands up and says he wants me to apologise to his missus next time I see her, so I just say, 'All right,' and that's the end of it.

We do meet again – on the night of the Liverpool players' Christmas party when we're all in fancy dress! Jamie and me have hired the biggest gangster suits we can find and we've stuffed them with clothes to make them even bigger. We're as fat as fools when we meet at Est Est Est for some food, and then walk across to the Moat House Hotel where we've a room booked for karaoke.

We have these massive suits on and these tiny little heads hanging out of them as we struggle to walk across the road when a car comes screaming up behind us and does a handbrake stop like something out of *The Sweeney*.

This bloke gets out of the car and it's only the heavy again. I'm a sitting duck. I can barely move in the fancy dress suit and I reckon all he has to do is touch me and I'm going to hop down the street and bounce across the tarmac. It'll be bong, bong, bong as I hit the ground.

Instead he just stands in front of me and says, 'You can apologise to my missus now.' The window of the jeep rolls down and the woman is there right in front of me. I'm shaking and I don't even recognise her, I wouldn't know her even now, but I say, 'I'm sorry if I offended you in the club. I'm really, really sorry for it all.'

She just goes, 'All right, nice costume,' and the bloke says, 'Be seeing you,' as he gets into the car and disappears into the night.

That's the last I ever see of him. I hear afterwards that John Smith warned him not to touch me or look for anything other than an apology from me.

The heavy ended up going a bit mental apparently. He was last seen walking down the motorway out of Liverpool on the wrong side of the road!

Another time, four lads did try to bundle Jamie into the back of a car as we came out of Cream, but we got him away just in time. We still don't know what that was about, and it was scary at the time – but not half as scary as meeting a gangster when you look like Mr Blobby in a pinstripe suit!

Chapter Seventeen

It's Sunday night and we're out as usual in the Albert Dock. We've our regular table in Est Est Est, a few floors below Jamie Redknapp's apartment. I order pizza.

'Four slices or eight?' asks the waiter when it arrives.

'Four,' says I. 'I'd never manage eight.'

The 1996 European Championship finals are in England, and my plan is to stay around for the summer and support Robbie, Macca and Jamie in their bid to win the tournament on home soil, thirty years after Bobby Moore lifted the World Cup at Wembley.

We've been out of the tournament since the Anfield play-off debacle against Holland, and Mick McCarthy's the new Ireland manager. I'm happy with that. I never played alongside Mick for Ireland, but I met him at the World Cup finals when he was in and around the camp in Florida, and he seems like a decent bloke.

Jamie Redknapp's brother Mark has invited me to stay with him in London for all the games and to tag along with his dad Harry and the rest of the family. So that's exactly what I do after Ireland's end-of-season tour to the States.

Because of the Redknapp connection, we end up as close to the England squad as you can possibly get without actually being a part of it. We're everywhere, outside the dressing room after the games, in the hotel, basically anywhere the players are.

Their boss Terry Venables is brilliant with me. One night outside the Wembley dressing room he walks by me with a big grin on his face, has a look at me and asks, 'How are you, Irish? You'd be playing for me now.' Then he just laughs. He's clearly brilliant with his players and I can see the atmosphere is great within the England camp, probably as close as they can get to what we had with Ireland and Jack at the 1994 World Cup.

My only issue with Terry is his persistence in using Teddy Sheringham up front as Alan Shearer's strike partner instead of Robbie. Shearer is on fire and untouchable, but I'd have Robbie in there beside him, not sitting on the bench waiting for the chance to make an impact.

For me, Robbie has everything you want in a great centre-forward. I can sling balls forward at Liverpool and he'll score when he has no right to. Like Rushie, he has this knack for being in the right place at the right time and he can pull something out of the bag when our backs are up against the wall. That's why Roy Evans is able to let Rushie leave Liverpool this summer. Robbie's a carbon copy.

Robbie doesn't get the recognition he deserves, and the way he's being treated by Terry with England is part of the problem. He should be the star of the show alongside Shearer and then the world would see him at his best in a side that has Macca in top gear and Gazza playing the best football he's managed since his knee injury.

It's all going swimmingly well for England until they meet the old enemy, Germany, in the semis. And it goes to penalties and more cannon fodder for the Pizza Hut marketing guys. Maybe Robbie would have scored in that penalty shootout with the Germans. Who knows? But I'd have played him in every game.

The one player who does catch the eye as far as Liverpool are concerned is the Czech Republic striker Patrick Berger. Roy buys him on the back of his Euro performances and straight away he's the great white hope as far as our title chances are concerned.

There's a lot of speculation around the place as well. The papers say Roy wants the Argentinean striker Batistuta, and he's even linked with Everton's Duncan Ferguson. There's talk of a bid for the big Leicester defender Matt Elliott as well, but that comes to nothing. In the end, Patrick Berger is the one big signing, along with a kid from Australia called Nick Rizzo none of us have ever heard of.

Roy still has this vision of building a young team to challenge Manchester United, but the reality is that he is still cleaning up things left behind by Graeme Souness. As a lifelong red, I didn't enjoy the Graeme Souness reign at Anfield. For me, there was too much change. The first thing he did was clear out Ronnie Whelan and Stevie McMahon and that destroyed the engine room of the team. He didn't stop there either, and by the time the board finally gave Roy the job, rebuilding the team and the club was almost an impossible task. But Roy is trying hard to get the winning mentality and the boot-room spirit back into Liverpool Football Club.

The feeling within the dressing room ahead of the 1996–97 season is that we have something positive to build on after a third-place finish in the league and the FA Cup final defeat to United. The only thing still holding us back is our lack of consistency.

The season starts well enough as we go eight games unbeaten, but the Spice Boys tag is still hanging around and a headline writer labels David James 'Calamity James' after a howler.

We are top of the league at Christmas, but it's a false dawn. A month later we start to slip down the places.

Our defence is still a problem and it's only when the goals dry up – we score just five times in seven games – that it comes to a head. Stan Collymore is acting up as well. When he first signed from Forest he decided not to move to Merseyside and used to drive up and down from Cannock, just north of Birmingham, every day for training. Ronnie Moran doesn't like the arrangement, but Stan is such a strong-willed character that Roy lets him away with it. But when he starts to turn up late for training and becomes increasingly more difficult, Roy drops him, but all that does is weaken the team at a time when we badly need his goals.

It's all starting to crumble. The beginning of the end for the season comes at the end of January in a fourth-round FA Cup tie at Chelsea, just days after we hammer them 5–1 at home in the league. Macca is on his game down at the Bridge, and we're 2–0 up at half-time when they throw Mark Hughes on. They murder our defence with Sparky throwing his weight around up front. He changes everything. We concede four goals in the second half and our cup run is over before January is done with us.

The Newcastle home game in the league is re-fixed for March. It should have been one of the first games of the season but was cancelled. When one of the secretaries rang me to say the match was off and I asked her if the pitch was waterlogged or something, she told me to switch on the television. Princess Diana had just died!

The talk ahead of the re-fixture is all about the 4–3 game a season earlier and the chances of a repeat. The odds against it are huge and stretch even further when we're 3–0 up. Newcastle are battlers, though, and they get it back to 3–3 late in the game. Roy is losing it with us on the sideline, when Robbie pops up with a last-gasp winner and another 4–3 scoreline is secured in our favour.

We've done them 4–3 on the spin at Anfield, but Roy lets rip in the dressing room afterwards. He knows we're up to our old tricks again and, sure enough, United come to our place in April and we lose 3–1. After the defeat to Coventry the league is gone for us and we're done – even though, technically, we finish joint runners-up with Arsenal and Newcastle, but we're seven points behind United. Goal difference has us down to fourth and it hurts. This is the Liverpool team that should have won the league. It was there for us and we blew it, all on our own.

It's worse than the previous season when we'd been chasing it. This time we were leading the way at Christmas and failed to sustain our momentum. It's been Liverpool's failing for years and it shows no sign of going away, no matter who the manager is.

Europe's no better, all promise and no delivery. We get all the way to the semi-finals of the Cup Winners' Cup, beating MyPa of Finland, Sion of Switzerland and Brann from Norway on the way. It's taken a long time to get to the semis, but when we play Paris Saint-Germain in April, our confidence is low. We've all but conceded the title to United, and Roy's plan going to France is to play our own game and try to win it. We could have gone for the draw but didn't, and we end up losing 3–0.

The semi-final second leg is one of the great floodlit European nights at Anfield, and goals from Robbie and Mark Wright get us within sniffing distance of extra time. Mark has a chance right at the death, but it goes over the bar and that's it, Europe and the season is over. It's all much ado about nothing, again.

My only real personal achievement for the season is in March – my first league goal for the club in a 2–1 win against Arsenal. Robbie is through on David Seaman when they clash, and the ref gives a penalty. Robbie tells the referee it's not a penalty, that Seaman got a hand to the ball and not to him, but the ref is sticking by his decision. Robbie hits the penalty and Seaman gets a hand to it, but I put away the rebound, even with a bloody big bandage on my head thanks to a challenge from Dean Saunders against Forest a week earlier when he caught me with his elbow and left me with a wound that needed fourteen stitches.

This season, the only bonus for Liverpool fans is the emergence of a young striker called Michael Owen. He played in the last two games of the season, scoring against Wimbledon, and he has the look of a player who's going to be around the first team for a long time to come.

Roy does splash the cash in the summer. Paul Ince arrives from Inter Milan in a £4.2 million deal and that causes a bit of a stir, not least because he's a former Manchester United player who loved rubbing Liverpool's nose in it when he could.

Incey is clearly out to lose the Man Utd baggage and he also wants to remind everyone in England that he's still a midfield enforcer. Even though time is catching up on him, Ince fancies himself as the new Graeme Souness, and Roy knows the fans believe we're too light in the middle of the park. He can add a bit of steel to the flair of Barnes, Redknapp and McManaman.

Karl-Heinz Riedle also arrives from Borussia Dortmund to bolster the attack and the Norwegian international Øyvind Leonhardsen, a lifelong Liverpool fan, comes in from Wimbeldon to strengthen the midfield.

Riedle is a timely addition because Stan Collymore is still causing a few problems. We're on a pre-season tour of Ireland, staying at my old Nuremore Hotel haunt ahead of a friendly against Dundalk, when Stan blows his top again. He's rooming with our reserve keeper Tony Warner and the story goes that he's told Tony to hang his suit up for him. Tony tells him to behave. Then they come down for dinner and there's no chair where Stan is supposed to sit. Again he tells Tony to give him his chair. Again Tony tells him to behave himself.

Next thing Stan goes to punch Tony. Big mistake. Tony turns into Mike Tyson. There's blood all over the hotel dining room. Joe Corrigan, our goalkeeping coach, jumps in. David James joins in. Roy Evans steps in to stop it and gets punched right on the nose. I can see Stan Collymore's Liverpool career ending here, right in front of me.

Stan has everything you need to be one of the best centre-forwards in the game and should have been. He's physical, he can run, he's good on the ground and in the air and he has an appetite for goal. Sadly, he also has an appetite for destruction, and the dining room chaos in the Nuremore proves it.

Roy needs a new room-mate for Tony when the dust settles, and I volunteer. He's clearly a hard man who will protect me, and we become great friends. He even stands up for me when they vote me Egg of the Year again for being the daftest player in the squad.

Pre-season isn't going very well for me. The 1997–98 league season is only around the corner and I'm very nervy. Rob Jones has been the regular right-back in the friendlies as we go back to a back four, and I'm in and out of the team, too much for my liking.

We open the league against Wimbledon and, sure enough, I'm left out. I'm a bad spectator, so it's a nightmare for me – and for Roy Evans. I want to be on the pitch, and I let him know. Regularly. I start falling out with Roy, almost on a daily basis.

He's an approachable fellow but sometimes will just tell you what you want to hear. Roy Evans doesn't do confrontation. He tells me I'm great and I'll be back in the team next week, then he leaves me on the bench again. I love him to bits but I know he's just trying to keep me happy.

Roy is Liverpool through and through. He's been here all his life and he deserves the chance to be manager after doing every other job connected with the team. His knowledge is second to none and he's a real legend of the club, but he finds it hard saying no or dropping players. He just doesn't like upsetting anyone and that's sometimes the last thing you need when you want to mount a title challenge, never mind trying to react when your chances of the Premier League are slipping away by the week.

I can't get a straight answer about my future from Roy, and I'm in and out of the team like a yo-yo. Rob Jones is his regular choice on the right, and when I finally do get into contention and back into the starting team, I only go and break my leg in a home game against Blackburn at the end of January.

We're attacking towards the Kop and I'm about to cross the ball when I change my mind in mid-action and put all the weight on my standing leg. It just snaps under the strain and the noise tells everyone around me that I've broken a bone, the tibia as it happens. The shock glosses over the pain. Robbie comes over to check on me. They're loading me onto a stretcher and I tell him I've broken my leg. He tells me I'll see him in the Conti later.

I do get a standing ovation from the Kop, but I don't make it to the Conti. I get to the hospital and the doctor tries to cut my boot off and I nearly kill him with the pain. The x-rays confirm the break and the club decide the best thing for me while I can't train is to send me on a holiday. The club offers me a holiday so I go to Barbados with two mates. We'll have a bit of that, thanks very much.

When we get back from the Caribbean I have to ask Roy if it's okay for me not to attend the games at Anfield. I just can't bear to watch them when I should be out there with them. Even checking the results on teletext is painful.

The only game I watch live on the TV – with David James' missus Tanya and her family – is the second leg of the League Cup semi-final against Middlesbrough. Tanya makes a great chicken-and-rice dinner but I'm nearly sick when we go two down inside the first four minutes to a Paul Merson penalty and a goal from Branca. We lose 2–0 on the night and 3–2 on aggregate, and another Wembley chance is gone.

A month before that, Dion Dublin and Coventry had already sent us packing in the third round of the FA Cup, 3–1 at Anfield, and while we'd knocked Celtic out of the UEFA Cup on the away-goals rule, we'd lost out to Strasbourg in the second round just before Christmas.

It's not a good season all round. Michael Owen scores eighteen league goals to cement his place in England's World Cup squad for France, but Robbie is out injured for a long spell and Arsenal are emerging as a real force under Arsène Wenger, Bruce's replacement at Highbury. Arsenal win the league by a point from United, and though we finish third, we're a staggering thirteen points behind the winners, and well off the pace. It's not good enough. Something is going to have to give.

At least Michael Owen gives us a reason to be cheerful in the summer. He's the star of England's World Cup bid in France and he adds to his value by the game and by the goal. We have a real gem on our hands in this lad. He could be the new Robbie Fowler – and we already have the old one, not that he's old or anything, like.

We're now into another summer of conjecture on Merseyside, fuelled by the rumours that the board want Ronnie Moran to retire. They seem hell-bent on destroying the boot-room culture that is Bill Shankly's legacy. Ronnie can be grumpy at times, but he's our grumpy Ronnie.

There's not a player in that dressing room who wouldn't die for him.

The board is also making noises about bringing someone in to 'help' Roy Evans as manager, whatever the hell that means. There's a story going around that John Toshack is going to come back to Anfield as director of football and operate over Roy's head. Kenny Dalglish has just been sacked at Newcastle and he's been linked with this director role as well.

The King might stick me in the reserves just to prove a point, but I'd welcome Kenny for two reasons. Firstly, he knows this club inside out and knows what we need to win things. And, secondly, he rated me highly enough to offer money for me when he was at Blackburn, so his opinion of me as a player can't be all bad.

The board does make its move eventually, but it's not Tosh or Kenny. It's a bolt from the blue when we discover that some French bloke called Gérard Houllier is going to be 'joint manager' alongside Roy. I've never heard of him. And he's never heard of me. He makes that perfectly clear on the pitch before a pre-season friendly at Crewe when he asks me if I've played any international football for England. I kid you not! Turns out he was the manager who failed to get France to the 1994 World Cup finals in America.

He clearly hasn't done his homework on the squad he's about to work with, which is a bit of a surprise, because those who do know of him inside the camp, few as they are, tell me he's a former schoolteacher who is renowned for his attention to detail.

He's a diehard Liverpool fan as well, apparently, who came to the city in 1970 as a trainee teacher in Alsop and saw the Reds hammer Dundalk in a European Cup match at Anfield. That's the night he fell in love with my club.

It looks like our board has been watching too much television. Arsenal won the league with a French manager and France won the World Cup. The French are all the rage in football, so they go and get us our very own Frenchman.

Houllier soon makes it clear that he's not a fan of flash footballers. This is the manager who lambasted David Ginola for putting in the cross that led to a breakaway goal as Bulgaria knocked France out of the USA '94 qualifiers. And he's never been fond of Eric Cantona. He certainly won't like the Spice Boys and our white – sorry, cream – suits.

After swapping teaching for coaching early on in his professional life, Houllier did enjoy some success with Lens and Paris Saint-Germain, so he must have something going for him. From the day we meet him for the first time, however, I'm pretty sure it's not a Liverpool something. I soon realise not to trust him.

He's supposed to be working with Roy as a joint manager, but he seems to be all about himself as far as I can work out. He's definitely not into the boot-room mentality, and he makes it clear from day one that he's going to change things.

We've always been an expansive side in my time here, playing to the strengths of Macca and Robbie and Michael Owen. That's Roy's way of playing football. Keep the ball, pass the ball, move and score. As long as we score more than the opposition, we'll be fine.

Houllier's approach is at the complete opposite end of the spectrum. The first training session with him is defensive from start to finish. He points out that we haven't won the title because we can't stop conceding goals. Fair point. He's going to get rid of that frailty at the back and he's going to turn us into real title contenders.

So we work and work and work on our defence. In that search for defensive strength, Houllier takes the glamour out of the Liverpool game. We were always at our best going forward under Roy Evans. But that is no more.

The transfer dealings that summer hint at what's to come. Razor Ruddock is farmed off to West Ham for a hundred grand. Michael Thomas is exported to Portugal and Benfica on a free transfer. Steve Staunton comes back to the club from Aston Villa, again on a free, but he's the only player we sign in England. Everyone else is a foreigner – Rigobert Song, Djimi Traoré, Vegard Heggem and a German striker with the wonderful name of Sean Dundee, who's supposed to qualify for Ireland as well.

The so-called Spice Boys are now under real threat, and I'm one of the chief targets, probably because I'm openly in the Roy camp. I'm left in the reserves at the start of the 1998–99 season and Houllier doesn't even bother to turn up to watch the games. I ask this new French coach he's brought with him, a guy called Patrice Bergues, why I should burst my guts in the reserves when Gérard can't even have the manners to come and watch me. If he can't be arsed, why should I be?

Bad and all as my relationship with Houllier is, poor Roy Evans doesn't stand a chance. This becomes clear to me in November when we go to Valencia for a UEFA Cup match. As far as I'm concerned, I'm in the team. The pointers in training have all been good and I know I'm going to play from the vibes around the dining table at the pre-match meal. When I get back to my room I get the call from Roy, 'Come and see me.' That's never a good call to get so near to us leaving for the stadium.

My heart is in my mouth when I knock on Roy's door. I know what he's going to say, that I've been dropped. What I don't expect is that Roy is ready to open up his heart to me about his problematic relationship with Gérard Houllier.

'Do you know things are bad between us?' he asks.

Of course I do, we all do. He looks and sounds like a broken man. He wants to play me but Houllier is having none of it. He's insisting I be dropped and that Patrick Berger starts in my place. Roy is apologising to me for dropping me, telling me that he no longer has the stomach for this constant battle with Houllier. He can't fight my case for me. He can't fight with Houllier anymore.

'I'm not going to do it, I can't do it, Jason,' he says.

It's fucking horrible. I'm upset that I'm not playing, but I'm more upset about what Houllier has done to Roy Evans, my manager, the man who brought me to this great football club.

Houllier was supposed to be there to tell me the news alongside Roy, that had been the deal. He left Roy to do the dirty work on his own. I'm so hurt for Roy, so worried about his behaviour. He looked like a man with no fight left.

The game doesn't help Roy's cause. We draw 2–2 with goals in the last nine minutes from Macca and Berger, of all people, getting us through on the away-goals rule. The French ref does us no favours all night as he sends off both Incey and Macca late on. We're fuming with him.

After the match Houllier takes the media conference and all the glory and leaves Roy back in the dressing room with the players. Then there's a massive row when Roy and Doug Livermore discover that Houllier wants some Liverpool shirts for the French ref. He wants us to give him the shirts off our backs! In the end, Houllier just tosses the shirts back at Roy and Dougie. Roy knows his number is up.

The following week, when we lose 2–1 to Derby in the Premier League and then 3–1 to Spurs in the League Cup, we all fear the worst for Roy. Sure enough, our day off is cancelled after the Spurs match and we are told to report to Melwood first thing.

When we get there we realise it's serious. There's no training gear laid out so something is up. Roy walks in with Dougie and Houllier, and he lets it all out. He's leaving, quitting the club altogether and taking a break from football.

Roy's in tears now. So am I. He'd first reported for duty at Liverpool Football Club thirty-five years earlier as a fifteen-year-old kid. He's been at the club man and boy and he's done every job there is, and now he's out the door.

Houllier stands motionless beside him, ice cold. There's no hint of remorse, no suggestion that he's had anything to do with breaking this great man, this great Liverpool man. No compassion and no feeling. He's in sole charge of LFC now. I'd say he's made up. He's won the battle and now he can prepare for war.

The tea and toast at the training ground in the morning is the first victim of the Houllier regime. He's changing the times we train at, how we train, what we wear for training

– everything. There's a science about everything now, he says, and there was me thinking science was all about blowing things up at school!

Training becomes a grind, and that's never been the Liverpool way, going back long before my time. I used to go to training with a smile on my face. I was the first one through the gates, the first one in for a chat with the girls in the canteen and a brew. I used to be the last one off the training ground, always looking for something else to do. Now I'm the last one in for training and the first one out of Melwood. Houllier has robbed the spirit from the club, he's taken the team element out of it for any of us who were there before him. He wants to control everything.

One Saturday we have a home game, and he insists on bringing us to a hotel near Wigan after the match so that he knows exactly what we are doing. He doesn't let us back to our families until the Sunday evening. Some of the lads have young families and they are livid at being kept behind for over twenty-four hours after a game. It's schoolteacher stuff all right.

He seems determined to break up Roy's team, ignoring the fact that he's breaking up the Liverpool way, the club's tradition, in the process.

The arguments are endless. Paul Ince stands up for the lads. David James is always arguing with Houllier and Phil Thompson, who is now on the staff. Robbie Fowler just isn't the same bloke anymore. With Roy gone, it's getting to the point where I don't want to be a part of it. I'm close to not wanting to play because of this manager, and it's breaking my heart. My time here is coming to an end. I know it – Gérard Houllier wants me to know it.

In November we've an Ireland game away to Yugoslavia for the 2000 Euros, and I can't wait for the temporary escape from my French hell. The trip is everything I want it to be, a glorious release from Houllier and the madness at Melwood.

We're at the airport, waiting for a bus that seems like it's never going to arrive, when I get chatting to Quinny about it all. He asks how I'm getting on with Houllier and he has to stand back as I let it all out. I start laughing, then I explain that it's hell with him in charge, how he has changed everything from the canteen at the training ground to making us stay in hotels on the night after a game, to not turning up to watch the reserves and the players trying to force their way back into the first team. I explain how he got rid of Roy, how it seemed like he wanted sole charge from the moment he arrived at the club. Quinny's in shock as I rabbit on, but little do I know that there's an English-based journalist, a Scot, listening to my every word and taking notes, delighted with his surprise scoop.

Next morning the story is all over the paper: 'My Houllier Hell By Jason McAteer'. Houllier goes bananas. The club ring me in Belgrade, asking if I've seen the English papers – in fucking Belgrade! There's a war going on near here. I'm thousands of miles from Liverpool, of course I haven't seen the fucking papers!

I get back from the Ireland game, which we lose 1–0, to find Phil Thompson waiting for me with a summons to a meeting. Houllier's new assistant has been putting his foot down from the day he arrived, the day Roy and Doug Livermore left. He's always made it clear in the media, which he loves by the way, that he's anti-Spice Boys and of the opinion that such behaviour is not the Liverpool way.

David James and a few others don't click with Thommo, and Robbie had enough of him in the reserves not to want anything to do with him in the first-team squad. He's Houllier's man, though, and he's happy to call this meeting between the manager and the players before training.

To begin with Houllier starts rabbiting on about something or other in front of all the players when all of a sudden he pulls my article out of his pocket, shows it to everyone then asks me to explain it. I explain how I was stitched up by a journalist listening in over my shoulder at a bus stop. I've not done any article with any newspaper, they've printed their version of a private conversation they've overheard. The manager orders me to sue the newspaper. I will so.

Thommo, to be fair to him, stands up for me and says he doesn't think I would deliberately do something like this. I repeat that I haven't, that I said some things to the lads and I've been overheard. I've not slated anyone publicly. Houllier doesn't seem so convinced with my explanation. He makes it clear that I've crossed a line with him. I just know leaving that room that my days at Liverpool are numbered. Houllier is not going anywhere fast, but chances are I am.

It seems like my life is falling apart. Rob Jones is out injured again but Vegard Heggem is Houllier's first-choice replacement at right-back – I'm on the bench. I can't get near the team. My private life is taking a battering as well when my partner suffers a miscarriage and the world is collapsing around me.

When I signed a new four-year deal with Roy in 1996 I really believed I'd be here for life. I thought I'd end my playing days in the red shirt. Now I've fallen out with the manager and I have an international career to think of.

Hiding my emotions has never been my strong point. It's pretty obvious to all around me that I'm unhappy, and word soon gets out. There's speculation in the press that Spurs and Newcastle could rescue me from my 'Houllier Hell'. I come home one night to find a message on the machine from Ruud Gullit, the Newcastle manager, saying that Liverpool are looking for a lot of money but he is prepared to think about it and could probably match their demands. Spurs have a little sniff as well, but I don't really fancy moving to London and I'm not going to move to a club where I'm not guaranteed first-team football.

I'm not the only Liverpool player on edge. Macca's contract is up in the summer when he'll be available on a free transfer and there's plenty of interest from the continent, Spain mostly. Robbie's not a happy camper either, so there are lots of scouts and agents and rumours hanging around the place.

I've a new agent at this stage and he's keen to do a deal, not surprisingly. I wanted to change last year when Liverpool put that new deal on the table, so I let Ian Rioch go and asked Jamie Redknapp for advice. His dad put me in touch with one of these 'super' agents, a guy by the name of Pini Zahavi who landed on my doorstep and told me he'd sort it all out for me. He did, but for a hefty six-figure fee. I walked myself right into that one.

Pini's telling me to move on. He says he can make me a

good few bob with a move – and he won't do badly out of it either.

It's little or no surprise then when Houllier pulls me before training one morning and tells me that the new Blackburn manager Brian Kidd has made a four million pound bid for me. Houllier drives me himself from Melwood to training at the academy in Kirkby that morning to discuss the bid. He talks it through with me and tells me, I kid you not, that he doesn't want me to go. I think that's what they call irony. I don't want to leave the club either. I make that absolutely clear to him. But I also make him well aware that I am not prepared to just stay at Liverpool and pick up my money while sitting on the bench. I will not cheat the club or the supporters. I want to play for Liverpool. I want to be part of the team, his team. He understands that, but he can't make me any promises. He wants me to turn the move down on the one hand but he doesn't beg me to stay on the other. Not that I'm surprised.

Pini arranges for us to go and meet Brian Kidd at the Blackburn training ground. I've only ever known of Brian as Alex Ferguson's coach at Manchester United. This is his first job as a manager in his own right and he's keen to rebuild the Blackburn team that won the league under my old mate Kenny Dalglish.

I'm really taken with Brian. He is brilliant with me when we sit down and talk the move through. My mate Dave Lockwood comes with me – he's still recovering from his brain haemorrhage – and Brian really sells the club and his ideas to Dave, Pini and myself. It's an easy sell, mind.

I'm desperate to get away from Gérard Houllier so I'm an easy date prepared to take the first decent offer that comes along.

Blackburn make the offer. I won't have to move house either, which makes it easier. The deal is done within minutes of talking to Brian. And a part of me dies.

For the first time in my life I am treating football as just a job, a means to an end, a way to make money. The romance of my move to Bolton, the magic of my transfer to Liverpool, it's all forgotten. This is cold and clinical. This is just business. I'm a commodity and I'm going to sell myself to the highest bidder. I've no lifelong love for Blackburn like I have for Liverpool. There's no gratitude for giving me the break I dreamed of like there was with Bolton. I want a move and they want a player.

I like the feeling of being wanted but I'm using Blackburn. Just over four years ago my idol Kenny Dalglish failed to sell the club to me. Now I'm using Blackburn to get at Houllier, to get away from Houllier. They're a team in post-title decline with a coach trying his hand at being a manager for the first time, but I don't care.

Nobody in the room tells me to stop. I'm on my own now. There's an agent trying to make money from the deal. There's a manager who wants to buy me. And there's a mate. None of them are going to tell me what I really need to hear. None of them will tell me to shut the fuck up, get back in the car, drive back to Liverpool Football Club and pretend none of this ever happened.

I'm taking the easy option because it's the only option I can see right now. My heart wants me to stay with Liverpool, but my head is telling me to sign the piece of paper, do the medical and get it all over with. It's all happening too quickly and emotions are very raw.

That's what I do.

The deal is completed and the club call a press conference at Ewood Park to announce the transfer. First question in and someone asks me why I'm leaving Liverpool. I just look the guy in the eye and I break down in tears. I can't answer him. I don't want to answer him. I want someone to burst through the doors in the media suite and object to this marriage. Nobody does.

I'm making the biggest mistake of my life and I'm stuck with it now.

I could see Heggem off at Anfield. I could prove Houllier wrong and see him off the premises as well, but I don't. Instead I run away and take a pay cut on the twenty-five grand a week I'm on at Liverpool, down to eighteen grand a week at Blackburn on a four-year deal. I'm hiding from reality and burying my head in a blue-and-white quadrant shirt.

Ruud Gullit rings me again when I get home, but it's too late. The deed is done. Next morning, I go back to Melwood to collect my boots. Jamie hugs me and I burst into tears again. The tea ladies send me on my way and I cry all the way home.

I know that once you leave Liverpool Football Club, you leave for good. It never leaves your heart. It really is the best club in the world, but LFC never takes you back.

Chapter Eighteen

Hotel golf is big on the Ireland trips. We always pack a couple of eight irons and putters in Joe Walsh's skips. It's not enough for Babbsy and Mark Kennedy, however, on the double-header trip to Iceland and Lithuania. They see some lovely new Callaway Big Bertha drivers and woods in duty free at Reykjavik airport, and buy them just minutes before they get on the plane. The air stewardess ain't happy.

The clubs come out in the hotel in Lithuania. The lads forgot to buy balls to go with their new clubs, so we roll up paper. We set a bin up in the corridor as the hole and take turns at trying to chip in from twenty yards. We all fail miserably, and the physio Mick Byrne, a member at Hollystown, tells us he'll show us how it's done. Mick takes a massive swing, connects with the paper ball and takes a divot – out of the carpet. We fall around laughing and Mick panics. When we get up the next morning there's a big pot plant hiding his divot.

Mick McCarthy is the new man and the new start for Ireland, and for me that is a worry simply because I don't know where I stand with him. I never played with Mick and I've only ever met him when he's been around the hotel as Jack's guest for some of the games.

I do know he had a blazing row with Roy on a trip to Boston, just before my time. Every Irish player knows about it. Roy had gone for a drink with some of the players at Frank Gillespie's Blackthorn bar, and they held up the team bus for the drive back to the airport and the flight home. They were so late, Mick Byrne had to pack their bags for them and Mick, as captain, wasn't having it. Being the stubborn Yorkshireman that he is, he let Roy know what he thought of him keeping the rest of the players waiting. Being the stubborn Corkman that *he* is, Roy let Mick have it straight back with both barrels: 'I didn't ask you to wait.' How are they going to get on as Irish manager and captain, if Mick appoints Roy captain? It is going to be interesting.

I don't know how Mick is going to act as manager. I don't think he'll be the fatherly type like Jack, so I'm a little bit nervous about his appointment. At least Kenny Dalglish didn't get the job. Joe Kinnear seemed to be the only other viable candidate, but Joe thinks he's a viable candidate every time the Ireland job comes up.

What I do know about Mick is that he's an Irish legend, both as a player and a leader. He's a big character with a big voice in the dressing room and everything about him suggests power and strength.

The man who knows him best in my circle is Sparky. He worked with Mick at Millwall and actually babysat Mick's kids, which is an unusual one for an international footballer and his new gaffer. Sparky loves Mick. He can't speak highly enough of him and says he's always been like a father figure to him, which is music to my ears.

The one thing I do like about Mick's appointment is the fact that he knows what makes Ireland special. We are Ragarse Rovers and that's the way we like it. We live together, we drink together, we go down fighting together. We have a bond as a squad, and we have a bond with the fans that a foreign manager would want to scrap straightaway. I don't want the new man getting rid of Mick Byrne or Tony Hickey. I don't want an end to Gibney's on a Sunday night or the pictures on a Monday before the game. That's us. That's Ireland. And it works. Mick McCarthy knows that well from his own days as a player when he led us to the World Cup quarter-finals in Italia '90. He was there for the win against England at the European finals in 1988. He won't change it. He can't change it.

Wrong. The first thing Mick does is introduce curfews, and he sticks to them. He knows all the old tricks. He knows how we get out the windows at the airport hotel, how we send one man in to distract the manager while the rest of us get back into the hotel through the side door. We can't pull the wool over Mick's eyes, and he makes that clear from day one. The food changes, the cinema changes, even the training changes on the first day Ian Evans takes charge at the AUL. You can see Mick wants to stamp his authority on the team and I can't blame him for that.

The media never questioned Jack, but they're getting brave now the big man's gone and they're throwing their weight around. There's more of an English-type mentality creeping into the Irish press, and they want to assert themselves with the new manager.

They start by accusing Mick of being nothing more than a Jack clone. Bad mistake, that. Mick is always going to be his own man and that doesn't change whether he's dealing with us as players or the media, Irish or English. He's going to change the culture and he's going to change the squad.

Jack only did that when it was forced on him – if it wasn't for injuries, the likes of myself, Babbsy and Gary Kelly would never have got near the 1994 World Cup. Mick is different. Straightaway, Shay Given, a young lad from Donegal who left Celtic for Blackburn without playing a competitive game, is in the squad as the heir apparent to Packie. Gary Breen, David Connolly, Kevin Kilbane, Damien Duff and a young fellow from Tallaght with skinny legs called Robbie Keane start to appear around the place.

Brian Kerr's teams are starting to make real progress at underage level and there is talent coming through at last, some of it world class. For the first time since I started playing for Ireland there's pressure on the establishment. Mick wants the likes of Ray and Aldo and Cas around for their experience, but they know they are definitely on borrowed time.

The Roy Keane undercurrent is there all the time as well. I wasn't in America that time and I didn't witness the row, but we all know the tension is lurking in the background and is going to explode sometime in the future. It's bound to with all these new rules and curfews, and Mick's demand that we treat the international team with the same respect and professionalism that we treat our day jobs. Roy likes a pint when he's away with Ireland and Mick's changes are not going to sit well with him. He's not a mixer – he was never in line to be the fourth amigo – but when we'd end up back in the airport hotel after a night out, sitting by the hatch bar in the corner, Roy would be there in the middle of it, enjoying the craic with his own mates and his brothers and giving as good as he gets.

He never wanted to be our mate, though, and we didn't care, to be honest. He's his own man, but he's Roy, and we can't deny he's a great player, for all his peculiarities.

Part of his problem with us is down to the Man Utd–Liverpool rivalry, part of it is down to his row with Babbsy in a Manchester restaurant when we ran into some United players on a night out and he said something to John Scales and Babbsy. Phil said something back and next thing, they're squaring up to each other and ready to exchange blows until someone stepped in to break them up. I know Roy boxed as a kid, but my money was on Babbsy that night.

Another night, I arrive late into the hotel at Dublin airport after a club game on a Sunday and the lads are in a private room out the back of the restaurant for their food. I literally arrive as they're finishing up, so I throw my bag into the bedroom and rush back to the dining area. As you do, I go around all the staff and all the players, shake their hands, hug some of them and say, 'All right, mate.' I get to Roy and he's not exactly friendly. Did I get him at a bad time? Did I hell. He's just so inconsistent with his attitudes. Next thing, he could be my best mate in the world. You just never know which Roy Keane is going to turn up.

Mick didn't see a lot of either Roy Keane at the start. The best word to describe their relationship in the early days of Mick's reign is 'accommodating' – Mick accommodates

Roy, and Roy, as far as I could see, is quite happy to take advantage. It's not that he's abusing it, but he is taking advantage of Mick's generosity and hospitality.

Mick lets him go home to Cork when we're over for games and then travel back up to Dublin the day before the match. Roy is treated differently, there's no doubt about that, but we're not bothered. There are twenty-three of us to get on with it, and we'll put up with him so long as he delivers on the pitch. We don't miss him anywhere other than the pitch. He's not this larger-than-life character cracking great jokes. He's not hilarious. He's not a good laugh. He's not even a giggle. He doesn't add anything to the group away from the pitch, so we won't miss him if he doesn't want to be part of the group. We're away from home and we're cooped up in a hotel, but we don't need Roy Keane the personality to make life bearable, we only need Roy Keane the footballer to make us a better team. The rest of him and all his baggage we can live without until the night before the game.

That's when the real Roy Keane arrives back into the Irish camp. The match switch goes on in his head and a different character emerges from the darkness. That's when he is worth his weight in gold, when he switches back to being the Irish captain and the Irish team leader. That's when he *is* bothered, when he makes a connection and gets everyone worked up and ready for the game. That's when he's at work and when he's happiest. His head is in the game, and your head had better be with him.

The one mantra he preaches is total concentration and total commitment, and he won't tolerate anything less. That's when the genius springs into life, in the hotel the night before the match, when we go for the traditional lunchtime walk, on the bus, or in the dressing room. He is inspirational and leading from the front even before a ball has been kicked.

When we finish the game he goes straight back to being the Roy Keane who doesn't want to know the rest of us. And good luck to him. As long as he delivers as Roy Keane the footballer, we couldn't give a toss if we never see him from one match to the next.

He's a man of few words when he gets inside the Ireland dressing room, he's certainly not a shouter – but when he talks, you listen, when he says something, you pay attention. You can't afford not to, on or off the pitch. Give the ball away and he will give you a bollocking. I'm speaking from experience, trust me. When you take his criticism on board, you know he is talking sense, you know he demands respect on that pitch. Game over and he'll shake hands. He'll even accept the McAteer hug, but only because he's still in match mode, he's still the ultimate professional. Back in the dressing room and the other Roy Keane takes over again. *Blankety Blank* time, no emotion and no connection.

I don't know Roy Keane. Never will. I've met his missus a couple of times at games and she seems a nice woman, but I can't tell you how many kids he has or what their names are. He doesn't want me to know. Fair enough. I've never been invited around to his house and I don't want to be, I don't even know where it is. He's not my type of person, but he is my type of footballer and that's why he is irreplaceable for Ireland.

Turns out Mick McCarthy is great for me, and I love him

to bits. He's more like an uncle than a father figure, and even when things are going bad for me with Houllier at Liverpool he's there to help me through it.

We do have our moments, though, particularly around the time of one of the qualifiers for the 1998 World Cup finals in France, when he left me out of the team and I threw a strop. I was having a 'mare at Anfield at the time, and Mick clearly didn't fancy me for the match, but I knew that no matter what was going on at club level, I always came good for Ireland. Always.

If I'm honest, I knew in my heart and soul I wasn't going to play when I came over for the game, but you know me, I'm a sulker, and my head goes the night Mick picks the team and I'm not in it. I just go straight back to the room, order room service and swim in self-pity. That lasts all of five minutes until Mick bursts through the door and tells me to sort myself out. We have this big chat and I start letting it all out. Nothing is going right at home, nothing is going right with Liverpool and now he's dropping me from Ireland. He explains that leaving me out for Ireland has nothing to do with Liverpool or what is happening at home. He has a good tactical reason, and he explains it to me. That's the day he changes in my eyes. I could see him now for what he is – a bloody great man-manager, even when he drags me back up to the restaurant to eat with the lads. But that's Mick. I love him to bits and maybe there is a bit of that father figure thing there as well. I like parental-style influences in my life, and Mick is like that for me with Ireland.

One thing about Mick is his lack of sentiment. I know he has a reputation as a hard-man defender, but he's even harder as a manager. If something needs to be done, he will do it, and he makes that clear the minute he gets the Ireland job.

Having played with some of the squad still there from Jack's time probably didn't help him, but he didn't look for the easy option, he didn't leave it up to the players to retire for him. If you were good enough, you were young enough – if you weren't good enough, it didn't matter what age you were, young or old.

The Euro '96 play-off defeat to Holland hurt us as a team and cost Jack his job, so Mick knows it is time to start again and he's not shy about bringing kids into the squad. That means more responsibility on the Three Amigos to act our age – God help us – but some of these kids don't need much in the way of leadership. Like all kids, the good ones don't lack for confidence, and as far as Robbie Keane is concerned, they don't lack for cockiness either.

Duffer's a different kettle of fish altogether. He's so quiet, there are times when you want to shake him just to make sure he's alive, and he seems to spend way too much time in his room. We start to wonder if he's painting the walls black or something, he spends so much time up there on his own. Great kid, but dead quiet. That's not a claim to throw in Robbie's direction. He's just a cheeky kid from Tallaght and makes that clear the minute he comes into the squad and starts giving guff to everyone, young and old. A few times I have to tell Robbie to shut up and treat people with respect. I have to hammer him on a tour to America when he's really taking the piss out of me in front of the lads, but that's just his way of immersing himself into the group. He has to be big and brash and bold and heard.

Jamie Carragher's exactly the same at Liverpool. We were on a hospital visit once on Merseyside and I have this grey jacket on, so Jamie goes right down the back of the jacket with the marker pen he's using to sign autographs. I'm furious, so I make him give me the money for the jacket – and I never bought another one. I think he paid for a good night but he deserved to.

I was always seen as a bit of a messer in the Irish camp, but I never gave anyone cheek, not like these new kids – or maybe I'm getting old!

My first time on the training ground with Ireland, all I was short of doing was asking for autographs – and that was just from Jack. Keith O'Neill comes into the squad for the first time and goes right through Shay Given in his first training session. Mick goes ballistic with him and the lads soon put him back in his box. That's the thing with Ireland. Keith is probably the biggest 'big-time Charlie' I've seen in the group, the sort who thinks he's something, but you won't get away with that in this squad. There's always someone there to knock you down a peg and bring you back to normality.

Keith's a bit mad. He wore clear glasses once because he thought they made him look cool – and he's never shirked a dare. We were on a beach run in Portmarnock one day when he challenged Mick McCarthy to a race. Mick beat him. Keith had tracksuit bottoms on and halfway through they were sopping wet and covered in sand, so he just took them off and ran the rest of the race in his underpants. Mick still beat him.

Roy stood up to Keith another day in the dressing room. Players have different habits in the changing room before a game. Stevie Mac at Liverpool is a sitter. Five minutes before the bell, he'll still be sitting on the bench, reading the match programme, calm as can be. I'm a walker. I walk around the room and can't sit still. Roy is quiet and collected and when he has something to say, he will say it with authority. Keith's the complete opposite. He's more Keith Moon in the dressing room, a complete lunatic. He's lively, he's aggressive, he's banging things, he's shouting at everyone. As soon as the bell goes, he's round the room, shouting in your face; as far as he's concerned, he's getting you up for the match. One night he grabs Roy by the cheeks – he puts the palms of his hands on Roy Keane's face – and screams, 'Come onnnnnnnnnnnnnnnn.' Roy stands up and the whole dressing room freezes. He's going to crack him. It's one of those 'fucking hell' moments. Roy just shakes his head at Keith and gives him one of those looks. That's all he has to do to turn the lunatic into a wall of silence in an instant.

The 1998 World Cup qualifiers are a bit of hit and miss for us – hit being the appropriate word in my case when it comes to the match away in Macedonia in April 1997. That match *should* be remembered for the bright-orange shirt we're wearing, an Umbro creation that certainly made us stand out, but it *will* be remembered for my kung-fu kick and the red card that follows, the only red card of my international career.

My first problem comes when a ball is flicked into our box when we're 1–0 up through Alan McLoughlin, and it comes off the head of their centre-forward and our centre-back. It falls behind them and hits me on the arm. Penalty. Disgraceful decision. They score – the first of two penalties they get before half-time. Then Hristov hits a screamer into the top corner on the hour mark. David Kelly pulls one back with twenty minutes to go so we're 3–2 down and fighting for our lives.

The game is in added time when I can see David Kelly in space in front of me. If I give the ball a little flick, he's through. I jump as high as I can. There's a bloke coming into my vision, but this is my ball. Up I go, like a gazelle. I put my leg straight out for protection as I go for the ball. The bloke never jumps. He just stands there because he knows he's not going to win the ball. My foot is straight out now and heading for his throat – and I karate kick him in the chest. I get the ball to David, but the ref stops play.

The guy is lying flat out on the ground and the locals are none too pleased. It looks bad. A Macedonian player comes straight for me and Roy runs at him. Fair play to him. He's always the first man to defend his team-mates on the pitch, no matter what he thinks of you off it. He's roaring at the bloke and there's all hell breaking out around us. The Macedonian player is in my face now. He stands on my feet so I knee him in the bollocks. He's right in my face and I tell him to fuck off. The ref has no choice and the red card is the next thing in front of me. It all goes mental as I'm led off the pitch by Tony Hickey, the team security. We get to the dressing room and I'm so angry I kick the door to get in. It's locked and it's plywood. The caretaker comes around the corner to find a massive hole in his door and my foot stuck in the middle of it. It's all jagged and I can't get my boot out. Tony pulls me away and I get into the dressing room and throw my boots around the place. I'm sitting there with my head in my hands when the lads come in. We've lost 3–2. I'm gutted. Mick's not happy with me, but there's nothing he can say to me that I haven't already said to myself.

A few weeks later I get the bill from FIFA for the door and I've no choice but to pay it.

I only play three more games in the qualifiers for the 1998 World Cup, thanks to the suspension I got after the Macedonia game and injury. We go to Iceland the day of Princess Diana's funeral and win 4–2. The team decide to wear black armbands for the day because we all earn our living in England, but some of the lads 'lose' them in the tunnel before the match. David Connolly gives us the lead, but we're 2–1 down in the forty-seventh minute. Kevin Kilbane is thrown in at the deep end and struggles a bit before he's replaced by Denis Irwin, but he will come good. Roy drags us back into it with two goals in ten minutes and Sparky puts the icing on the cake with his first Ireland goal eleven minutes from time.

I get on in the second half and keep my place for the match against Lithuania in Vilnius on the Wednesday night, when two Tony Cascarino goals get us a 2–1 win.

The final qualifier sees Cas on the scoresheet again as we draw 1–1 at home to Romania. Hagi opens the scoring for a side that finishes ten points ahead of us as Group 8 winners and automatic qualification for France. We end up second, a point ahead of Lithuania, and we're into the play-offs again, this time against Belgium. I miss both games with injury. Denis Irwin scores in a 1–1 draw at Lansdowne, but the away goal from Luc Nilis proves crucial as we go down 2–1 in the second leg, and 3–2 on aggregate. Four years after America, our World Cup dream is over before Christmas arrives.

The qualifiers for Euro 2000 aren't too good for me or Ireland either. Thanks to injury, I only play in three of the games, home to Croatia and Malta, which we win 2–0 and 5–0 respectively, and away to Yugoslavia when we lose 1–0 in a warzone. Literally. Aer Lingus doesn't want to fly us there because of the fighting, but we just get on with it as we always do. The big thing for me that night is the penalty that never was. The referee bottles it and I can understand why because the atmosphere is as volatile as we've come across. They're throwing fruit at us, paper darts, anything they can get their hands on. I'm through on the keeper, he comes out and I nudge the ball past him. He's sliding down and his momentum pulls me down. Stonewall peno. I look around waiting for the referee to point to the spot and the only thing he's pointing to is the six-yard box for a goal kick. Unbelievable.

It's my last competitive game for Ireland for eighteen months. From the beginning of 1999 to June 2000 I manage just three friendlies, against Paraguay (2–0), Sweden (2–0) and Scotland (1–2).

The lads battle their way through to finish second to Yugoslavia in the Euro 2000 Group 8 table, dumping second seed Croatia out along the way, and get drawn to play Turkey in the play-offs.

The home leg in November 1999 is a tetchy affair. I'm on the bench but don't get on, not helped by the fact that Mick has to replace the injured Alan Kelly with Dean Kiely on the hour mark. Robbie eventually gives us the lead in the seventy-ninth minute, but it's short-lived and the Turks equalise four minutes later through a penalty, and the game finishes 1–1. We're not out of it, but the Turks are up to their usual tricks and bring us to the far-flung city of Bursa for the return leg. I'm not even fit enough for the bench for this one, and it all goes pear-shaped. The city is a shithole and we can only get there via a flight and a ferry. It's as out of the way and as inhospitable as they can make it.

The Turks know what they're at. Thanks to the goal in Dublin, they can shut up shop and make life as difficult as they can for us. Again, injuries don't help when Stephen Carr is forced off after just six minutes and replaced by Jeff Kenna. Roy is brilliant in the midfield, but the Turks are cynical and just as calculated. By the time Mick throws Big Cas on for Jeff with ten minutes to go, we are running out of options and going out of the tournament. There's ructions when the game ends scoreless and they go through. Roy is targeted by riot cops as the players leave the field. Cas gets pushed and shoved in the mêlée that follows and ends up with a red card and a UEFA ban that's still in place simply because he retired after the game. Yet again, UEFA does nothing about it, and the Turks get away with loads.

The play-offs have done us again, and it's time we did something about it.

Chapter Nineteen

I've come back from a shopping trip to London with Babbsy, who knows all the trendiest shops. I've this amazing leather jacket on and my mother wants to know how much it cost. I can't tell her the truth, so I say a couple of hundred quid. Then I do a magazine article and the girl asks me what's the most I've ever spent on clothes. I tell her about the two-thousand-pound leather jacket I bought in London. My mum reads the article, hits the roof and makes me take it back. All the way to London.

Brian Kidd is a great coach. His sessions on the training ground at Blackburn are the best I've come across. Better than Bolton. Better than Liverpool. He knows exactly what he wants on the pitch and he knows how to get it.

But Brian Kidd is not a manager. He's a coach. Like Roy Evans, he's too nice a human being to be a top football manager. He's missing the very qualities you can't coach or buy.

There's no sign of the ruthlessness I saw in Kenny Dalglish during those transfer talks in the Haydock Thistle

Hotel. There's no sign of the cold-heartedness Kenny displayed on our phone call after I signed for Liverpool when he told me to get used to Southport's home ground. There's none of the arrogance and none of the swagger that Gérard Houllier displayed from the minute he walked into Liverpool FC, ready to become the main man at Anfield. Kiddo doesn't do arrogance or ruthlessness or rudeness, and it's going to cost him.

That becomes fairly evident the minute I clock on at Blackburn Rovers in January 1999. Football's only a job for me now, which is unfair to him, I know, but I've left Liverpool for a team in freefall. This is a far cry from the side that won the title just four years ago.

Jack Walker is still pumping money into the club, but he's not been well of late and has other things to worry about. Roy Hodgson has come and gone as manager, the victim of the relegation battle that's still haunting us.

Roy and Brian both try to paper over the cracks with new players as the likes of Kevin Davies, Nathan Blake, Matt Jansen, Keith Gillespie, my Irish team-mate, Lee Carsley and Ashley Ward, who I didn't think was good enough for the Premier League, all arrive at Ewood Park. The aim is to build a team to win the Premier League, but the way we're going, we'll be relegated to the First Division.

Relegation is a new word in my football vocabulary. Promotion chases and Wembley appearances were the norm when Bruce Rioch took over at Bolton. Premier League title bids and FA Cup finals were the standard bearers at Liverpool. Scrapping for survival wasn't on my agenda when I signed for Brian – it's hurting me and the club.

Thanks to Jack Walker's millions, this is a club built for success. The training facilities and the ground are first class. The fans are passionate about the team and the owner is an absolute gentleman. We have a great coach in Brian Kidd and a decent assistant in Brian McClair, but we just can't make it work on the pitch. That's football.

Everything about Blackburn off the pitch points to glory. Everything on the pitch points to relegation.

This isn't what I left Liverpool for – but I know as well as the next fan that I should never have left Anfield. I can't see my Blackburn contract going the distance.

Injuries don't help. By the time we are relegated, after a scoreless draw with champions-elect Manchester United on the second Tuesday night in May 1999, I've played just thirteen games for Rovers and scored just one goal, in a 4–1 defeat to Sheffield Wednesday.

My football dream is dying a quick and painful death. There's no enjoyment in relegation and no relief when we begin life as a Division One side. Then an injury almost wrecks my career completely, twenty-five games into the 1999–2000 season.

It's all fairly innocuous when I turn on a ball in training and tweak my knee. I can feel something go and I head straight to the treatment room. One of the young physios decides to put a compression boot on my leg and ice my knee. He sticks the bag of ice inside the compression boot. When he takes it off twenty minutes later my knee has gone numb. I can't feel my toes. My leg won't lift. I want to move my foot and my brain is telling my foot to move but there's nothing happening. The nerve isn't responding and my foot isn't moving.

Something is badly wrong. The senior physios and the team doctor know it. Straightaway I'm sent to see a specialist in Manchester for a nerve conductor scan. He confirms my worst fears. I have drop foot. A physio had iced the wrong part of the knee and ended up freezing my peroneal nerve (which wraps around your knee).

My career is now on the line. All I can do is wait, wait for the nerve to grow again and hope that everything works as it is supposed to. It could be six months before we know if I can play again.

I'm a brutal spectator at the best of times, so this is hell on earth. We've a new physio at the club, a fella called Dave Fevre who Brian's attracted from Manchester United, and I become his pet project. The specialist has warned me there's a chance I'll never play again and Dave Lockwood, who's gone from being my mate to being my agent, is talking about suing the club for loss of earnings and career damage, but all I want to do is play. I persecute Dave Fevre to get me fit. I practically live with him for the next six months as he works really hard to get the feeling back into the nerve.

By Spring 2000 Dave's magic has worked and it's time to test it. I'm out on the training ground, like a child waiting for Santa. Dave kicks the ball at me. I trap it. I can feel it. I kick it. I'm back. My career is saved.

Brian Kidd isn't so lucky. The failure to win promotion at the end of our first season in Division One is followed by the inevitable sack. Brian has been persecuted in the media. His ability to pick teams and his transfer dealings have been torn apart by pundits and fans alike. I only ever speak as I find – Brian is a top-class coach who always treats me with respect, and is always keen to listen to my views on tactics and players. He's not a manager, and he'll probably admit that himself, but he's a top-class coach.

I'm still fighting my way back to fitness when Graeme Souness comes swinging in through the doors at Ewood Park with his faithful assistant Phil Boersma. They call Phil 'the Suitcase' because Graeme brings him everywhere with him!

I was never a fan of what Souness did at Liverpool, but I do welcome his arrival at Blackburn simply because I reckon I'm a Graeme Souness type of player: full of energy, commitment and honesty. The Liverpool connection can only help as well.

Wrong.

Souness arrives with a bang. He brings Brad Friedel with him to put pressure on my Irish mate Alan Kelly as our first-choice goalkeeper. And Dean Saunders is here to add experience to the strike force.

I stay out of the way to begin with as I work my way back to fitness. I begin to play with the reserves and train with the first team again. I'm still Trigger, still cracking the jokes and winding people up. Souness is not a fan of such behaviour and he lets me know it. He rules the roost with an iron fist, all authority.

It all comes to a head towards the end of the season when we go to Birmingham with a very young squad, including Damien Duff, who's coming up through the ranks. He's got a left foot to die for and he's going to be a superstar.

I'm the oldest player in this squad by a distance, but I'm fit again. At the very worst I'll make the bench and get my appearance money. Wrong again. I'm the only playing member of the travelling squad not to get stripped. The kitman has more chance of getting a game than me. I've played in World Cup finals, been sold for over eight million quid, and I can't even make the bench for a poxy league game at Birmingham with nothing at stake.

The next night I play for the reserves and get taken off after an hour. They're taking the piss now and it isn't funny. We finish the season in eleventh – Lee Carsley is top scorer with ten goals – but I only manage twenty-eight games in all and one goal, with most of those games and the goal coming before I was injured.

Souness does guide Blackburn to promotion the next season, but I'm beyond caring. As far as I am concerned, he's always applying the writing to the wall for me and events in and around an FA Cup third-round clash with lowly Chester City prove it.

The game is set for 6 January 2001, and I'm in the squad. I'm at home with my partner and our newborn son Harry the night before the game when the phone rings at around 3 a.m. It's my partner's sister. Their mum has been rushed to hospital with septicaemia and it's not looking good. My partner rushes off to the hospital and leaves me at home with our son, Harry.

The game against Chester is the last thing on my mind as I ring the club doctor Phil Batty and ask him for advice. It's the middle of the night, but he has no problem taking the call. He talks me through what might be wrong and tells me what's best for my partner and her family. He's brilliant. Phil assures me not to worry about the game the next day, it's only Chester in the FA Cup and he's sure Graeme will understand when he explains it all to him.

I'm already in the hospital at the bedside, when Phil rings me back. He's spoken to Graeme and Graeme is adamant that I have to report for first-team duty as planned and play the game. He tells Phil to look after my phone on the bench and if it rings and I'm needed back at the hospital, I can go.

I've no choice here. I have to go to work, I have to do what Graeme Souness tells me. I really don't think he's grasped the enormity of the problem, or maybe it's a misunderstanding. I leave the hospital, even though my partner's mum is deteriorating by the minute. The doctors say there is little they can do to stop the poison in her blood. My partner and her family are in bits and I'm leaving them to play a bloody football match.

I don't know how I get to the ground but I do. I'm sitting behind the wheel and I can't stop thinking about my partner's mum dying in that hospital bed. The game goes by in a blur. We win 2–0 with two late goals. I play the entire ninety minutes. The fans don't have a clue.

The final whistle blows and I'm down the tunnel, straight into a tracksuit and out the door. I'm straight back to the hospital. There's nothing I can do; her mum dies on the Sunday morning.

Phil Batty comes around on the Monday and helps me through it all, through the mourning and the funeral.

Two weeks later, my partner's dad falls ill suddenly. He's diagnosed with throat cancer. He'd had a couple of tests a few weeks before his wife became ill but when she died, it's almost like he lost the will to live. He gets his results back the week after the funeral and within six weeks he's died.

He comes to live with us for a short bit in between the operations but next thing we know, he's on a life-support machine. He never comes around after the final op, and my partner loses her mum and dad in the space of six weeks. I feel absolutely helpless. No words can console her.

It doesn't matter what money we have. It makes no difference that I make my living playing football for Blackburn Rovers and Ireland, that I know surgeons and doctors. My partner has just lost both her parents and there's nothing money can do for her, nothing I can do for her.

Graeme Souness does offer his condolences but I don't care. I've lost all interest in playing for Blackburn. In fact, I've lost interest in playing football.

We're done.

Chapter Twenty

We're just back from Amsterdam after the 2–2 draw with Holland and straight into Lillie's Bordello in our Ireland tracksuits. As we enter the piano bar, Jimmy White and Ronnie O'Sullivan are leaving. I can't resist saying something. So I shout across the room, 'Jimmy White, one hundred and eighty.' Breeny collapses.

There's a common misconception out there that the Harcourt Street Two are, in fact, the Harcourt Street Three. Wrong. I was nowhere near the garda's car, your honour! Let me explain.

In the summer of 2000 we go back to America for the US Cup, the tournament we always seem to qualify for when we don't make the European Championships or the World Cup finals. It's a nice little earner for the FAI and it's a decent end-of-season blowout for the lads. This time we draw 2–2 with Mexico in Chicago and beat South Africa 2–1 at Giants Stadium.

It's a great trip, helped by the fact that Mick McCarthy allows us to let our hair down. So we do. Quinny organises a day-long session in Manhattan and we basically turn up a bit worse for wear for training the next morning. That might sound unprofessional to some but, trust me, the trip is worth its weight in gold because it brings the squad together like the old days. The craic is back. Alan Kelly has a new watch his missus gave him for his birthday and the lads dip it into his pint to see if it's waterproof. In return, Alan takes Quinny's cowboy boots off him in O'Neill's pub and throws them onto Third Avenue. Oh for a photograph of Ireland's top scorer running around big yellow taxis trying to get his boots back.

The feel-good factor is back but, boys being boys, we take advantage of the fact that Mick is finally giving us a bit of rope – enough to hang ourselves, as it happens, when the summer ends and we report back to Dublin ahead of the World Cup clash away to Holland at the beginning of September.

Blackburn have a game on the Monday night, so I don't get to meet up with the squad until Tuesday morning. As a result, I miss the night out in Gibney's and Lillie's. Thankfully.

I get to the hotel on Tuesday before breakfast and go to dump my bag in the room, only to find Babbsy packing his cases and getting ready to go home. I've no idea what's up, so I ask him. He tells me he's been out the night before with Sparky and has given it a good go. They ended up in Copper Face Jack's on Dublin's Harcourt Street and were well tanked, so well tanked that they decided to race down the street à la *Starsky and Hutch* – on the bonnets of the parked cars. What they don't know is that Harcourt Street is home to one of the most high-profile police stations in the country, and one of the guards happens to be looking at them as they jump up and down on her bonnet. She does her own Starsky impersonation and books them on the spot. Mick McCarthy gets called out of his bed in the middle of the night to be told that two of his players are in the holding cells and will be up in front of the judge the following morning.

There's hell to pay. The two lads are released on bail pending a full court hearing in November, and Mick's agent Liam Gaskin has to come in and bail them out. Mick's none too happy and sends them packing – just as I arrive! And, yes, I would have been out there with them in different circumstances. But there's no way I'd have jumped on a car. Never!

We play Holland away in just four days, and Mick is livid. He makes the two lads apologise to the officer in public before he sends them home. Babbsy has never enjoyed the best of working relationships with Mick and this isn't doing him any favours at all. Mick has huge time for Sparky since their days at Millwall, but there are times when Sparky doesn't know where the line is, and this is one of those times. Another night, we were out with him in Manchester and went back to his apartment in the same block where the Beckhams lived. Mark had no key so he knocked the Beckhams up and got David down, in his pyjamas, to open the front door for us.

Mick is willing to give younger players a go and trust them on the pitch. That's why I'm sort of confident going to Amsterdam. The new team has been together long enough to deliver, and the likes of Shay Given, Stephen Carr, Steve Finnan, Robbie and Duffer have established themselves.

They are pushing for places and there's pressure on the likes of Quinny, Stan and myself just to get into the starting team.

I know I'm now an elder player, but I'm not going anywhere. I'm six years into my international career and I am really committed to the cause for this World Cup campaign. I've never refused to play for my country. The only time there's ever been an issue was when England went to Lansdowne Road in 1995 and wrecked the place. Liverpool all but told us not to go for that game. They knew there was trouble brewing and they didn't want their players there. It turned out they were right, but that's the only occasion I've ever had doubts about playing for Ireland.

Holland don't worry me. They've had a good summer as Euro co-hosts, but this is the perfect time to play them. We're a solid unit and we're galvanised after the Harcourt Street incident. Some of the press reaction to the court appearance has been over the top, but it's only made us more determined to cause an upset in the Amsterdam Arena on 2 September 2000.

We're staying in the Hilton where John Lennon and Yoko Ono had their famous love-in, but one of us is not feeling the love. We come down for pre-match on Friday night before we go training at the stadium, and there's soup and sandwiches in the team room. Roy's not happy and, typically, he lets us know it in his own inimitable style – by warming up on his own at the stadium, away from Ian Evans who's leading the rest of the group. When we get back to the hotel he's still livid and orders room service. Away with him.

The match can't come quickly enough for me, but I'm really nervous. The stadium is brand new, and it's amazing.

There's a sea of orange the whole way from the hotel to the ground, but when we get out there we realise just how many Irish have made this trip. There's thousands of them here with us and clearly still believing in us. It's a great boost to have them there and helps us be positive.

We start the game well. We're winning tackles, dominating possession and dictating play. I put a ball down the line for Stephen Carr and follow the pass. My marker stops and, as he does so, Stephen plays a great little ball in behind him. I'm on it again and I know there's only one place this ball is going. I don't even look up. It's that Mexico cross from the 1994 World Cup all over again. I hit the area and Robbie's there, waiting to jump like a salmon and bury the ball in the back of the net. This is beautiful. We've just scored in front of the stand where our own fans are standing, and we're one up against the mighty Holland.

We're still one up when we go into the dressing room for half-time. Mick is pumped and tells us just to carry on as we are. The crowd are getting on Holland's back and that's the way he wants it. We'd worked on a few things on the training ground that week – Mick was good for technical detail and very different to Jack in that regard – and we get an opportunity to try one of his ideas early in the second half when there's a ball played into Quinny and I get the chance to come in off the line, just like I had done on the training ground in Dublin.

Niall gets it around the corner to Robbie and even though he gets battered by the defender, he gets the ball out to me. I take one touch with my right foot and I have nothing else on now but a shot with my left foot. The ball is wet and slippery as I curl it into the corner – Edwin van der Sar can't get near it. We're 2–0 up against Holland, and I've scored. I don't know what to do.

It's almost too good to be true – and it is. We throw it away, you'd have to say. They get two late goals for the draw and the second one, from Van Bronckhorst, takes a wicked deflection over Alan Kelly with just six minutes to go. We've thrown it away but when we get into the dressing room, we're celebrating as if it's a win.

One man's not happy. Roy is livid inside that dressing room and, as always, he lets us know it. But, for the first time with an Irish team, I get it. We're celebrating a draw in a match we should have won. It's not the right thing to do. He wouldn't do it with Manchester United and we shouldn't do it with Ireland. We were two up and dominating the match against one of the best teams in the world, and we let it slip. How can we really be happy with that?

Personally, I'm thrilled. It's the biggest Ireland game I've played in for years and I've done my job. I've scored a goal and I've made a goal. I get into the mixed zone and they can't shut me up. I'm Mr Popular again and I'm going to milk it for all its worth.

We fly straight back to Dublin that night and we land not long after midnight. There's only one thing for it. Lillie's. Tracksuits and all. They won't have a dress policy for us tonight. We're back in the hotel for ten past one and in Lillie's by half past. It's the night I shout 'one hundred and eighty' at Jimmy White. I'm on fire!

A month later we go to Portugal and the Estádio da Luz for the real test. Roy's reaction in Amsterdam – and his rant over the sandwiches – is public knowledge and we're being talked down again. Portugal's golden generation are at the height of their powers, apparently, and we travel as lambs to the slaughter in some eyes. Not in our eyes, though. There's a real resilience in the squad, something we had when I was at Bolton and we were on those cups runs. We could be behind, as we were in the play-off final against Reading, but know we won't be beaten. We have that with Ireland and we're starting to believe Roy's theory that we can't be content with moral victories and score draws any more. We need to dictate matches and win them.

We play well enough early on in Lisbon, but they're running through us in the middle of the park and Mick decides to make a significant change at half-time when Quinny goes off and Mattie Holland comes into the midfield, leaving Robbie up front on his own. It doesn't make an immediate difference and we go a goal behind in the fifty-seventh minute to a Conceição effort – but we don't panic, and continue to press forward. I'm replaced by Duffer in the sixty-ninth minute, just after I get booked, and within four minutes Mattie has us level with a screamer from the edge of the box.

We hold out for the draw and, this time, we do celebrate it. It's a good result because Portugal are a better team than Holland and they're the ones to be disappointed.

It's too late to fly out of Lisbon that night, so there's no visit to Lillie's.

Estonia are next up in Dublin four days later, but I only last forty-five minutes. Duffer comes in for me again – there's a trend starting here – and we win 2–0 with goals either side of half-time from Mark Kinsella and Gary Breen. It's the final competitive match of the year, and we're sitting pretty in the group.

The World Cup qualifiers resume in March 2001, when we go to Nicosia and Barcelona for a double-header against Cyprus and Andorra. Mick's dad dies when we're in Cyprus, but he won't fly back to spend some time with his family until after the game. That's typical of him.

Roy is on fire against Cyprus in the GSP Stadium and grabs the first goal of a 4–0 win in the thirty-second minute. An Ian Harte penalty has us two up and cruising at half-time before Gary Kelly and then Roy again score in the last ten minutes to send the huge army of travelling fans off into the night happy. It's not a good night for me. I get hooked again, this time in the seventy-seventh minute for Mattie Holland, and it's no more than I expected. As I'm going down the tunnel, one of the British squaddies in the stand shouts, 'McAteer, you were shit.' I stare back at him with a scowl and I'm sure he's expecting a row. Instead I just look at him and say nothing more than, 'You're right, mate.'

It's not the end of my problems. We have a few beers by the pool at the hotel in Limassol on the Sunday, but I'm down in the dumps, so down that I'm not even interested when Richard Dunne sneaks out and goes to an Irish pub, of all places, to meet his family. My head's up my arse but even I know the last place to sneak out to is an Irish pub full of Irish fans on the beer!

Mick goes home to say goodbye to his dad and leaves Taff – Ian Evans – in charge for the transfer to Spain on the Monday. We've yet to train, but I know I'll be struggling to play on Wednesday in what is effectively Barcelona's third stadium. As a professional, I want to play, but I realise I'm not worth a place on my current form. Sure enough, Mick's dropped me when he names the team. I'm livid, but I can't have it out with him given the circumstances. And I'm also honest enough with myself to know it's the right decision for the team.

Duffer gets my place on the right side of midfield with Mattie Holland alongside Roy in the middle instead of Mark Kinsella. I sit on the bench for the ninety minutes, and we win 3-0 with goals from Ian Harte, Kevin Kilbane and Mattie.

We beat Andorra 3–1 at home in April – after the shock of going a goal down – but I'm out with an injury and have to watch it on the telly.

At the beginning of June I'm back on the bench for the double-header against Portugal in Dublin and Estonia in Tallinn. Portugal's the big one and, again, we can't beat each other. Roy gives us the lead in the sixty-eighth minute and Figo equalises ten minutes later. I get on for the final few minutes and the place is rocking. It's a significant result, and means it's still all to play for between ourselves, Portugal and Holland for those top two places.

We're away to Estonia the following Wednesday and, again, I'm only listed amongst the substitutes. Mart Poom from Sunderland is in goal – one of the nicest blokes in football – but there's no room for sentiment in a game that sees Robbie Keane left out of the starting team as well, with Duffer alongside Quinny in a bold move by Mick. The stadium we play in is only half-finished, but goals from Richard Dunne and Matt Holland have us two up at the break and the job is all but done. The summer holidays beckon and we end the international season with a beer or three or four in the beautiful old town of Tallinn.

In August the new season begins with a friendly at

home against Croatia, which we draw 2–2, in which I make another substitute appearance, but the big one, and we all know it, is three weeks later against Holland. Portugal are starting to pull away from both of us – they beat Cyprus 6–0 in June and Andorra 7–1 in September – so their goal difference is looking untouchable.

We have only two games left and if we can beat the Dutch and then Cyprus, both at Lansdowne Road, we can book a place in the play-offs at the very least. It's a tall order, but it's where we want to be. It's where I want to be as well. Away from the Ireland team, my life is a mess. I'm hardly playing at Blackburn, but Mick's always been fair to me. He's been to see me play in some of the games I *have* managed, so hopefully he knows I'm in decent form.

The last week of August in the build-up to the game against Holland, he takes a different approach and brings us down to Kilkea Castle in Athy, a great hotel run by Shane Cassidy, just to get us away from the hype. It's the game everyone wants to see, the game the whole country wants us to win, and we need to stay cool and calm and collected and away from the eye of the storm.

Closer to the Saturday, we move up to the Citywest Hotel just outside Dublin, and we can feel the tension rising as we get nearer to game time. I'm rooming with Lee Carsley for the week and he's brilliant for me. He is such a positive person and he passes that on to those around him twenty-four/seven. Lee knows I am dubious about playing, but he tells me to believe that I'll start – even though he's one of the guys who will more likely than not be on the bench. That's Lee, 100 per cent committed to the Irish team whether he's playing or not.

Turns out Lee is right about the team. Mick pulls me on the Friday and tells me I'm in. He wants to play with Robbie and Duffer up front against the Dutch. He saw Chelsea play two quick forwards against Jaap Stam at United, and it really unsettled him. He wants to do the same thing and he needs me to protect the right side behind them and support them when we have the ball. He says it's a match made for me and that I'm not to let him down. I promise I won't. I want to kiss him, he's no idea what this start means to me.

I'm not the only one up for this match. Roy's game face is as intense as I've ever seen it in the dressing room. He's heard the stories from the Dutch camp like the rest of us, and he wants to shove them down their arrogant Dutch throats.

They've already booked their flights to the World Cup.

They've their training camp and their hotel sorted for the finals.

They've already decided we're beaten and out of the running.

Clearly they haven't met Roy Keane and Ireland in this humour or encountered a bad day at Lansdowne Road. They're in for a Ruud awakening!

They get it after just sixty seconds when Roy hits Marc Overmars with a tackle as powerful as a Mike Tyson punch. He could have been sent off for it, but the referee hasn't got the bottle to make that big a decision with just a minute gone. The Dutch know we mean business and know there's plenty more where that came from.

Hofland and Zenden are in German referee Hellmut Krug's little black book before Gary Kelly gets his own yellow card seven minutes before half-time, after following Roy's lead and smashing Overmars. Roy's set the tone with that early tackle and the crowd rise to it. The old East Stand at Lansdowne is visibly rocking with the emotion of it all. Turns out, Roy didn't hit Overmars hard enough. He's on my side of the pitch and he's hard work for me and Kells, who's playing behind me. The fact Kells is now on a yellow means he's also on a tightrope, and that's not good against a player of Overmars' quality.

I smash Arthur Numan but there's nothing malicious about it even if he ends up with a load of stitches in his head. Quinny nods one down for Robbie but van der Sar saves it.

We're on the back foot for the rest of the first half. Van Nistelrooy misses a great chance and he's not alone – they're creating chances, but they're not taking them. When we get into the dressing room at the break I tell anyone who'll listen that this could be our day. We can't play with any fear in the second half. We don't.

Kells and I still have our hands full with Overmars. He's long enough in the game to know he can be cute with Gary after that yellow card. Kells and I have a good understanding. We've played on that right side together as far back as the German friendly before the 1994 World Cup. He's got great pace and he knows how to attack from his time as a striker with the Leeds and Ireland youth teams. He has this trick of getting ahead of me when we're attacking and I just know to drop back and protect him defensively. It's definitely something Mick was thinking about when he picked this team, because we have to give the Dutch something to worry about down this side as well.

Overmars tries to isolate Kells as often as he can. With about an hour gone, Overmars goes outside him again, and Gary's first instinct is to hit him hard. That's exactly what he does and as soon as he's done it, we all know what's coming next. I'm first on the scene and pleading with the referee. *No, no, no.* It wasn't reckless and it wasn't stupid but it wasn't fair either, and the referee's already let Roy off a red card. Kells has put the decision entirely in the referee's hands and the inevitable second yellow card – followed by a red – is produced. Kells is distraught. He's almost in tears as he heads off the pitch with Mick Byrne's arm around him. Gary thinks he's let the whole country down but, you know something, he's probably done us a favour.

It is ten Irish players and the noisiest fans we've ever heard at Lansdowne Road against the world. Not just the Dutch – the world.

Mick responds quickly and takes Robbie off. Steve Finnan goes in behind me at right-back and we switch to a four-four-one formation. Instead of retreating into our shell and playing for a draw, we start to have a go at them. We have nothing but the World Cup to lose now – so why not?

We win a corner under the East Stand and I go out to take it. It gets punched away by van der Sar and Roy picks it up on the halfway line. He's just played the ball into Duffer when he gets whacked, but the referee waves the play on. It's the best decision he ever made. It's a great position for a free kick, but the ref gives us the advantage and Duffer gets on the ball. He plays it wide for the overlapping Stevie Finnan, who loses the chance to cross first time and checks inside. I'm on the far side now, still there from the corner, and I'm waiting for Stevie to get the ball in. The Dutch haven't picked me up, so when the ball is floated across, I'm unmarked and waiting. Duffer tries to flick it on and, thankfully, he misses. If he got even the slightest touch to it, I'd have had to control it. Instead it comes my way and is sitting pretty. I know exactly what I'm going to do. It's sitting up at exactly the right height and the right speed – all I have to do is smash it past van der Sar and into the net. There it is, dropping, dropping, dropping. I tense my body, get my weight behind it and smash it. The technique is bloody brilliant, even if I do say so myself. Van der Sar is watching it hit the net, but I'm already off on a lap of honour.

The East Stand is shaking with the noise. I don't know where I'm going and I don't care. I'll cover every inch of Lansdowne Road if I can. Roy's the first up to throw his arms around me. I'm smothered in bodies. The crowd is going berserk. We're back in our half now, waiting for the restart. The Dutch look shell-shocked. Mick's fist is pumping the air. I'm the hero. A real live hero. I can't wait to get back to Blackburn, and show them who's the king of Dublin.

I've got the goal and the rest of the match is a blur. We've won the must-win match. We're all but guaranteed the runners-up spot in the group, and the play-offs for Japan and Korea at the very least, if we beat Cyprus in Dublin next month.

Back in the dressing room I bawl my eyes out again. It is all very emotional, and I just need a minute to myself so I go into the loo, close the door and sob. I've just scored the goal to put the Dutch out of the World Cup and I can't stop crying. That goal means so much to me because of everything that's going on in my life, on and off the field.

There are messages coming in from everywhere. Mick Byrne is obviously looking for me and, as always, he throws his arms around me when he finds me trying to escape the maddening crowd. Mick has the ability to make me cry at the best of times, but this time I have the perfect excuse.

He is made up for me and explains that Bono wants me to head to Slane Castle and go on stage with U2. He even has a helicopter sorted to get me there – we played in the afternoon so there is plenty of time – and he wants me to get up there and celebrate the goal in front of the crowd at the castle.

Mick does know U2, to be fair, but he also has some bizarre stories, a bit like the Churchill dog on the TV ad. He'd be there telling you he had tea with George Bush or shook hands with the Pope – he did shake hands with the Pope – so I'm not quite sure if this is a tall story or a fact. Anyway, I'd got Aldo tickets for the game and promised him I'd go on the ale with him afterwards no matter what happened – win, lose or draw – and I'm not going to break my promise to one of my best mates. Not even for Bono.

Mick just says, 'Fine, I'll ring Bono and tell him you can't make it.'

I never believe it is anything other than Mick trying to make the goal celebrations even bigger and give me more reason to be proud of myself at a time when my life is falling apart outside the Ireland camp. That would be typical Mick.

A few years later I'm in Las Vegas for a stag party – John Oster from Sunderland is the host – when I bump into an Irish fan who'd been in Slane that day. That's nothing new. Ever since the goal against Holland I am always meeting Irish people who were either at the game or in Slane, or both. Sometimes I even wonder if the crowd at the match was bigger than the crowd for U2.

This lad explains that he had been at the gig and had only just bought the DVD of it and had been watching it a few nights earlier. It brought back memories of the goal simply because Bono had grabbed an Irish tricolour from the crowd and walked up the stage when someone kicked a big inflatable ball at him. He kicks it and says, 'Pretend I'm Jason McAteer', and the whole crowd goes absolutely mad. The fan says everyone went mental and they were all waiting for me to walk out on stage. He said he was sure at the time that I was going to appear from the side of the stage and join Bono and the flag, but I never surfaced.

So the invite was real and the story was true after all. Sorry, Mick!

World Cup fever is back in Ireland with a bang, but Mick McCarthy leaves me out for the 4–0 win over Cyprus in the final qualifier in October, when it's confirmed that Portugal have won the group and we're runners-up, ahead of Holland. It's a wise decision on his part to rest a number of us that night. I'm on a yellow and he needs me for the play-offs, possibly against Ali Daei and Iran, if they beat the UAE.

Iran do win, with Mick and Taff and our travel agent Ray Treacy watching in the stands. They'll come to Dublin for the home leg on a Saturday night in November followed by the prospect of a nice little trip to Tehran for the return match five days later.

Graeme Souness does open one more door for me at Blackburn before the play-off – the exit door. I'm a Sunderland player by the time we face the Iranians in Dublin, and I couldn't be happier. I know if I am playing first-team football at club level – and I am with Sunderland – then Mick can't even dare to think about dropping me for the Iran match after that goal against Holland.

The big debate in the build-up concerns Roy Keane's availability. Some of the clubs in England are nervous about the political sideshows concerning a match in Tehran, and there's a story doing the rounds that Roy is carrying an injury. Some reports say Alex Ferguson will only allow him to play in the home leg, but I doubt Alex Ferguson is going to stop Roy Keane playing for his country if he really wants to. There's even talk that he will play the first game and not travel if we are guaranteed qualification after the result in Dublin.

I'm not having that.

We are a weaker team without Roy, everyone knows that, and no matter what happens in the first leg, we have to put out our strongest team going to Iran. This is the World Cup finals we are playing for – who is going to miss out on playing for Ireland in another World Cup finals?

Roy can do what he wants – and he normally does – but we need him in that dressing room and on that pitch in Tehran if we are going to see this job through. We've done really well to get this far but nobody knows better than us what the play-offs mean. We've lost to Holland, Belgium and Turkey, and we can't afford to go through that again. Personally or collectively. I don't think I could play international football again if we lose another play-off. That's how much this means to me and, I hope, to all of us.

The one advantage going into the play-offs is the fact that the first leg is in Dublin. Just as we will be going into the unknown in Tehran, Iran will be playing in a venue far removed from what is the norm for them. That's the beauty of Lansdowne Road, which looks every inch like the oldest ground still used in international rugby when you first see it.

It's concrete and wood and far from pretty, and it's made for Ireland. Foreign teams come here and they don't know what to make of it. The Dutch probably brought their own mirrors with them in September. Paraguay came here once and they came out for the warm-up with long sleeves and gloves on. We were baking and wearing short sleeves. We knew then they didn't fancy it and that gave us a head start on them in the warm-up. And I doubt the Iranians, most of whom play their football at home, will like it either.

The one thing I don't like in the build-up to the game is the pressure. The expectation is massive and you can feel it in the air. There are fans all around the hotel and they want us to win this for them. Jesus, *we* want to win it for them – and for us. But the theory that Iran will be easier opponents than the likes of Belgium or Turkey doesn't sit well with me. I know we have to make the home leg really count for something on a dark and damp Saturday night in Dublin. We do.

Shay is brilliant again. He kept us in it against Holland in September and he performs heroics against Iran with a great save from Ali Karimi late on, when we are hanging on to a two-goal lead and desperate not to concede.

This is a big game for me personally and, again, I deliver. I'm the happiest I've been on and off the pitch for a long time, and that translates into my performance as I make a major impact in our bid to get the ball past Mirzapour, their erratic goalkeeper. It's a penalty that gets us on the way just before half-time and I win it – deliberately – when I get the ball around the defender Rezaei. I see him coming at me as I head into the box and I know exactly what I'm going to do as the ball breaks into the penalty area. I suck him into the tackle because I know I'm going to get there first and I know he's going to commit the foul. There's no way out of it for him. I play the man, not the ball, and he falls for it. He comes right through me. I don't even have to dive to get the penalty. I'm lying on the floor as the referee blows his whistle and points to the spot. I gesture at the crowd behind the goal – a fist-up, victory-style salute. I know, and they know, that this is going to be a goal. Ian Harte doesn't miss penalties. He has the best left foot in the game and he beats Mirzapour with a sweet kick high into the top right-hand corner.

The goal settles our nerves and Mick tells us there's another one there for the taking when we get into the dressing room at half-time. He's also adamant that we cannot afford to concede a goal.

I set up the second goal for Robbie five minutes into the second half when I hit a free kick into the box and Breeny has a header blocked. The rebound falls to Robbie, who hits a sweet half-volley into the net. Quinny, Killer and Robbie get close to the third goal that would make it impossible for Iran, but it just won't come. Instead Iran almost score twice in the closing minutes when Shay makes two stops from Karimi, one of them world-class. We hang on for the win, and there's a real sense of relief around the ground and within the squad. We know it's going to be tough in Tehran – it's going to be tough *getting* to Tehran – but we have a two-goal cushion and we haven't conceded an away goal. It's half-time, but we're in the driving seat.

There's no night out tonight. We're ninety minutes away from the World Cup and we know it's not the time to party. Back at the hotel we regroup and start to plan for the eight-hour flight on Monday morning. Quinny's back is in bits and there's no way he's going to play, but he's adamant he is travelling. If nothing else, he wants to be a supporter out there. He's quite happy to sit in agony on an Aer Lingus plane for eight hours knowing full well that he won't play. That's what playing for Ireland means to us, and Quinny's presence will make a big difference off the field, even if he won't be on it.

The story with Roy is a bit different. The injury talk is alive again, and there's a suggestion that United don't want him to travel. There's no word when we train on the Sunday, but the news comes through that night that he's not coming with us. It's a blow. We all feel we need his experience on the pitch. Even a half-fit Roy Keane would make a difference in a game this big. He'd intimidate the Iranians if nothing else.

Intimidation is a big part of the second leg and that's apparent the minute we arrive at the airport. Turkey is the closest atmosphere I've experienced to this. There are people everywhere, milling around us and looking for autographs as we go through arrivals. But to be fair, there's no fingers-across-the-throat gestures like we had in Bursa. They have placards with 3–0 written on them and all we can do is smile at them as we get onto the bus for the drive into town.

The hotel isn't up to much, but it's as good as we are going to get. All they seem to offer us in the dining room is this manky chicken and I'm convinced they're budgies rather than chickens, they're that small. Mick Byrne has his usual, and endless, supply of Snickers and Mars bars and Tayto crisps. Our chef has brought lots of beans with him as well. I live on Taytos and beans for the week.

It's not the most exciting place in the world, this hotel. When I look out my room window I can see the biggest prison in Tehran. One of the staff tells me it's where the Ayatollah used to send political prisoners. Some of them never came back, apparently. I tell Breeny that's where we're heading if we win on Thursday night. That's about the most exciting story from the build-up to the game. We have the usual DVDs and card games to keep us entertained. We even have a game of *Who Wants To Be A Millionaire?* on the Monday night – amongst a group of millionaires!

On Tuesday night we train at the stadium but only for about half an hour. There's this massive tunnel under the ground into the dressing room and, inside it, everything is dark and damp. There's nothing palatial about the surroundings, but the pitch isn't that bad and the centre circle is far enough away from the stands not to get hit by missiles. That's where I'm staying tomorrow night – in the centre circle.

Mick McCarthy does his press conference back at the hotel after we train, and they're stirring it up. Miroslav

Blazevic is in charge of the Iranians and he has them all well up for it. The Iranian media bombard Mick with questions about Roy. They seem to think we are a one-man band and that we haven't a hope without our captain. At one point a local journalist asks Mick if the team is 'the Republic of Roy Keane or the Republic of Ireland'. They seem adamant that they're going to win 3–0, simply because Roy is back in Manchester. Good luck with that one, lads.

The morning of the game we go for a walk with Tony Hickey minding us, but it's shorter than usual. There's no great anger towards us around the hotel, but Tony's taking no chances. We sleep in the afternoon, have our pre-match meal in the hotel and then we're on the bus and on our way. The ballads are playing and Sean South is giving it loads as we get into the ground. There's a real buzz about the squad – this is thirty or so Irishmen against all of Iran. Bring it on!

When we get to the dressing room, Johnny Fallon is putting the kit out with Joe Walsh. It's a good two hours before the game and Johnny says the ground is already packed with over a hundred thousand people. They've been shouting and screaming for an hour already, even he got shouted at when he went out for a look earlier on. Someone from the FAI says we don't have to go out for the warm-up if we don't want to. The Iranians don't seem that keen for us to go out there either. There's a warm-up area under the stand and there's nothing in the rule book that says you have to go out onto the pitch.

Ian Evans has his war face on and says, 'Fuck that, we're going out.' He wants us to stand up to these guys, to look them in the eye and prove that we mean business. We're with you, Taff – but, heroes that we are, we let Taff lead the charge. And we get mullered on the way out to the pitch. We can hear the noise as we leave the dressing room but nothing prepares us for what follows.

The minute Taff appears from the tunnel, the place just erupts. They're firing things at us, they're hissing at us, they're trying to get across the fence. It's like we've put two fingers up to Iran just by coming onto the pitch to warm up. I've seen nothing like it in my life – nothing. There's ninety minutes to kick-off and they're going mad. Fireworks are blazing, bottles are flying and we're in the middle of the pitch, as far as we can get from the crowd, and sniggering to each other as we try to take it in.

The warm-up doesn't take very long, but it's the right thing to do. We won't be surprised now when we come back out for the main event and that's a real bonus given what we've just witnessed.

It doesn't get any better when the match starts. We're calm enough in the dressing room before the referee's call but you just know this is huge for all of us. We're on our own, but we're within sniffing distance of the World Cup finals. It's time to stand up and be counted – just as Taff said.

The Iranian players are no better than their fanatical supporters. I smash the left-back just by the halfway line and he spits at me as he gets up off the ground. I just think, *You dirty bastard*, but that's only the start of it. Spitting is the most disgusting act in football, but he just laughs at me as he walks away – and then spits on the ground in case I was in any doubt about how he felt.

The same player ends up being a human shield for me when we clash again under the stand and the fans bombard me with fruit and bottles. I have the defender behind me and the linesman in front of me, and they shield me. The linesman gets hit with an apple and I can only laugh at it all.

Iran are no great shakes. We smother them in midfield and they offer little in terms of a real threat in spite of all their promises of a 3–0 win. We attack when we have to, defend when we have to, and keep our composure and our shape, just like Mick told us to. He's calm at half-time, reminds us we're forty-five minutes away from the World Cup and tells us to carry on as we are. They do up the tempo in the second half and finally get a goal with only minutes left on the clock, but it is too little, too late. The final whistle goes and I've never felt elation like it.

This is up there with everything I've ever done in football, probably even better. We're off to the World Cup after surviving a night in Tehran in the most intimidating atmosphere I've ever encountered. I can't control myself. I'm jumping up and down with Johnny Fallon. I'm kissing Mick Byrne. I'm hugging Tony Hickey and Mick McCarthy and Ian Evans. We've done it. I'm bawling my eyes out again! And I never want this moment to stop. A few Iranians, only a few, offer handshakes, and good luck to them, but this is our moment, this is about us. Chances are we're never going to see them again and I just want to savour this moment with the players and the staff who are here. And with the few Irish fans who have been brave enough to make the journey. I'm the last off the pitch. I stay out there for about fifteen minutes. I know this is never going to happen for me again and I'm not letting go.

By the time I get back to the dressing room, the place is rocking. We've cracked open the orange juice – this is Iran, don't forget – and the songs are flying. Poor old Sean South won't get a rest tonight. I get the chance to ring home. My mum's delighted. The family is thrilled. We're going to the World Cup finals again.

There's a text on my phone from Babbsy. He's delighted for me. He's in limbo with Ireland now after the Harcourt Street shuffle, and he's in Lisbon with Sporting. I'm gutted for him because we've been through so much together, but he's made up for me that we've qualified. That's Phil for you.

The journey out to the airport is incredible. The streets are paved with broken glass. The home fans didn't take defeat too well and break every car window they come across. They're still out on the streets in their thousands but we're not the problem now. They have their own team to take issue with and they leave us alone. The most intimidating thing we face is a stern-looking policeman at passport control. We've burst his bubble, that much is obvious. The flight's delayed and some of the lads jump on a private jet sent out by David O'Leary and Leeds for Robbie, Hartey and Gary Kelly. I'm disappointed for them, they're going to miss the party.

The Aer Lingus pilot congratulates us the minute we get on the plane. Then he apologises. He can't open the bar under international aviation rules until we clear Iranian air space and that won't be for a couple of hours. We're gutted. We qualified for the World Cup hours ago and our lips are as dry as the desert below us.

Five minutes into the flight he comes back on the PA. Great news. The plane has taken on Concorde qualities and we've cleared Iranian air space in just minutes, not hours. The bar is open and the champagne is on Aer Lingus. I'm sitting next to Dean Kiely in the big seats and the craic is ninety. Kenny Cunningham gets the singsong going, the whole plane is partying. There's a conga led by Paul Howard in the section behind us occupied by the journalists. The drink and the songs flow all the way back to Ireland. It should be in the *Guinness Book of Records* for the longest party in the air ever.

There's more to come. We land at Dublin in the early hours of the morning and there are thousands of fans there to greet us. I get carried through arrivals on someone's shoulders. This is what it means to play for Ireland. This is what makes us so special. We'll never be England or Holland or Brazil – and we don't want to be.

Chapter Twenty-One

Sunderland are playing Chelsea not long after Ireland have beaten Holland to the 2002 World Cup finals. There's a bit of a push and shove in the tunnel. Jimmy Floyd Hasselbaink is giving it loads, big-time Charlie.

I stand up to him, look him right in the face and snarl, 'At least we're going to the World Cup in China, Jimbo.'

Breeny has to step in and remind me we're going to Japan. And he's right. Wherever it is – we're going to the World Cup and Holland aren't.

The World Cup is still months away. There's lots of football to be played for our clubs first, with games to be won and wages to be earned before we can even think about the trip to Japan, even after the draw puts us in against Cameroon, Germany and Saudi Arabia. The draw is no more or no less than we expect. When you qualify for the big tournaments you want to play the big teams. Cameroon are a quality side. The Germans are one of the favourites for the tournament. The Saudis are the unknown quantity, but it's unlikely they'll be up to much.

There's a bit of doom and gloom about the place after the draw, and the inevitable 'Group of Death' headline appears in more than one Irish paper, but I'm not too worried. We've already played class sides to qualify and we've even managed to send the Dutch off to their beach holidays ahead of schedule. We've been to Iran and finished the job, so why should we be scared of anything that can come our way in the summer or worry about it?

First up we've the bulk of a difficult season to get through with Sunderland. I try to park the World Cup and forget about it for a while at least.

I'd moved to Sunderland in October 2001. Things still weren't going well at Blackburn, but I knew the end was nigh when I got back on the Monday morning having scored against Holland and made headlines all across the football world. All the staff were hugging me and high-fiving me. Julie in the office was thrilled to bits for me. She's typical of the reaction from everyone at Ewood Park – everyone except Mr Souness.

As I made my way to the dressing room that morning, Graeme was walking towards me. I open the door, ready for him to say something like 'great goal' and give me a big bear hug at the very least. But there's nothing, not as much as hello. We might not see eye to eye. It might be a clash of personalities, but he was still one of my heroes and that hurt.

I'd had enough. I thought about quitting football. I rang Mick McCarthy for a chat. He told me not to be stupid, to stick it out and prove them all wrong by getting Ireland to the World Cup finals in Japan and Korea. Mick is right, as always. The World Cup is a big enough incentive to keep me going and to keep me sane – but I have to sort out what's happening at Blackburn.

I marched down to Graeme's office after training one day, shaking with trepidation. I was also livid. He was one of the hardest men in football as a player, and he's still tough as old boots as a manager, but he's really pissed me off.

When I knocked on the door, he said he was about to get into the shower and that I should come back in ten minutes. I'd psyched myself up for this big showdown, and now I had to wait another ten minutes.

When I got called back to his office he was sitting with his feet up on his desk and this tiny, I mean tiny, towel wrapped around his arse. His knackers were hanging out of the towel, staring me in the face. It was like looking at a grandfather clock.

Trying hard not to look at his tackle, I let him have it.

He gave as good as he got. I want out. I don't want to play for him again. That's fine by him, but the ultimate decision will lie with the club. If they decide to keep me, he'll keep me. But there was no promise about playing me. That was his decision – and only his decision. He didn't budge an inch as he beckoned for me to leave his office.

I didn't care. He could do what he wanted to me at Blackburn, but he could never take that Holland goal away from me. It was mine, and I'll dine out on it for the rest of my life.

Dave Lockwood sorted a meeting with John Williams, the Blackburn chief executive. John's a decent bloke. He knew I was good to the club when I took a pay cut to move there. He knew that I couldn't go on with Graeme anymore. He agreed to let me go when a reasonable offer came in. And I know just the man – Niall Quinn.

He'd been on at me for ages to move to Sunderland. He loves the manager Peter Reid and everything about the club and the football folk on Wearside. He's forever telling me that I'd love it up there in the northeast. It was time to find out.

Quinny had a word with Peter Reid and, sure enough, six weeks after that goal against Holland I head up to Sunderland for a million quid – finally rid of Blackburn and their manager. I was on cloud nine as I left Blackburn for the last time, and I fell back in love with football. Thanks, Reidy.

Quinny and Kevin Kilbane are dead right about Sunderland and the manager. It's the perfect antidote to my Blackburn fallout at a time when I really need to love club football again, for the sake of my international career. The deal is worth sixteen grand a week to me, down two grand a week from Blackburn, but I gladly take it to get away from Ewood Park. And there's a five-grand bonus every time we win a game.

I've another World Cup to go to and I need to be playing, but more than that, I need to be happy.

If I'm honest about it, I'm not in a great place when we move up to a new house and a new start in Durham. My personal life is a nightmare. I'm really struggling on the home front and the expectations of 40,000 fans every other game at the Stadium of Light weigh heavily on my shoulders.

They've enjoyed two great seasons under Reidy and a seventh-place finish in the Premier League at the end of the 2000–01 season, so the relegation struggle I join isn't to their liking. Peter Reid is brilliant with me. Everything Niall said about him as a man-manager is spot on. It's my last chance with a big club. I know it, and Reidy knows it.

He has this way about him. Like Mick McCarthy, it's all about the group and not about any individual, no matter who you are or where you came from. Even though things are going against us on the field, there is this massive belief, this great atmosphere in the dressing room. There's a bond between the players and the staff just like there was at Liverpool when Roy was manager and like there's always been with Ireland.

The Saturday after we beat Iran, they wheeled myself, Quinny and Kevin Kilbane onto the pitch to offer their congratulations. That's how good that club is. Peter Reid is delighted for us.

The main problem I encounter early in my time at Sunderland is injury. I've a hamstring that's taking forever to heal and I'm not all that much use to Peter in my first season as we avoid relegation by just a point.

This 2001–02 season isn't an easy time for Peter Reid. We can't score goals – we manage just twenty-nine for the season, at the time, the lowest of any club in the Premier League – and we're involved in a relegation scrap from start to finish. Eventually we finish fourth from bottom, just four points clear of Ipswich, who are relegated along with Derby and Leicester. Even the cups go badly for us. We're sent packing first time – in the League Cup at Sheffield Wednesday in September and in the FA Cup at home to West Brom in January.

International football is a welcome relief from the stress levels at the Stadium of Light when Ireland's World Cup year kicks off in February 2002 with a friendly against Russia at Lansdowne Road. It's ironic that we're facing the Russians again for the first time since my debut in 1994. Mick's having a look at a couple of players, knowing that he can only bring twenty-three of us to Japan in the summer.

Richard Sadlier of Millwall, a big striker Mick knows well from his time at The Den, and midfielder Colin Healy, a young Corkman at Celtic, both get their chance and make the most of it, so much so that Colin wins the Man of the Match award despite only playing as a substitute for the second half. My involvement is brief, very brief, on a night that Mick hands out twenty-three caps and uses the same number of players he can bring to the finals. If you're doing the maths in your head right now, you'll probably have guessed that means one player comes on as a sub and is taken off again – and guess who that is? Yes, me! I replace Steve Finnan in the seventy-first minute at right-back and then make way for my Sunderland team-mate Niall Quinn in the dying seconds. Even by the time I get onto the field, the match is well and truly over thanks to first-half goals from Steven Reid and Robbie Keane.

Mick's advice after the match is to carry on doing what we're doing with our clubs. He'll be watching from the stands and he's adamant there's plenty to play for, even for those on the fringes of the squad.

Like us, Mick knows injury is a constant danger in the cut and thrust of the Premier League and I soon learn that lesson when we play Arsenal away and a young Ashley Cole comes in right over the top and smashes me. I lose the rag with him, remind him I have a World Cup to go to and point out that he's put my chances of playing in Japan at risk with his recklessness, throwing in tackles like that. I've no problem with a fifty-fifty tackle, no issue with a fair tackle even if it ends with an injury, but I can seriously do without a young upstart like Ashley Cole going over the top. For ten minutes after the tackle I chase him around the pitch. I want to smash him – but I can't catch him. I'm like a headless chicken and Reidy is getting annoyed with me.

The half-time whistle blows and Cole's down the tunnel before I can grab him and give him a piece of my mind and the old McAteer one-two made famous by my uncles. Reidy and Bobby Saxton try to calm me down in the dressing room, but I'm having none of it. One more tackle like that and I'm going to miss the World Cup finals. Ireland might not get to another World Cup in my playing career, and I'm not going to miss out because of a reckless challenge by an idiot. Reidy's heard enough and decides to substitute me at half-time. He explains it's safer for Ashley Cole and it's definitely safer for me. He's probably right. It's only on the coach going home that I realise he's done me a favour. I'd either have got sent off or carried off, that's how worked up I was. Reidy's done me a turn.

I know better than most how precious this World Cup is. When I first came into the Ireland set-up, the hard work for 1994 was done. We'd already qualified and I thought we'd be in every major tournament, World Cup and European Championships. I'd no idea how hard it is to qualify from a group as a second or even third seed. I just expected qualification every time after 1994, but all I got was heartache and most of it in the play-offs. I kept missing out by a goal or two, a game or two, and it hurt like hell. That's why this World Cup means so much to me. It's my last chance. It's probably the only chance I will ever get to bring my son to the World Cup finals when I am playing. I'm a father figure in the squad now as well. I'm needed in Japan, and there's no way a young wannabe like Ashley Cole is going to keep me away.

I know I'm going, by the way. There's talk in the papers when we come in for the next game against Denmark in March that Mick has a couple of places up for grabs, but mine's not one of them. He tells me as much when we go to the cinema as normal on the Monday night. It's like a joke between us – don't-be-worrying-about-your-seat-on-the-plane sort of thing, but I know exactly what he means. I know and he knows that he can't leave me out after the goal against Holland, but there's always that little seed of doubt. In my mind there's always a doubt or two – 'Thanks for that goal, Jason, now do one, I'm going to bring a younger player to the World Cup. Thank you. See you!'

We muller Denmark 3–0 and I play for sixty-five minutes before I'm replaced, by Steven Reid this time. Hartey has us 1–0 up at the break, Robbie scores yet again and Clinton Morrison stakes his World Cup claim with the third. Colin Healy is excellent once more but the star of the show is Duffer. He's on fire. Even the few Danish fans in the crowd applaud him off just before the final whistle.

We know Stephen Carr won't be going to the finals. He played in that first game over in Amsterdam, but he's been injured for ages and Mick knows the best thing is to make the decision and let everyone come to terms with it. I'm gutted for him and just glad, like everyone else, that I'm not in the same boat.

I don't play in the April game, a 2–1 win against the Yanks at Lansdowne on a mucky, mucky night. Mark

Kinsella and Gary Doherty score and the winning warm-up run continues. You can sense the buzz of expectation about the place. We're almost there.

We've two games left to play before we fly off to somewhere called Saipan for the start of our preparations.

Quinny's been granted a testimonial by Sunderland and he's caused a real stir by announcing that all the proceeds will go to charity, to two children's hospitals in Dublin and on Wearside. I know sweet FA about testimonials. Apparently you get one after ten years with the same club. Means nothing to me, I've never been at any club long enough to even hear mention of the word.

His decision to give all the money away causes a bit of a stir. Some of my greedier colleagues in the game are upset that he is setting a precedent. They might be obliged to do the same thing when their turn comes and they're not impressed. Many of them see the testimonial as their last big pay day. There are a few guys who have even been at clubs long enough to get two of them, but that's not as common as it used to be.

I'm not surprised Quinny's going to give the money away. That's the sort of guy he is, and it's fitting that Ireland will provide the opposition for the game because the only place in the world that comes close to loving Quinny as much as Ireland does is Sunderland. They might even love him more up here, if that's possible.

The squad for Quinny's game and the Dublin friendly with Nigeria is the squad for Japan. It's down to twenty-three and the usual suspects are all in there. There's no real surprises but Gary Doherty, Colin Healy and Steven Reid miss out and both Richard Sadlier and Stephen Carr are out through injury. It's tough, and you feel for them, but part of you is just glad you're in. You don't really care about anyone else. It's cruel, but that's football.

Niall's game is on a Tuesday night in the middle of May at the Stadium of Light. We meet up in the Marriot Hotel on the Sunday, which is dead handy for me.

The itinerary is quite specific: we'll have a couple of meetings to get everything in place for the build-up to the opening game against Cameroon and everything to do with the World Cup will be explained on the Monday night. We're also getting sorted with boots, clothes, training gear, etc., so it'll be a busy few days. Adidas is in and they give me about ten pairs of Predators to bring with me. I'm not contracted to anyone, but I like Adidas – although it was a Nike boot that scored that goal against Holland.

At the meeting on Monday night, the day before Quinny's game, Mick sets the agenda for the next month. He's going to have a look at a few things during Quinny's testimonial. Mark Kennedy is struggling with an injury and you can tell just by talking to him that he's walking a fine line. He has to prove this week that he is fit enough for a World Cup finals, never mind Mick. Steven Reid is on stand-by according to my moles in the coaching set-up, and I think Steven's been unlucky not to make the squad.

After Sunderland we're going to Dublin to play Nigeria in the farewell game, the hundredth international soccer match at Lansdowne Road. That's on Thursday night. We can have a few beers in town after, and then we fly to Amsterdam to pick up a KLM flight to Tokyo. It's the very same flight the Dutch team had booked before some spoilsport upset their plans with the winner in Dublin.

From Tokyo we go to Saipan, an island in the Pacific – a bit like Hawaii, according to Mick McCarthy. We'll be there for five or six days to acclimatise to the heat, to rest up after the long season and to get used to the time zone. It's past Japan, so we'll be well-adjusted by the time we move to Izumo for the proper training camp. Mick says Saipan is as much about R&R as it is about anything. We'll be doing some training every day, but only to keep us ticking over. I'd be happy just to park my arse on a beach and chill out but the advice is we can't just sit around for the few days. It'll all be light and fun, a bit of a break, almost a thank you for getting to the World Cup. That's fine by me. Izumo will be where the real business of getting ready for the opening match against Cameroon begins. Mick says the set-up at the training ground in Izumo is better than anything we've experienced with any Ireland team, so it must be good.

There is, however, a bit of a storm brewing in the background before Quinn's testimonial. Our captain is missing. We don't pay much attention to it. Roy is well capable of turning up an hour before the game as if nothing is amiss. That's the way he is, and, like I've said before, as long as he's right on the pitch, he can be as odd and as aloof off it as he wants to be. He's not there when we meet on the Sunday, he's not there when Johnny Fallon gives us all our casual gear for around the hotel, and he also misses the team meeting on the Monday night, but I don't pay any attention. I just assume he's going to turn up in Dublin when he doesn't show on Tuesday. Maybe he has family commitments. Maybe he's carrying a knock. Maybe he doesn't like Quinny. Who cares, as long as he's on the plane on Saturday morning.

Quinny's match gets almost 30,000 fans into the Stadium of Light and it's going to net over a million pounds for the two hospitals. It's great. He plays the first half for Sunderland and most of the second half for Ireland and we're warned not to kick him. No chance. We're days away from flying off to the World Cup so the most physical danger we're going to be in over the next few days is in Lillie's Bordello.

Jack Charlton along with Sunderland and Ireland legend Charlie Hurley are the guests of honour, and I can't help but hug Jack when we meet. Thanks to him I'm off to the World Cup for the second time and I make sure he knows it. He says he'll never let me forget it and I tend to believe him.

Mark Kennedy is on fire. He opens the scoring after three minutes of a 3–0 win – David Connolly and Kevin Kilbane also score – and by the time he goes off in the eighty-fourth minute he's knackered. I play for Ireland in the second half and manage to stay out of trouble. One game down, one to go – and then we're off.

Back in the hotel there's still no sign of Roy and the papers are starting to make a fuss. They're calling it an anti-Niall gesture and claiming it points to a fragile relationship between the captain and his manager, and the captain and his team-mates. To be honest, we'd become used to the papers enhancing the problems Mick and Roy had.

Sparky goes to see Mick when we get back. He's been brilliant in the match but he's struggling with the injury. There's something not right and he's honest enough to say it. Other players would readily have said nothing and carried on to Japan before declaring the full extent of their injury. Not Sparky. He's too loyal to Ireland and to Mick to bluff this one. He's out of the World Cup and he's in tears. I'm gutted for him. Steven Reid gets the call to replace him – just as he's in a taxi on the way to Gatwick airport and a holiday in the Caribbean.

We fly to Dublin and our captain sees fit to join us – like nothing's happened. There's no explanation, no chat. Normal service with Roy has been restored.

Nigeria is the send-off party but no one told them. I start on the right side of midfield with Roy and Mattie Holland inside me, and Killer on the left. This looks like the World Cup midfield to me. Steven Reid scores in the sixty-ninth minute in front of a sell-out Lansdowne but we're 2–0 down at that stage, and lose 2–1. There's a lap of honour at the final whistle and everyone is wishing us well.

We do our own lap of honour in town, and we get rat-arsed. When we check in the next day at Dublin airport, Stan is see-through with the reddest eyes in the world. Roy is giggly, which is how he gets with a few beers on him, but he has that face on him. There are guys dressed up as leprechauns everywhere and the snappers are trying to get Roy to pose with them. He's having none of it. He doesn't even get up when the Taoiseach Bertie Ahern comes over to shake his hand. It's a real messy mood we're in. Some media suggest Roy is snubbing the Taoiseach, but personally, I'm just not sure he can stand up! I'm not far behind him, by the way. My head is thumping.

Get me to Amsterdam. Get me onto that Dutch team flight. Get me to the World Cup, and quick.

Playing for Ireland was one of the best decisions I ever made.
International friendly, Ireland v Russia, 23 March 1994

Playing against the world's best, Paulo Maldini.
1994 World Cup, Italy v Ireland, 18 June 1994

The Three Amigos press conference
– part of the best six weeks of my playing career.
1994 World Cup

Jack Charlton throwing water
bags at us – some of the lads
found the heat in America
too much.
1994 World Cup, Mexico v
Ireland, 24 June 1994

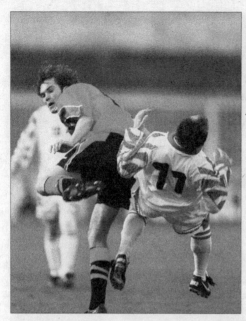

Not one of my proudest moments in an Ireland shirt.
1998 World Cup qualifier, FYR Macedonia v Ireland, 2 April 1997

Messing around with Mick McCarthy. Mick was more like an uncle than a manager, love him to bits.
Ireland training camp, 5 October 1998

A friendly against Paraguay was one of only three games I played for Ireland in the eighteen months from the start of 1999 to June 2000.
International friendly, Ireland v Paraguay, 10 February 1999

The Nike Cup in the US was always an enjoyable tournament.
Nike Cup, Ireland v USA, 11 June 2000

The feeling when you score for Ireland is amazing. The crowd that day played their part, they were definitely our twelfth man.
2002 World Cup qualifier, Ireland v Hollland, 1 September 2001

The play-off against Iran in Tehran was the most intimidating atmosphere I've ever played in.
2002 World Cup play-off, Iran v Ireland, 15 November 2001

My angel, Mick Byrne.
International friendly, Ireland v Nigeria, 16 May 2002

Mick and Roy, you could always feel the strain in their relationship.
2002 World Cup

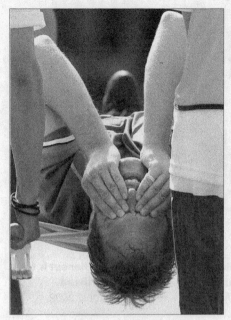

As soon as the tackle was made, I knew my World Cup was all but over.
2002 World Cup, Ireland v Hiroshima, 25 May 2002

My knee was in bits, but I had to give it a go.
2002 World Cup, Ireland v Cameroon, 1 June 2002

Press conference with Mick McCarthy. The greatest honour is to captain your country, which I did on my fiftieth cap.
International friendly, Finland v Ireland, 21 August 2002

What a way to go out.
Playing against Ronaldinho and Brazil in my final international.
International friendly, Ireland v Brazil, 18 February 2004

Chapter Twenty-two

My journalist mate has handed me a copy of the Roy Keane interview in the Irish Times. *They've had it faxed out from Dublin. It's lethal. He's called out Mick and he's had a right go at loads of us. Thanks, Roy. Mick has called a team meeting. We're out of here tomorrow to go to Japan, but Mick wants to clear the air and set a few rules for the rest of the trip. I'm getting a ringside seat for this one.*

We're waiting at Schiphol airport to board the plane to Tokyo and Roy's having a go at two journalists, Philip Quinn from the *Irish Independent* and Billy George from the *Examiner* in Roy's hometown of Cork. He's not happy with the way they portrayed his absence from Quinny's testimonial, telling them it wasn't a snub to Mick or to Niall. The scrapy head from Dublin airport is gone and he has that face on him again, the war face. We leave him to it – it's his argument, not ours. We've a plane to catch and a World Cup to prepare for.

We're sat upstairs in the big leather seats on the KLM jet, where we'll be for the next twenty hours, and I'm dying. My head is up my arse. A night on the town and a real nervousness about long-haul flights has me in bits. I'm fine hopping across the Irish Sea, but don't ask me to sit in a metal tube for any longer than that. There's no drink now. Water it is. We have to rehydrate but even the mineral water is upsetting me. We land, eventually, in Tokyo and the first thing I do is get to the toilet and throw up everywhere. I'm blaming it on travel sickness. I feel terrible.

A few hours on another plane and we're almost in Saipan. Gary Kelly is hosting a quiz on board – name a song for every day of the week. 'Blue Monday' seems right for me, even though I think it's only Sunday our time. 'Sunday Bloody Sunday' if you ask me. When we land in Saipan, the local girls are out in force to greet us with their garlands – I did ask someone what they were called – made up of local flowers which they try to put over our heads. Some of us do it for a laugh. Some we won't name just scowl at the idea of a ring of flowers over their heads and a photo opportunity for Sportsfile's Dave Maher and Inpho's Donall Farmer, the snappers who've travelled with us from Dublin.

It's early Saturday morning local time, the middle of the night as far as my body is concerned. The hotel is brilliant when we get there. 'Idyllic' is the word they'd have used on one of those travel programmes. It's right on the most beautiful beach, with everything you could want for some R&R, but all I want right now is my bed and a decent kip. It's Saturday evening before I wake up, just in time for dinner.

Joe Walsh, the kitman, has a bit of news for us. The training gear was sent on from Sunderland when we went to Dublin and it hasn't arrived yet. They've got the dates wrong and there's conflicting stories about who is to blame and when it's going to arrive. We still have the balls and stuff from the Nigeria game in Dublin, but we're to wear our own T-shirts and shorts for the first light training session the following morning. Some of the lads are livid, and I know from the look on Mick McCarthy's face that he's not happy at all. Much and all as we love the notion of Ragarse Rovers and Ireland being the Dog and Duck team in international football terms, there is a time and a place for everything. And this is not the time and certainly not the place for shambolic organisation.

Jetlag makes it difficult to sleep on the first night in Saipan, and I'm up early to haunt Mick Byrne for a strapping before breakfast and before we go to train. He has his gear with him – there's no fear of Mick Byrne being caught unprepared.

It's already roasting as we get on the bus – a school bus by the look of it – for the short journey to the training ground, if that's what you want to call it. It's a school sports ground for want of a better term, and the grass is like all that Bermuda stuff you come across when you go to play golf in the States. It's bone dry on the surface and the grass is way too long. We try to have a light-hearted session, but the ball won't move properly because there are pitch marks and divots and potholes everywhere. Never mind the ball, you could go over on your ankle very easy in one of these potholes and the World Cup could be over after day one in the training camp! It's a short workout and it's sort of sharp.

Pretty soon that first training session is over, with little or no work done. Back on the bus, Mick McCarthy reminds us we're having a barbecue with the twenty or so journalists in the team hotel in the evening and then we're out for the night, our last blowout before the World Cup itself. Mick is anxious to build bridges with the media, to throw them an olive branch ahead of anything up to six weeks together, and he wants the gesture to be embraced by the players. Most of us don't have an issue with the barbecue. The media have been great to me since I got into the squad, and I prefer it when we are all in it together and no one has to look over their shoulder in case there's a camera or a microphone pointed at them. I know it's changing. The English tabloids have a greater presence than ever in Ireland and some of the Fleet Street ways have come with them. Some of the lads hate the press, and Roy in particular is livid with the idea that he has to sit and break bread with them at a barbecue thousands of miles from home.

When the entertainment act introduces a samurai sword during the cabaret, I'm sure I hear him shout, 'Cut their fucking heads off,' as various journalists volunteer for the act. That's the only hint of unpleasantness on the night. Afterwards, most of us head for the Beefeater, a pub around the corner from the hotel that the press guys have found, as they do. Roy heads back to his room and no one bats an eyelid. That's just the way it is.

What he misses is a cracking night out. Clinton Morrison is hogging the pool table and Richard Dunne, with a bottle of Bud in one hand and a cigarette in the other, is arguing with Neil O'Riordan and a couple of the press guys about why they have it in for him and his lifestyle. I kid you not. It's a good night as far as I'm concerned, a throwback to the old days, the sort of thing we should do more often. If you're paranoid about the press, chances are they'll do you no favours. If you play the game, they'll be as good as gold. I'm always happier playing the game.

Again, I can't sleep on the Sunday night. I'm up at the crack of dawn on Monday and head down for coffee and some early breakfast. In the lift I meet Roy, who's heading down the beach, so I decide to go with him. We walk down the end of the beach in front of the hotel and back, and it's the first time we've ever had a proper conversation. We're talking about everything, family and football, the World Cup, the barbecue and, God help me, but I actually think there's a bit of mutual respect. I've never got that from Roy before. I've never felt anything other than disdain from him and that whole United–Liverpool rivalry of old. This is different. Roy wants to talk to me. He wants to warm to me. He wants to know me. Wow. I wasn't expecting this. A few of the lads join us for coffees at the beach bar, and he's in cracking form.

After brekkie on the Monday morning, we go to train again. It's worse. Mick had complained the day before that the pitch was too dry so they flooded it. It's like a swimming pool. We try another light training session and it's over as quick as the previous one. Mick's livid now and Roy's face tells its own story.

On Monday afternoon they bring us on a tour of the war sites in Saipan from the days of the Japanese occupancy during the Second World War. We visit the suicide cliffs and the caves where the Japanese hid the guns, and it's fascinating. Who'd think such a small American enclave in the middle of the Pacific could have such a part to play in one of the world's greatest conflicts?

On the Tuesday, Roy joins the rest of us on the bus, but he's in a funny humour and ends up having a row with Packie Bonner and the goalkeepers when Packie takes the three lads – Shay Given, Alan Kelly and Dean Kiely – off to train on their own. There's murder between him and Packie – and they played together for so long! He's still fuming when we get back to the hotel and Mick Byrne spends ages up in Roy's room, trying to calm him down.

A rumour starts to gain momentum that Roy is going home. He wants out of the training camp and out of the World Cup. He's told Mick McCarthy as much and the lads start to speculate on his plans. One of our squad had heard before we left for Saipan that the England players were betting on his going home before a ball was kicked. The United lads were stirring that one, apparently they claimed, with good reason. Not what you want to hear four days before you fly to mainland Japan for the tournament proper.

We're sure he's going when we get up for training and there's no training kit outside his door – the skips have finally arrived, by the way. That's it so, he must be quitting on us. Then he comes down for breakfast and wants to know from Joe Walsh where his training kit is! We don't know what to think now. He's in the medical room when I go in for my strapping before training, and I ask him if he's going back to England. Roy just laughs at me.

Then, Mick McCarthy is having breakfast with Roy, and all seems well with the world again. They seem to have made their peace, and Roy is even laughing and joking over his cornflakes. Only for Mick Byrne, he'd probably be gone.

We do some more work on the training ground – the grass is the right length at last – and a few of us do some press stuff at the media hotel with the FAI's media officer Brendan McKenna and John Givens from the sponsor Eircom. We're days away from flying to Japan and the real training camp in Izumo and, to be honest, I just want off Saipan at this stage.

When I see Roy afterwards, he's sitting in the booths in the restaurant area doing interviews with two journalists. I'm just hanging around, killing time, and he's talking to some of the few journalists he wants to talk to these days. Fair enough.

Dinner on the Thursday night is the same as usual. There's a three-piece band trying to get us to sing along and the lads are having none of it. Mick's in and out of the room like a yo-yo, and at the end of the dinner he tells us to be back down in an hour for a team meeting, no exceptions.

My dinner's done at 6.30 p.m. and I've half an hour to kill before the meeting, so I mooch around reception with Kells and Hartey. The press lads are starting to gather and one of them hands me a fax with the interview that Roy had done the previous day with the *Irish Times*. The journo tells me I have to read it and that it might have something to do with the meeting!

I read it quickly and I know straightaway – this is definitely what the meeting is all about. Roy's only gone and slaughtered practically everyone in Saipan preparing for the World Cup with him as our captain. He's lashed the FAI. He's lashed Mick.

I know it's all going to go off in this meeting. Mick and Taff have had a good read of the article, and they've copied it. The staff know what Roy has said about them, and we're about to find out what he's said about his team-mates.

I head back into the dining room for the meeting, and Roy's still there. I grab a coffee and sit down right next to him. I want a front-row seat for this one. The hotel three-piece, with the sombreros and the big guitars, are back and giving it loads with their 'Guantanamera' song. They're even trying to start a conga with the lads – not the wisest move. Mick comes in with Taff and Tony Hickey and leaves the band be for a minute or two, before Tony politely asks them to leave.

Everyone's arrived, and the lads think this is the last big meeting before we leave for Japan. How wrong they are. Some of us know what it's really about. I've read the article – so have Quinny and Stan. We can sense what's coming.

Mick stands up when the band has moved the conga back to the main dining room and tells us all what time we're leaving in the morning, what time to check out and what time to pay all our bills. Tonight preferably. Then it's the dress code for travelling. It's the casual Umbro polo shirt with the white collar and trackie bottoms – and we're to make sure it's all clean and smart. There'll be press waiting for us at the airport in Izumo and we're to be polite to them. We want to make the right impression with our Japanese hosts and get them on our side for the World Cup.

Then he adds there's one last thing. He turns to Roy and says that he has to ask him about the *Irish Times* article that's just been published back in Ireland. He has the article in his hand and the blood is rising in his veins. Showtime.

Mick says he can't believe what's been published in the *Irish Times*. He can't believe what he's just read. Roy shifts back in his chair and makes some room for himself. Mick unravels the paper and starts quoting from the article. He starts quoting what his captain has said about his team-mates, about his manager, about his coaches, about his football association. We're all getting it.

Roy leans forward in the chair and tells Mick, 'I'll stop you there.' He says, 'Everything' – and he repeats the word 'everything' – 'I said to the *Irish Times* is true.' He tells Mick he is a shit manager with a shit coach. He's off on one and nobody's safe. The coaching is shit. The training ground is shit. The preparation has been shit.

Mick is standing up. We're in shock. The two of them are going at each other hammer and tongs and it's like we're not there. We're spectators to the biggest row I've ever witnessed in a football meeting and it's surreal.

I'm in the box seats, right next to Roy. The vein on his temple is throbbing. He's trading insults with Mick. Tony Hickey moves between them. It looks like one of them is going to throw a punch.

Roy keeps telling Mick what he thinks and that's what he believes.

Mick tells him to fuck off home.

Roy says, 'I'll give you your excuse for when you get knocked out of the World Cup.'

He's at the door, looking at us all, and he's saying, 'You can blame Roy Keane, you can blame Roy Keane.' Then he's gone out the door. Our captain has just left the room, a couple of weeks before the World Cup starts. He says he's going home and slams the door shut.

There's a stunned silence. No one knows what to say or what to do. No one. I knew it was going to kick off but I never saw this coming. I never thought about our leader, our captain, our best player quitting on us.

Mick breaks the silence. He wants to know if anyone has anything to add to Roy's words, if anyone has anything else they'd like to say about his management or his training or his coaches.

Dean Kiely puts his hand up and quick as a flash he says, 'I just want you to know, Mick, if you need someone in centre-midfield I can do a job for you, I can fill that position.'

The room bursts out laughing. It's the perfect riposte for the nonsense we've just witnessed. Mick repeats what time we're leaving in the morning, and tells us we're free to go back to our rooms.

Fucking hell. What's just happened? Why did Roy behave like that? Kells and myself are dumbfounded. I reckon Roy knew Mick had the article and had his response ready just in case. It was all too well planned, too thought-out in his strange head. He knew exactly what he was going to say and do when Mick produced the article. He had his defence of the article ready. He had his response ready. It was almost like he wanted Mick to make a big deal of it in front of the lads and give him an excuse to get out of Dodge. He almost had it all itemised from the interview. It's like he'd been waiting years to get it all off his chest.

Like most of the other players, I'd known of their row at the US Cup in Boston when Mick was still playing and Roy went on the beer with Frank Gillespie instead of packing for home. I'd seen him hammer Mick in

Amsterdam about the pizzas and the pre-match and all that I-bet-Jimmy-Floyd-Hasselbaink-isn't-eating-pizza-right-now nonsense. He wasn't, by the way, because he wasn't in the Dutch squad that night!

There is history between Mick and Roy, and there has always been that undercurrent between them. This was the argument waiting to happen and when it happened, there was no holding them back. It was pure hatred. That's the only way I can describe it – hatred.

Everyone is stunned. Some of the lads go back to their rooms. Ian Harte goes off to see Roy. I want Roy to stay but I'm disappointed with the things he's said. He's hammered us all in that article and, for me, it was just days after we had been getting on so well.

We've worked so hard to get here, all of us. Roy wasn't on his own in Amsterdam, despite what people think. He didn't beat Holland on his own in Dublin. He wasn't even in Tehran when we really needed him. And now he's gone.

There's a time and a place for a row with your manager. There's a time and place for slagging your coach and your team-mates in a newspaper article. Here, the night before we leave for the World Cup finals is not it.

I'm gutted for Mick. No matter what we do now, this is going to follow him to the grave.

I want to have it out with Roy. I do go to his room with the idea of getting back some DVDs I'd lent him but my real motive is to see if Roy is really serious about going home. I get to his room and knock and he answers the door quickly. I can see Mick Byrne just inside the room. I ask for my DVDs back but it's obvious that Roy doesn't want to have a conversation with me so I leave them to it.

Maybe I should have stepped in when he started ranting at Mick. Maybe I should have said to him that I wasn't happy with the training ground either, that the balls should have arrived on time. I wasn't happy about any of it, but I wasn't going to let it jeopardise my World Cup. I'd waited eight years for another World Cup – just like him – and I wasn't going to let myself or the team or the fans down just because a training pitch we'd be using for five days was crap or just because the FAI couldn't get our training gear out in time. I'd too much respect for myself, for Mick and for the Irish team to do that.

When you're with Ireland you get through anything that comes your way and you thrive on it. That's the way we are. That's the way we've always been. In some way, I felt it was part of our DNA. It made us fight a bit more. I get what Roy's argument was about, but I don't think it would have made us any better. We've a World Cup to play in. And now we have a World Cup to play without one of the best midfielders in the world. And no DVDs!

Brendan Menton from the FAI calls a press conference. Quinny, Alan Kelly and Stan offer to join Mick at the top table and show solidarity with the manager. It's their decision. There's no players' meeting or anything like that. There's only David Connolly would have a problem with Mick, aside from Roy, and even he has nothing to say at the minute. The three lads just want to be there to protect Mick, I suppose.

It's frantic in the conference room, but it's not packed. There's only the Irish journalists with us. Fraser Robertson from Sky has already left for Tokyo to send footage back to London. Bad timing that.

I sneak in down the back. I love watching press conferences, but I don't want to be part of this one. Mick's not helped much by the FAI – no surprise there – but the three lads make it perfectly clear that the rest of the squad is 100 per cent behind the manager. Roy's gone now and we have to get on with it. We've a plane to catch in the morning and a World Cup to get to.

Our travel agent Ray Treacy is already making plans to get Roy off the island and back to Manchester. Chris Ryan from the FAI has been on to FIFA for the second time in four days to ask about getting Colin Healy in as a replacement for Roy Keane. There was still time to do that the first time Roy said he was going home, but now the deadline for naming the World Cup squad has passed. I can't see Roy changing his mind a second time – and I'm not sure the boys want him to.

Chapter Twenty-three

The fans outside the hotel in Izumo all have their phones in the air as we arrive on the team coach. What the hell are they trying to do, phone us? We've made headlines all over the world after Saipan, but why would they want to phone us? One of the lads asks our Japanese guide what they are doing with the phones. 'Taking photos,' he says. It's a new one on me.

There's no sign of our captain at breakfast early the next morning. We've a flight to catch to Izumo. He's a flight to catch to Manchester.

So it was all true, it did all happen. I didn't dream that Roy Keane decided to leave us on the eve of the World Cup finals.

Mick has twenty-two of us to look out for now, and that's his big concern as we get ready to leave Saipan and head for the media circus that is going to be Izumo airport's arrivals hall. Like all football squads, the lads are already getting back to normal and ready to carry on regardless. I realise as much when I get on the bus and Shay Given has stuck a 'Roy's seat' sign on the seat where Roy always sits. No one's allowed to sit there, a joke that we're going to carry with us through this World Cup. But it still seems wrong that we're leaving without Roy Keane.

I know this World Cup trip is never going to be the same again. That dream I had of another American adventure, of the Three Amigos, the sequel, has been blown out of the water. The next few days are going to be hell and we're going to have to get used to being the centre of attention. At the airport, one of the journos tells me that we've made the front page of the *New Delhi Times*. We're making headlines in India? Jesus.

Sure enough, the world and his mother are waiting for us after the two-hour flight from Saipan. And his mother has cameras, lots of them. This must be what England players go through all the time, all the attention and all the questions.

We nod politely when we get through immigration in Japan and get straight onto the bus. The hotel isn't far away and it's decent. It's also behind a bloody big gate and an armed guard, not a bad thing considering Mick has told us not to talk to anyone until everything dies down. He wants us to stay away from the press as much as we can. Any of us with columns for the newspapers will have to get them checked. The FAI and Mick, with Liam Gaskin now at his side to finally give him some help, want to control what's coming out of the camp, and that's fair enough. They're getting hammered back home from what we can hear.

After lunch on the first afternoon in Izumo we leave for the training ground and there are hundreds of local fans waiting for us outside the gates at the hotel. They all have their phones up in the air. It looks weird and I can't figure out what they are doing. Are they trying to call us? Are they trying to record what we're saying? Turns out they all have new camera phones and want to get photos of us. I've never seen a phone like it before, but where else are you going to see your first one if not Japan?

The training ground, the official training ground for our World Cup preparations, is about twenty minutes out of Izumo in the sticks and, I have to say, it is class. The local mayor is there to welcome us at an official function and he can't do enough for us. The pitch is perfect. The dressing rooms are perfect. The support facilities are perfect. If only Roy were here, even he'd be happy with everything on offer. It's as good as anything I've ever seen with either club or country, and that's saying something. Why didn't he wait until he got to Japan and had a look at all this before venting his anger? I can't get my head around it.

The camera phones are still flashing when we get back to the hotel and the TV cameras are outside as well. Roy is on his way back to England and Mick is the centre of attention. It's funny that we spent the 1994 World Cup watching the O.J. Simpson drama unfold on the TV and now we're watching the Roy Keane drama unfold at the 2002 World Cup. It's that big.

This is so different from the 1994 World Cup experience. Eight years ago we were getting videotapes from home of the whole country celebrating and partying and enjoying the World Cup. Now all we're seeing is the country at war over the row between the Ireland manager and his captain.

It's endless.

Tony O'Donoghue from RTÉ is being called Kate Adie by

his colleagues and being asked where his flak jacket is as he broadcasts from the roof of the hotel. We can't really leave the hotel, and when we do, we have to have security with us and avoid the media. We're starting to feel the pressure and we're starting to doubt ourselves in this vacuum.

Should Roy come back? Should we ask him back? Was he wrong? Was Mick wrong? We're talking about professional footballers here. We're not a Sunday pub team. We know how to act and how to behave as professionals on and off the field, but nothing has ever prepared us for something like this. There are kids on this team, Duffer and Robbie for instance, and it must be putting them under huge strain.

Mick is ageing in front of our eyes. He's good on the training ground, and Taff is acting like nothing ever happened, but the press conferences are starting to take their toll. Mick's now spending hours in there telling the world why he did what he did and what he's going to do next. Roy is back in England and walking his dog. Triggs he's called the poor Labrador who has to accompany him on these endless walks when he thought his master was going to be away from home for at least a month. The lads cop the dog's name and they give me a good ribbing about it. They reckon Roy's named the dog after me! And they don't let up on it. Every time the camera pans to Triggs on those walks, they start pointing at me.

At least we can laugh about that, but it is all getting out of hand so close to the start of the tournament – and Mick knows it. He calls a meeting at the end of the first week in Izumo and he puts his cards on the table. He's under real pressure to take Roy back. The whole world seems to want him to take Roy back. He doesn't know if Roy will come back, and he's heard nothing from Roy or Roy's camp to suggest he'd even consider it. But Mick has a squad to think about, not just himself, and he feels duty-bound to the country and to the fans, who will start arriving in Japan any day now after spending a lot of money on their journeys. He's on the spot and he has to make a decision.

The country is divided and Mick wants to know if the squad is divided as well. He tells us he can take Roy back, but the decision has to be made by the players. If we want him back, if we'll have him back, then Mick will bite the bullet and do what's best for the team, not what's best for him. It's typical Mick. The team is always bigger than the individual in Mick's eyes.

Mick and the staff leave, and Quinny takes the chair. He puts Mick's question to the floor. There are twenty-two players in that room and when Niall asks who wants to bring him back, there's a silence. You can see the strain on the lads' faces. They all have different relationships with Roy – some good and some bad. Just two hands go up. One goes back down pretty quickly. The lads are torn, and it's a difficult decision, but everyone feels that Roy made his choice and we'll do it without him. We don't want him back. The vote is twenty-one to one – we don't want him back.

Mick could have made that decision on his own, but he didn't, and I understand why. He wanted us – the players left behind, the ones who will play against Cameroon next week – to know exactly where we stand. He needs to know where we stand as well, after all the debate and all the pressure of the past week. If he doesn't bring Roy back, then all the blame will be on him. If the players vote against it, then it is a collective decision and we all carry the can.

It's not Mick's decision. It's still his problem, but he hasn't had to make the call on it. He's given the responsibility to us and we've given him our answer.

News of the meeting gets out fairly quickly. The RTÉ cameras have been in Manchester and Tommie Gorman does his infamous 'think of the kids' interview with Roy. Bits of it are getting through to us, but nothing coming from Roy's mouth sounds like he wants to come back to us anyway. It's like he's made his bed and now he's going to lie in it, and sod the begrudgers, which is typical Roy, backed into a corner with no way out.

What would have happened if we had voted to take him back? What would have happened if he'd told Tommie Gorman that he was ready to apologise to Mick and ask to be brought back into the fold? We'll never know, but the night he finally announced he wasn't coming back, it was like a weight was lifted off all our shoulders.

The media all go out that night, and most of them get hammered in a karaoke bar, given that the speculation and the guessing are finally over. I wish I was with them.

Chapter Twenty-four

Quinny's organised a breakout from the team hotel in Seoul. We make for an Irish bar and have a great night. Mick McCarthy knows nothing of it all and we get away with it. Next night, Mick is out for a few beers with his wife and some mates. He walks into the Irish bar and there's giant posters of us all over the walls, drinking in the same bar. We're fucked!

So Roy's gone and we can get back to the closest thing to normality that will ever be associated with this Irish team and this Irish manager from here on in. He's back in Manchester, walking Triggs for miles and miles and miles. We're in camp in Izumo, preparing for a warm-up game on Saturday against Hiroshima, a J-League side.

The FAI and Mick arranged the game to get us acclimatised for Japan but if anything, it's cooler here than it was in Saipan and we're flying on the training ground. The conditions are no problem at all, and the game is going ahead in a local college stadium. They've sold a good few tickets and all the local schoolkids are coming to have a look at a real live World Cup team.

The big thing for us is not to get injured. We're too close to the tournament now, only a week away, to run any risks. The squad's already down to twenty-two, so the last thing Mick needs is an injured player.

I'm all but over my ankle injury and I'm eager to play. I want to prove to Mick that the injury is behind me and I fancy nailing down that right-hand-side role in his midfield before we get any closer to the real action. Mark Kinsella is the man to replace Roy in the centre of midfield, and I start the Hiroshima game on the right. So far, so good.

We're pinging balls around on a decent surface and we're battering them. It's coming up to half-time and there's a ball played down the channel. It's heading out of play. I can slide in here now and keep it in play, but there's a guy charging down on me and if I slide, he'll slide. No thanks. I just carry on running when I realise he's already committed himself to the sliding tackle. The ball's going nowhere when he clatters into me from behind and smashes my knee. The pain is instant. I've been here before and I know it's bad. I'm fuming as I hit the floor.

He's risked conceding a corner when the ball was on the way out of play, just to get at me, just to tackle me for the sake of tackling me. He's wrapped his big legs around me and scissored me as he's come across. No one has any doubt he meant it – he may play his club football with Sanfrecce Hiroshima, but he's from Cameroon, the country we're facing in our opening group game in a week.

My knee's given way and I just know I'm in trouble even before Mick Byrne and Ciaran get to me. I'm fucked and

I know it. That's all I can say to Mick Byrne when he gets
out to me. 'My knee is fucked, Mick. It's gone.' It's numb
and they stretcher me off. Mick Byrne's trying to get at
the lad as they put me on the stretcher. He's fuming. He's
shouting 'stupid idiot' at him, giving him loads of stick,
asking him what the hell he's doing that for in a friendly
game. I'm too sore to even look up, but I can hear Mick
bashing him. They get me to the dressing room and they
get me into the shower. The warm water does some sort of
a trick and the numbness dies down. I can start to feel my
knee again – maybe it isn't so bad.

I hobble out to watch the second half and there's real
concern for me on the Irish bench. I'm putting a brave face
on it when Mick McCarthy's around. 'I'll be grand.' I keep
repeating it. 'I'll be grand.'

Tony Hickey comes up to me in the dressing room
when the game is over. The bloke is outside and he wants
to apologise and swap shirts. 'Swap fucking shirts? Tell
him to fuck off, Tony.' So he does. He looks this big bloke
straight in the eye and says, 'Fuck off. He doesn't want
your apology and you're not coming in.'

Back in the hotel I all but lock myself in the room. I can't
let Mick McCarthy or any of the lads see the pain I'm in.
Mick Byrne gets me all sorts from Martin Walsh, the team
doctor. My knee has swollen up like a balloon. I'm popping
pills for fun all night – anti-inflammatories, painkillers –
I'm dosing up on anything I can get my hands on. I'm not
going home. I'm not missing my last World Cup. No way.

The doc has another look at me the next morning. My
knee is so swollen he can't even send me for a scan. So
it's more painkillers, more anti-inflammatories and more

ice than the bars on Grand National day at Aintree. Mick
Byrne's as distraught as I am. He's saying prayers for me at
this stage. He's on about some Child of Prague he's going
to fly out. He can pray to Roy Keane if it gets me through
this one.

Mick McCarthy is good as gold with me. He knows I
won't let him down, knows I'll be honest with him. For the
first few days after the smash, he tells me to take it easy,
to let time take its own course. By the middle of the week
I can jog and do some light work. Back in my room I'm
overdosing on pills.

By Friday Mick needs an answer. We've said our
goodbyes to Izumo and flown down to Niigata. We're in the
match stadium for the traditional visit twenty-four hours
before the game when Mick pulls me aside. He needs an
answer, he needs to know where and how I stand before he
finalises his team. He wants me to play, but he wants me to
be honest with him. He can't expect anything less.

We have a light training session and then a five-a-side at
the end of it. There's no hiding place now. I join in because
I have to, but it's sore. My knee is still swollen and it's only
the pills that are getting me through it all. I blag my way
through the game, but Mick's not so sure, even though he
knows as well as anyone how desperate I am to play.

He asks me again how my knee is. I say it's fine. I use
that word 'grand' again. I've been using it all week. He
wants to test it. We go down the tunnel and he has me
block tackle the wall with a ball in between me and my
foot. I have to smash the stationary ball against the wall
with the side of my foot. The look on my face will tell him
if the knee is good to go or not. My knee hurts like hell.

I'm sure I must be rattling with all the pills inside me, but I grin and bear it. This is not the time to break down in front of the Ireland manager.

I smash the ball. Smash, smash, smash. Inside I'm dying but all Mick can see is determination and commitment. When he asks one last time how it is, I smile. 'It's grand.' I'm in the team to play Cameroon. It was worth the lie to Mick McCarthy.

The morning of the match can't come quick enough for me. The pills are popped and my game head is on. Mick McCarthy's more nervous than we are. I can tell. We've been inside a bubble since Saipan and now we're about to step into the public arena for the first time since he sent his captain home. How will the fans take to him after everything that's happened? What sort of reception will he get? We're not worried in the same way. Roy's gone as far as we're concerned – he doesn't exist on this match day because he's not here. Like all football teams, we can only play what's put in front of us and we can only play with the players on the pitch with us.

Any worries Mick had about the fans are soon put to bed. The minute we get out there for the warm-up, they welcome us like Green Gods. There's a real Irish party going on behind one of the goals and nothing's going to stop us. They're here for the World Cup. They're here for us now. And for Mick. Everything else can be parked for the next ninety minutes.

He's calm in the dressing room beforehand, goes through the game plan one last time and tells us to enjoy it. Then he's out the door ahead of us.

As I make my way down the tunnel, Mick gives me this little nod and a wink. It's his way of telling me it's going to be all right. My knee will be fine. The match will be fine. The World Cup will be grand.

Cameroon are decent. They have to be with a young Samuel Eto'o in their side. They're strong in the middle and they have pace. They're going to put us on the front foot early on. They're going to test us in all departments. They go a goal up through M'Boma just before the break, by which time I've been booked. I put my hand on this guy's shoulder and the Japanese referee goes straight for the yellow card. It's soft. But it's not the only thing worrying me. My knee is in bits. It's swollen again and it's killing me. I can't wait for half-time.

We get back into the dressing room and Mick McCarthy is straight over.

'How are you?' he asks, but he knows the truth as he looks at my leg. All I can do is yell at Mick Byrne to get me some ice. I'm telling Mick McCarthy it'll be okay and I'm screaming at Mick Byrne for ice and painkillers. Mick McCarthy just turns around as he walks back to the centre of the room, looks at me and shakes his head. I'll never forget it. He knows I'm fucked. He knows my World Cup is over. He knows I should never have started the game in the first place. I know what he's going to say before he even says it.

'I'm taking you off, Steve Finnan's in at right-back.'

Stevie is warming up as I'm protesting. I know my World Cup's as good as over, and I'm fuming.

The others are on their way back out as I hobble into the shower. When the door closes behind them, I break down.

I start crying and I can't stop. I know this is the end of my World Cup, maybe even the end of my time with Ireland.

I'm on the bench when Mattie scores the equaliser seven minutes into the second half and I'm made up for the lads, but part of this World Cup has just died for me. That's the killer part of all this. I'm jumping up and down like everyone else when Mattie's shot hits the back of the net. I want to be a part of it and I want the team to get something from this game, but football's taught me to be a selfish bastard as well. I'm shouting on the outside and bleeding on the inside as we escape Niigata with a 1–1 draw.

My head's back up my arse now. I want to punch that bloke from Cameroon who smashed me in Izumo last week. I want to shout and scream and have a go at anyone who gets in my way. I don't have long to wait for the opportunity.

We fly to Chiba City, just outside Tokyo, straight after the game, so there's no time to see my dad or Harry afterwards – I'll catch up with them tomorrow when we've a day off. First Mick wants a word in his room. He's not happy, and he's not alone in that regard.

I start lying again. I tell him that he was wrong to take me off, my knee was fine, I'd have made it through the second half. But he's fuming. He took a chance on me and, as far as he is concerned, I let him down. He reckons I wasn't fit for Cameroon and I won't be fit for Germany in Ibaraki, the second game in the group. That's like a red rag to a bull and I lose it.

But I'm wrong. I am so out of order when I tell Mick McCarthy, the one manager who understands me better than anyone, that I might as well go home right now if he's not going to play me against Germany. I do a Roy Keane on him, and I'm not proud of it. I know I can hurt him. I know what he's been through with Roy and how vulnerable he is, and this is my chance to stick the knife into the man who is denying me my World Cup chance. I know I'm like his son – Roy's not – so this is really going to hurt him. He's not showing me any loyalty as far as I'm concerned and I'm going to make him pay.

When he really needs me to be more truthful with him than ever before, I opt for petulance. He knows exactly what I'm doing and why. He knows I lied to him when I said I could play against Cameroon, and he has to know that I am lying to him when I say I can play against Germany.

He's asked me twice if I am fit and twice I've lied to him. My knee is still killing me, but this is the World Cup. It's not a league match with Sunderland or a friendly match with Ireland. It's the World Cup, the finals my goal against Holland got us to. It's the World Cup and I deserve to play, even if I can barely walk. Mick owes me that much after the Holland goal. Ireland owes me that much after Lansdowne Road. Delusions of grandeur!

Our meeting comes to an abrupt end. Mick agrees to disagree, but he warns me that he won't change his mind. I won't be in the team for the Germany game and he won't even think about Saudi Arabia until after Ibaraki. The Germans beat the Saudis 8–0 in their opening game so Mick has enough to be worrying about. I'm back on my own now, isolated in a twenty-two-man squad, and I'm not a happy camper.

The lads can sense it. I tell one of them I've been living a lie since the injury in Izumo and next thing it's on the back page in big, bold letters. 'McAteer's Lie' reads the headline, with a story that basically tells it the way it's been for me. It's not even been mentioned in my *Sunday Independent* column, so I'll bet they're not best pleased. I'm gutted it's got out, but quietly I have to admit to myself that it's true. I've cheated Mick but I can't regret it. I only did so because I was desperate to play in the World Cup finals.

I'm now spending loads of time with my guardian angel, Mick Byrne. I'm getting all the treatment I can get ahead of the Germany game, and I'm telling anyone who will listen that I'm fit. It's still a lie, of course, and Mick won't be fooled again. The night before the match, he names the team and my name is missing, as promised. I know it's coming but I'm livid nonetheless.

I'm up to see Mick again and, this time, I'm going home. There's no point being here if he doesn't want to play me. I'm losing the plot now. 'Piss off, Mick. And fuck the World Cup if I'm not wanted.'

He just goes, 'All right, if that's what you want.'

And that's it. He doesn't fight back. He doesn't tell me to fuck off. He doesn't send me home. He just lets me at it. He knows he can't win when I'm in this frame of mind.

I storm back to my room – we room on our own in Japan, which probably doesn't help me in this situation – and I pack my bags. Literally. Mick Byrne comes flying into the room and I have all my gear on the bed, ready to jam it into my Umbro kitbag. He's asking me what I'm doing when it's bloody obvious – I'm packing my bags and getting out of here. My angel can't believe it. Without actually calling me a spoiled brat, he lets me know that I am causing the gaffer more grief than I am worth. Tony Hickey's in the room now and he's telling me the same thing. They're telling me to cop on, to grow up, to treat Mick with more respect. And they're right. I know they're right, but it is hard to admit it. Mick McCarthy is as close to a dad as I have, and he doesn't deserve this.

I've seen my own dad a couple of times this week. He's finding it hard with the language barrier and he's struggling with the Japanese culture, so he's delighted to meet up for a brew in the team hotel and discover that there's a tented village for the Irish fans not far from where we're staying. It's clearly a Godsend for him because, a couple of days later, one of the press lads approaches me with a bit of a tale. He's only met my dad on the train back from the fan village and my dad has spilled the beans to him about the whole Roy Keane incident in Saipan. He says I'm lucky that he's not the sort to run the story based on hearsay. I'm not that lucky though. The next day it's all over the back page of one of the papers and they've only quoted my dad. I bleeding hammer him the next time I see him. He's only gone and killed me by opening his mouth to the press at a time when I'm already in Mick McCarthy's bad books.

At least Mick knows I'm hurting badly when we get to the stadium in Ibaraki the night before the game. As we walk out for the first time, he makes sure to follow me and he just puts those big arms around me and gives me a hug. He's let me have my sulk, and now it's time to make up. That hug sorts out everything in an instant. I just smile and he knows we're good again. I feel a part of it again. The strop is over.

I'm not in the team, but I am on the bench and part of me thinks I have a chance of getting on after that hug the night before. I keep looking over at Mick and giving him that look, that I'm-here-if-you-need-me-boss look that every player ever put on a bench knows how to do. It doesn't work. Instead I am an Ireland fan for the night – but what a night to be an Ireland fan.

We're slow to start again, just like in the Cameroon match, and we concede when Miroslav Klose scores in just the nineteenth minute at Kashima Stadium. We get back into the game after that early setback, but we can't get at Oliver Kahn in the German goal for all our possession. We're crawling towards the World Cup exit door as the second half heads to a conclusion and we just can't get the ball into the German net. It's not that we're playing badly – we're playing some great stuff – but we can't get that final touch.

Mick does turn to the bench in his hour of need – well, in the seventy-third minute to be precise about it – but it's Steven Reid and big Quinny who get the nod, and in Quinny's case, literally. His flick for Robbie in the final seconds of two minutes of added time is enough to inspire a Christy Moore song. Robbie buries it past Kahn, and we're up off the bench. Olé, olé, olé. He's already doing his bow-and-arrow celebration as we race onto the pitch. The ref barely has time to blow his whistle after the goal, and the game is over. We've drawn with Germany and we're still in with a chance of getting out of the group stage. A win against the Saudis – who lose 1–0 to a Samuel Eto'o goal for Cameroon in their second game – and we're through.

My anger has gone. I'm with the lads who didn't play and we're kicking every ball, we're dissecting every pass and every chance just like the fans. We have time for all of this, mind – Robbie's been selected for doping control and he can't produce a sample. Eventually we leave the ground without him. And we start the party back in the hotel without him too.

Stan has just become the first Irish player to win a hundred caps. We've all chipped in to buy him a Cartier watch to mark the occasion, and the FAI, thanks to the generosity of our favourite treasurer John Delaney, has thrown the bar open back at the team hotel. Sod the cost is John's attitude. It's a great night. Duffer's kid brother has the guitar out, the fans are in the thick of it and it's like the good old days all over again. And to think I was going to walk away from all of this!

The smile is back on my face but I'm not getting excited about playing against Saudi Arabia. I've been kicked in the teeth once too often by this World Cup and I'm not going to let it happen again. I've come to my senses and realised that it's time to do whatever is best for the team and for Mick. If that means sitting on the bench again, then so be it – if I can play a part, all the better, but I've got to be there for Mick now. We've survived one scrape against the Germans and the important thing is to take advantage of it against the Saudis, who have nothing left to play for but their pride.

There are no worries on the performance front. We're in the driver's seat from start to finish against Saudi Arabia. Robbie does what he always does and scores for Ireland, this time in the seventh minute. Gary Breen sends the fans wild – they keep singing about a team of Gary Breens – with the second in the sixty-first minute and Duffer scores one of the great Ireland goals three minutes from time and celebrates with a bow to his adoring audience. We win 3–0 and I even get a late run as a sub, on in the eightieth minute for Gary Kelly. I swear to God I am not expecting it when Mick tells me to warm up and then calls me back to put me on the field. I'm back and it feels great.

Maybe I can get back in the team now that we know we are definitely going to play in Korea in the second phase of the tournament.

First we have to get to Seoul. And it's not pleasant. The plane journey is probably the roughest the Irish team has had. But even though I'm a terrible flier, I don't mind it so much. Maybe I've been taking so many pills that I'm hallucinating!

Korea is certainly different to Japan. It seems more Westernised, more suitable for our families. And it gives us a night out with a week between the Saudi and Spanish games. A night out that Mick only finds out about by accident by the way.

It's the night of Spain's last game in their group and, if they win, they'll be next up for us in a city called Suwon, about an hour or so from Seoul.

Mick wants us to see the game, and he knows we could do with a bit of a blowout as well so he says it's okay to watch the match in the Irish bar – of course it's an Irish bar – in our team hotel. We can have a few beers watching the game but nothing stupid and no sneaking out. He specifically says no sneaking out – and there's the challenge.

Quinny, not for the first time, takes on the role of entertainment officer. The hotel is the centrepiece of a massive shopping mall and there are all these rows of shops working off the hotel on the ground floor. We do watch Spain qualify for Suwon and we do take note of their performance. We also take a few beers on board and they all taste of more.

The talk starts about breaking out of camp, about going over the wall if you like, and sneaking out just like Mick told us not to do. Quinny's argument is a simple one – if enough of us go out, Mick can't send us all home. There's no way he can send the Seoul Twenty-Two on their way.

It's a reasonable argument. And it takes hold. We're up to fifteen volunteers when the call to arms is sounded. Niall's plan is to make our own way back from the hotel bar in dribs and drabs so as not to raise any suspicions, and then meet down in the basement, on the shopping level. Problem is, there's four entrances to the mall at basement level and he's after telling everyone to meet at Entrance B. Funnily enough, the signs are all in Korean and none of us know which door is Entrance B. There's fifteen Irish footballers walking the mall in the basement of this hotel and none of us know where we're going. It's like the lingerie department scene in *Father Ted*.

Eventually we all hook up, and Niall brings us off to this other Irish bar he's heard about – as he would. The bloke who owns it clears out the bar and there's just us lot and the one and only Michael Flatley from *Riverdance*. The owner is delighted with himself and takes loads of photos of us lot in his pub. He's made up that Michael Flatley is there as well, but they're both sworn to secrecy. Mick must never know we broke curfew!

It's fair to say a great night ensues but no one gets into any bother and we're all back in the hotel in one piece, ready for some sleep and training the next day. Taff knows we've had a few pints in the hotel, so he runs the bollocks off us. What he doesn't know is that fifteen of us had a few more and are really suffering.

That night Mick and Taff go for a few pints with Mick's wife, his agent Liam Gaskin, the solicitor fellow Gerald Kean and a few other mates. There's only one place for them to end up and that's the Irish bar. Mick walks in, and there's photos of his players plastered all over the walls, beer in hand. The bloke's only gone and blown up the photos he took to poster size and put them on any piece of wall he can find. He's proper made up when the Irish manager arrives in the next night and the camera is out again. He even tells Mick he's never taking the photos of the Ireland players and the Ireland manager off his wall.

Mick could have torn strips off his wall there and then. Instead he threatens to tear strips off us at training the next day. He starts with a casual question about our 'night off' and asks if we had a good time. Quinny says we just watched the game in the hotel, the game was all right, we had a few beers and we went to bed. Mick starts breaking his arse laughing. He could have slaughtered us, but instead he said there were some photos of a lookalike team that looked well in the Irish bar. He knew we needed that blowout.

I've convinced myself and Mick Byrne that I am going to start against Spain. My knee's settling down and I'm buzzing about the place in training and Mick gave me that ten minutes against the Saudis, so he obviously fancies me again. I'm not worried about the Spanish either. They've good players, don't get me wrong, but they looked like a side in transition when we watched them the other night and nothing Mick has shown us on DVD should scare us.

I don't start. Mick tells me before he names the team the night before the game and, this time, there's no strop. At least I know I've a chance of getting on, but it never comes. We concede the first goal again, something we've done in every match bar the Saudi one at this World Cup. Morientes gets it after just eight minutes, when he nips in front of Breeny to head past Shay. Once again we've left ourselves with a mountain to climb. We're not helped when Hartey misses a penalty, won by Duffer when he was chopped down by Juanfran. Hartey's normally so reliable from the spot, I'd have put my house on him to score. Again we play well without inflicting real damage.

Kevin Kilbane does have one shot saved off the line by Hierro and Robbie and Mark Kinsella have chances but again we leave it till the last possible minute to get the equaliser when Hierro manhandles Quinny, a second-half replacement for Gary Kelly. The Swedish referee Anders Frisk, the man who awarded Turkey a late penalty at Lansdowne Road in the Euro 2000 play-offs, is on our side this time and points immediately to the spot. Robbie's big enough and bold enough to take the responsibility from Hartey and he buries the ball past Iker Casillas.

We're into extra time now and the Spanish are struggling. They've already used three substitutes when one of them – Albelda – limps out, but we just can't get the golden goal to send us through to the quarter-finals.

Instead we face a penalty shootout – and we've already missed one penalty. Robbie scores. Mattie misses. David Connolly misses. Killer's effort is stopped by Casillas. Stevie Finnan scores when he has to. Valerón and Juanfran have missed for Spain, so it's down to Mendieta to decide it with the final kick of the shootout.

He stops before he shoots. He moves to replace the ball.

I can't bear this on the line. I'm shrinking by the minute and I'm not even out there.

Mendieta scores and the World Cup is over.

I'm gutted. I had wanted so much from this World Cup. I had expected so much from this World Cup – but it just hasn't delivered. From Saipan to Suwon, it's been one let-down after another, for the team and for me. I know I'll probably never see this stage again. I might never play for Ireland again. That's a thought running through my head as we traipse around the pitch to say thank you to the fans who never lost the faith, no matter what was going on off the pitch. They've spent fortunes to get here and we've done our best, considering. Maybe it *is* time to move on and let the next generation through.

Maybe I set the bar too high this time. Maybe I thought it could be 1994 revisited when I was young and innocent, and had Babbsy and Kells with me on the trip of a lifetime. Babbsy's not been here and Kells is Robbie's mate now. He's got his Leeds United clique and they're his new amigos, Robbie and Hartey. I've not really enjoyed this World Cup. What Roy did was poor. What happened with my knee was shit. Telling Mick I was going home was shit on my part. The World Cup's been spoiled for me. And I'll never get the chance now to put that right.

That's the biggest disappointment. Back in 1994 I thought I'd be at every World Cup with Ireland and every European Championships. Now I've probably just been to my last big tournament with my country, and it hurts to end it like this. It hurts like hell.

Chapter Twenty-five

There's a girl I fancy who's been travelling with the Irish team. We're checking into a hotel for a match the next day. I'm single now, so why not try my luck? I throw the bags into the room and come back down to reception. She's there. Time for a chat.

'Tonight's your lucky night, get the key to Room 250 from reception and I'll be up to you in ten minutes,' she says.

I can't believe my luck, get the key and sprint to the room. I turn the key, walk into the room and realise I've been done like a kipper. It's my room and the only one waiting for me tonight will be Babbsy. He's no chance.

Mick McCarthy is standing at the top of the bus on the way back to Seoul from Suwon and thanking Stan, Quinny and Alan Kelly for their contribution to Irish football after their retirements in the wake of the defeat to Spain. It's news to Alan that he's retiring. Quinny and Stan had said as much in the dressing room after the game, but Alan has told nobody except his missus that he's going to call it a day. He thanks Mick for making his mind up for him! I'm thinking about calling it quits, but Mick asks if anyone else with a decision to make can take some time about it. He's right.

I know there's talk that he might go himself after the whole Saipan affair and there are very few managers who stay on after the World Cup finals anyway – it's a well-known fact that most international managers either quit for a club job or get the sack after the World Cup. I don't know where I'd stand with a new manager and I still don't really know if I want to retire. I'm on forty-nine caps after the Saudi Arabia game and fifty has a nice ring to it. The lads might even chip together and buy me a Cartier watch, like we did for Stan.

There's no rush. I've a holiday with Harry to look forward to and then a late return to pre-season with Sunderland. My knee is still sore – don't tell Mick – and I need to get that sorted out as well. As soon as I get back to the club, they send me down to Bradford for a scan and it looks like there's a bit of cartilage damage. There's definitely a tear there. I should never have stayed for the World Cup and I should never have played against Cameroon. The surgeon doesn't mince his words and I know, again, that I misled Mick before that first game, but that's history now. I have two choices – surgery, which will keep me out for months, or an injection that will give me at least a year before they have to think about an operation. The injection sounds good to me. I need to start the season in the Sunderland team, for my own sanity if nothing else.

At the start of the 2002–03 season we're still not winning much, or scoring much. Reidy's answer to the scoring crisis is to throw money at it. He buys Tore André Flo from Rangers for a club record fee of £6.75 million and Marcus Stewart from Huddersfield for a good few bob, but it doesn't do us any good.

I've had a groin op to try and sort out my injury, but I'm still travelling with the team and sitting on the bench with Peter and the coaching staff, watching and learning. I fancy this management business down the road and this is the perfect opportunity to learn from a master.

Results in the season mean the Sunderland board don't share my view of Peter Reid as a master manager. After we get beaten 3–1 at Arsenal at the start of October, Reidy has a paper on his knee in the dressing room, pretending to read it as the players get showered and changed. The paper's upside down. He's staring through the page and down to the floor. I look at him and I reckon he's losing it.

Quinny has another of his many birthdays that day, and we stay down in London for one of his great 'nights on the town', which involves visiting all his old haunts from his days as a young Irish kid in the big city with Arsenal. The old haunts all serve beer.

Next morning, we're on the train back to Durham when our mobile phones start hopping. Reidy's been sacked and the big rumour straight off is that the chairman Bob Murray wants Mick McCarthy for the job. I'm right behind that one. Mick would be made for it and I know from talking to him that he'd be keen to discuss it with Bob and the board. I tell the lads they'll love Mick.

The fixture list for the season is a good read. Ireland have a friendly in Finland in August ahead of the Euro qualifiers, and we play Manchester United at home in the Premier League a week later. That's Roy Keane's Manchester United. His book is just out and, sure enough, he has slaughtered Mick, Quinny, me and anyone else who had the cheek to stay on for the World Cup. We're all Muppets and Quinny is Mother Teresa. The game at the Stadium of Light is going to be a little bit spicy by my reckoning.

The northeastern press can't wait to get hold of me before the United game. 'Will I be buying Roy's book?'

Will I bollocks.

'Will I be reading Roy's book?'

Will I bollocks. 'I'd rather read Bob the Builder.'

My response just what they want to hear and it makes all the headlines.

I'm not bothered. Roy can take it any way he wants. And I don't have to buy his book anyway – Gavin McCann kindly has a copy of it waiting on my space in the dressing room when I get to the ground for the United game. How very thoughtful of him.

The lads get a great laugh when I pick up my towel and the book falls out. This is too good a chance to turn down. I get one of the apprentices and tell him to stand outside the United dressing room with the book and to ask Roy to sign it when he gets off the bus – but not to mention it's for me. Sure enough, Roy signs the book and the apprentice brings it straight back to me in the dressing room – I still have it at home, somewhere.

There's no words between any of us and Roy before the game, no shaking hands, no contact. United go one up early on, but we settle back into it and I set up the equaliser for Tore André Flo.

I'm enjoying this, and I'm having a right ding-dong battle with Roy in the middle of the park. Eventually we have a go at each other – and it's my fault, to be fair. I've taken a heavy touch and he's nipped in front of me and robbed the ball. So I pull him back, illegally, and he's not best pleased. I'm out of order, and he gets the free kick – but then elbows me in the head. I push him back and he squares up to me. He's going to rip my fucking head off, apparently. He's going to do this, that and the other to me. So I tell him to put it in his next book, and I make the gesture with a pen and a piece of paper. 'Write it down and I'll read it in your next book,' I tell him. He's fuming.

The game is all but over when he finally gets me back for mocking him. He just runs past me from behind and elbows me in the side of the head as Beckham comes at me. He's run into me from the blind side and he's caught me square on the head. I'm not expecting it and I end up on my arse. The referee Uriah Rennie is straight over with a red card for my mate Roy, who's mouthing off again. John O'Shea is over trying to calm things down. Beckham's accusing me of diving, rich! The ref was two yards away, he saw what happened, and how it happened.

Alex Ferguson starts shouting and screaming and Quinny, who's been substituted at this stage, comes running about forty yards onto the pitch to have a word with Roy. Roy just fobs him off before Fergie tells him to sit back down. It's all nonsense. Roy knew exactly what he was doing and he deserved the red.

The Ireland game in Finland is still a week away and the *News of the World* want me to do a big piece on Roy for the Sunday before it. They offer me three grand to tell my story about what happened before the World Cup, not just in the Sunderland–United game. They've also got wind of the fact that I was one of only two or three players to knock on his door that night in Saipan, and they want to know what I said to him. I opt not to talk to them. It's probably for the best.

The row with Roy is still big news when we meet up in Dublin the following Sunday before heading out for the friendly in Helsinki. Mick's curious about what he said, and most of the lads who were at the World Cup have a good laugh about it. Not for the first time, Roy gives us something to talk about.

Mick has news for me on the Monday before we fly to Finland. He wants me to captain the team in honour of my fiftieth cap. I'm dead chuffed. I don't even get to captain a quiz team down the pub, so to captain Ireland on the night I make my fiftieth appearance is something very special.

It's a mixed squad with most of the lads who were in Japan and Korea and a few young lads looking to break in, the likes of Cliff Byrne and Jim Goodwin and Tommy Butler, who Mick wants to have a look at. Jari Litmanen, who'd played for Liverpool, is the Finland captain and that adds to it for me.

I do the press conference the day before the game, as the captain always does, and the lads want to know what I am going to say to the players before the match. I joke that I've always liked the huddle that Celtic do pre-game, and one of the reporters tells his readers I'm more likely to have a cuddle before kick-off. He isn't far wrong.

We do have a huddle, and I just tell the lads to enjoy it. I might even say something beforehand about enjoying their Ireland career as much as I have – something for the new kids coming into the squad. We win the game easy enough, 3–0, with goals from Robbie, Colin Healy and Graham Barrett, so my record as captain is 100 per cent success. Played one, won one, drew none, lost none. Not many Irish captains can match that record.

Mick never says I'll only have the armband for the one match, but I know it. By the time we get to Moscow in September for the first Euro 2004 qualifier, we'll have a new captain in the seat.

Sure enough, Kenny Cunningham gets the job as Roy's replacement on a permanent basis, and the cuddle is replaced by a proper huddle at the Stadion Lokomotiv in Moscow. It's not a good night. We lose 4–2 in our first competitive game since the World Cup. I get replaced by Gary Doherty not long after the hour mark and Babbsy scores an own goal to finish the scoring, on what is his return to international football and his last appearance for Ireland rolled into one. To make matters worse, the Russians give some of our fans an awful beating before the game. Not the start we want in the bid to reach Portugal.

Ireland play again in October, but I'm not around for what turns out to be Mick's last game as boss. I do my groin at Sunderland and it takes months to recover, so I have to watch on television as the Swiss win 2–1 at Lansdowne Road. They take the lead through the great Hakan Yakin on half-time, and we pull one back through a Magnin own goal twelve minutes from time, but the writing is on the wall for Mick when Celestini scores the winner with three minutes to go. Straightaway some of the crowd start singing that there's only one Keano – and it's not Robbie they are referring to.

With two defeats from his opening two European Championship qualifiers, Mick has no option really other than to fall on his own sword. Saipan is still hanging over him; as he says himself, he will always be known as the bollocks who sent Roy Keane home from the World Cup. There is this ridiculous belief growing that we'd have won the World Cup if Roy had stayed or come back. Others seem to think that Roy will be straight back in as soon as Mick is out. Roy is an easy stick to beat Mick with and I've no doubt Roy is enjoying that particular role.

It's all rubbish of course. We were never going to win the World Cup, not even with a team of Roy Keanes or Gary Breens, but it is all so easy to have a go at Mick, clear him out and get the next man in.

Brian Kerr is the next man in as it happens, and I find it a strange appointment. I don't know him from Adam. I know he's been successful at underage level with Ireland but that doesn't mean he can work with senior professionals who've been to World Cup finals, two of them in some cases. He's appointed in January 2003 and one of the first things he does is set about getting Roy back into the fold.

I seem to be some part of his master plan on that front because he rings me before his first match in charge, away to Scotland, and asks me to come in and meet up with the squad. I explain to him that I still can't play because of my groin, but Brian wants me over to do a press conference with him and Roy. Let's put all our differences to bed in front of the press, answer all their questions about Saipan and bring an end to the whole saga. He makes it clear to me in the phone call that he wants to start off as Ireland manager with a level playing field, and getting me and Roy together for the media, with him sitting beside us, will help sort it. I'm convinced he's having a laugh, but he's dead serious. I'm not interested and I make that clear to him – which doesn't go down well, as you can imagine.

I don't go over to meet the press before the Scotland game, and I nearly fall off the chair the night before the match in Glasgow when Roy issues a statement to say he's retiring from international football full stop – less than twenty-four hours before the man who's going to bring him back has his first game in charge. With friends like that, who needs enemies?

My relationship with Brian never really improves after I refuse to go along with his press conference idea. It takes me months to get fit enough to play for Sunderland again, and even when I'm back playing in the Premier League he puts me on standby for one of the Ireland games. I take that as an insult but finally get back into the squad for a friendly against Brazil in February 2004, almost eighteen months after my last cap and seventeen months after Mick quit.

I know going to Dublin that this will be my last game for Ireland, and Brazil at Lansdowne is the perfect get-out game. I don't say it to anyone bar myself before I head over, but I know getting on that plane that I won't be doing this again.

The minute I meet up with the squad, I know it's definitely time to go. It's all changed under Brian, and not for the better. Tony Hickey and Mick Byrne have been cast to the wilderness and I'm not comfortable without them. I feel there's a lack of respect for Brian from the players from what I can see, and some of the training and the set-up is Youth-team to say the least. This is a man who can manage kids OK, but put in charge of grown men, and it doesn't seem to work. I know it's over for me and I don't think it's going to get better for the Ireland team anytime soon.

At least I get a good laugh before I leave. It's my first game back at Lansdowne since the World Cup finals and because I know it's my last game for Ireland, I want it to be something special. I want to savour every moment and remember every minute of the international experience one last time, so I let all the lads go out ahead of me for the warm-up and then enter the playing area last, hopefully to a little cheer just for me from the Irish fans. They've always been good as gold with me, more so than ever since the Holland goal, and I want to feel that love once more.

Out the lads go with me hanging on behind them. I'm last out and for the first ten seconds or so after I come out of the tunnel under the old West Stand there's nothing. Silence. Then all of a sudden this roar goes up and the fans in the East Stand across from me take to their feet. This is more like it. They've seen me now. They know it's me. It's an amazing sight and sound and I just stand there with my hands over my head, clapping them in return. Only thing is, the ones I can see aren't really looking in my direction. I turn to the end we're warming up at and it hits me – the Brazilian team are swarming out the tunnel. They're the ones getting the standing ovation. Roberto Carlos is doing stepovers on his way out. Ronaldinho is grinning like a Cheshire cat. Kaká and Ronaldo are laughing out loud. The cheers and the ovation are for the Brazilians. I'm history now. And I know it.

Brian helps the retirement decision move along when he starts me as a sub and puts me into the centre of midfield for Andy Reid in the sixty-fourth minute. Then he pushes me out right ten minutes later.

He's taking the piss here as far as I am concerned, letting me know who's boss. Who's the joker, more like.

I just don't know what he's doing managing Ireland. Johnny Fallon gets me a jersey – Brazil don't swap shirts so he goes into the dressing room and tells them it's for one of the players who's retiring and comes away with number thirteen, the shirt no Brazilian will wear.

I ring Brian when I get back to England and leave a message to say I'm retiring. It takes him ten days to get back to me – the story actually breaks on Sky before he has the courtesy to return my call. I've played for Ireland for twelve years, played in two World Cup finals and he doesn't even have the decency to phone me.

He should never have got the job as far as I am concerned, but the media love him and they campaigned for him.

It's all ended for me in a bit of an anticlimax but I will never regret a minute of it. The day I told Jack Charlton I'd be happy to play for Ireland was one of the best days of my life. I had the best of times with Ireland – and nobody can ever take that away from me. I will always look back with a massive smile on my face. There were good times and sad times but the people I met on that journey, I'll remember forever.

Chapter Twenty-six

It's Monday night and we're deep in the bowels of the Stadium of Light. We've just been beaten by Crystal Palace in the semi-finals of the promotion play-offs. Mick wants to see me on Wednesday morning. He warns me it won't be good news. A few months ago he offered me five grand a week for a sixteen-month contract extension. Now he has nothing to offer me. Sunderland are broke and I'm out the door. It's over.

There's a break in the Premier League for international football at the start of October 2002, and the lads not involved with their countries – or the injured souls like me – are given a long weekend off. Some plan quick trips to Spain or Portugal with the families.

No one gets away. The training ground on Thursday is buzzing with a rumour that Howard Wilkinson, the old Leeds and Sheffield Wednesday boss, is getting the job. He's been seen at the Stadium of Light, and those in the know say he's a shoe-in.

I'd spoken to Mick on the Tuesday night and I'm still convinced he's coming but, sure enough, the board announce that Howard is the new gaffer, with the Wimbledon Crazy Gang member Steve Cotterill as his assistant.

They arrive at the training ground on Thursday morning and cancel our weekend off. That's their introduction to the lads – and the lads ain't happy. Instead of sitting in the sun, those not on international duty spend their weekend doing fitness tests and bleep tests and all sorts of other nonsense. Cotterill runs the bollocks off them, and they're not happy about it. I'm not happy – and I'm injured!

I don't get his appointment. Howard did win the league with Leeds a few seasons back, but everyone in football knows Alex Ferguson and Manchester United threw that one away. The rumour mill has it that Bob Murray rang Howard because of his involvement with the League Managers Association to ask about his opinion on Mick McCarthy, and then discovered that Howard was interested in the job.

At least Howard makes it clear that he knows who I am when he arrives, unlike a certain Frenchman at Liverpool. He wants me fit and in his team. Trust me, Howard, I want to be fit and in your team.

Steve Cotterill is another matter altogether. He's got all these great ideas and schemes but he doesn't have the basics needed to be a good coach as far as I can see. If anything, he strikes me as clueless. It's fairly obvious from day one that he fancies himself as the next manager of Sunderland. He's here to learn the ropes under Howard then take them over. His big thing is his past as a member of the Crazy Gang at Wimbledon. He's always telling us about it, trying to make out that he was the craziest of the crazies, not a story I've ever heard before from any former Wimbledon player.

Howard is definitely the brains of this operation and Cotterill is the bad cop – but I don't like the way he talks to us. He's too condescending, often talking down to us. When he's not being critical, he's trying too hard to be your mate. That just annoys me from the start. I'm not looking for any more mates. He's punching way above his weight here and there's too many cute heads in the dressing room, the likes of Gavin McCann, Thomas Sorensen and Stefan Schwarz, not to see through him.

Howard tries his best to rally the troops with an inspirational speech one morning. Results aren't going well and we're struggling to cope with the relegation battle. Players are finding it difficult to grasp the moment and play without fear. Howard's way of showing us to grasp the moment is to put his hand in a plastic bag of stinging nettles, which he tells us won't sting him if he grabs them firmly. His face goes bright red and his hand comes out red raw with white dots all over it where he's been stung a hundred times by the nettles. Another thing that didn't go to plan.

At least Howard has the sense to listen to me when I tell him to sign Phil Babb from Sporting Lisbon. Two of the Three Amigos are back in harness, and we have the perfect watering hole to get away from the trials and tribulations of life with Howard and Sidekick Steve.

There's a pub in Seaham called The Phoenix run by a mate of Quinny's called Aidrian, and we have our very own *Phoenix Nights* in there on a regular basis. It's an escape from the Zig and Zag of management and a relief from the endless relegation battle we're in.

At the start of 2001 Sunderland were second in the Premier League; it's now the end of the 2003 season and we're relegated, having only won four games. Howard Wilkinson and Steve Cotterill leave the club in March 2003 after only five months in charge. After they leave, Bob Murray finally sees sense and calls on my mate Mick McCarthy, who's been out of work since he quit Ireland after the Euro qualifier against Switzerland.

The club is waiting for some good news, and Mick's appointment is great news as far as I am concerned. The feeling is mutual as he hands me the captain's armband, but that groin injury is still causing me grief, even after the operation. I eventually manage to find some match fitness towards the end of the 2002–2003 season.

We get to the semi-final of the FA Cup the following season and play Millwall at Old Trafford on 4 April 2004 with Manchester United awaiting the winners in the Cardiff final.

I've a bit of history with Millwall in general, and Dennis Wise in particular. He's hard work as far as I am concerned and I have no problem saying it to his face. Our pained relationship goes back to a league game at the New Den – when he was running alongside me and falls over, holding his face and screaming in agony. He's moaning at the referee and trying to get me sent off. If I had elbowed him, and I've often felt like it, then fair enough, but trying to get a fellow player red carded is despicable.

It must be a Millwall thing, because they're in our face from the off at Old Trafford. Kevin Muscat has a bit of a go at me so I tread on him. The yellow card I get is justified – it could easily be red, but referee Paul Durkin gives me the benefit of the doubt. We're chasing the game in the final minutes when Stephen Wright sells me short. Neil Harris gets in behind me and I put my hands on him. I'm a goner. The ref has no choice as he calls me over and I apologise to him for having to send a player off in the FA Cup semi-final.

Dennis Wise tries to shake my hand as I go off. Fuck off, Dennis. We're losing and I've been sent off. This is probably my last shot at Wembley, and it's gone. Last thing I want is Dennis Wise anywhere near me.

Sunderland are struggling financially and, like most of the senior pros, I need something to happen on the pitch to get a contract extension from Mick. He did approach me earlier in the season and offered me a sixteen-month contract, but for five grand a week, the win bonus when I joined. I opted then to hang on to the end of the season in the hope that we'd get back to the Premier League, then the TV money would come rolling in and we'd all know where we stood.

A cup final would have done the bank balance no harm at all, but at least we're still in the frame for promotion. We do make it to the play-offs and the score is 0–0 to Crystal Palace in the first leg when Mick hauls me off at half-time at Selhurst Park. What? He's taking me off!

I'm fuming, and I let him know it.

He says I'm not dictating the midfield the way he wants me to. I kick up a right fuss in the dressing room at half-time, kicking and screaming and all. 'You're taking me off! Are you sure?' It's the biggest row we've ever had. It's like fighting with your mum and dad, but in front of a dressing room full of grown men. Palace score in the last five minutes to win 3–2, just to make it worse.

We're still rowing as we head back up to the northeast on a flight out of Gatwick. I've had disagreements with him before and I've done what I always do, go off and have a sulk then come back with my tail between my legs and kiss and make it up with him, and he'd remind me why he had fallen out with me in the first place – my fault most of the time.

This is different. There's real anger in my voice and he's not one for rolling over and waving the white flag. We have another pop at each other on the plane and the build-up to the second leg three days later is tense to say the least.

Mick calls me into his office on the morning of the match. He's dropping me. I'll start on the bench as we chase the game, 3–2 down from the first leg.

I can't believe this but it's time to be strong with him, not stroppy. I remind him it's the biggest game of the season. He needs players who can handle the situation, who've been here before. We're close to promotion. He needs my experience, he knows I've done it for him before in the past. I got the goal that got him to the World Cup finals.

He looks me straight in the eye and says, 'Yeah, but I'm not playing you. I've made up my mind and that's it.'

For once with Mick, I stand my ground. I tell him he can't drop me. He shouldn't drop me. I'll run the game for him, I'll dictate the midfield like he wanted me to do down in London. He says his mind is made up. I say change it, one more time. And he does.

Having persuaded him to change his team on the morning of a game – something he never does – he warns me not to let him down. I won't. I promise.

It's not easy to keep the promise. We get battered for the first twenty minutes by Iain Dowie's team, but when I play a long, diagonal ball into the box, Kevin Kyle takes it on his chest and volleys it home. We're 1–0 up on the night from my assist, and 3–3 on aggregate.

Three minutes later I whip in another ball and Marcus Stewart scores with a header, it's another assist. I start to boss the midfield. I do exactly what I told Mick I would do. I can smell the play-off final at Wembley. I can smell a new contract.

The referee is Dave Pugh from the Wirral, like me, and this is his final game before he retires, but no one has told him what this game means to his neighbour. We're a minute away from victory when our keeper Mart Poom is tripped by Neil Shipperley as he goes for a cross. The ref ignores it and they score at the far post with our keeper sprawled on the six-yard line. The referee makes the biggest mistake of his life and allows the goal to stand.

The match goes to penalties. I miss mine. Jeff Whitley misses the final kick. We're out of the play-offs and I'm out of work.

As captain, I have to do the post-match press conference and I give it to the referee with both barrels. I also offer

Bob Murray some advice. If the chairman of Sunderland Football Club has anything about him at all, he will give Mick McCarthy some money, let him keep this team together and invest in it. We have a lot of players – like me – who are out of contract, and I know Mick's hands are tied by the chairman.

Mick is still fuming with the ref when we get back into the dressing room. The season is over and he has to organise who's staying and who's going. It's late on Monday night and he's telling players to come and see him on Tuesday and Wednesday.

I'm on the Wednesday list, and it won't be good news. I know that already.

I'm right. Mick has nothing for me, not even the five grand a week he offered me earlier in the season. It's not his fault, and I tell him I know that. I'm not going to fall out with Mick McCarthy over a decision by the Sunderland chairman. I owe Mick too much to let Bob Murray come between us.

He's showing me the door and there's nothing either of us can do about it. My career could end in this room. It's horrible.

There's no more to say. I give Mick the biggest hug ever and I feel myself filling up. I can't help it. I'm a lost soul now with nowhere to go. Two years after I'd gone to the World Cup finals with him, Mick is bringing the curtain down on my top-flight career. Cruel business, this football.

Panic sets in when I get home and realise how close the end is now. I tell Dave Lockwood to get me a club, but the stats from Sunderland won't do me any favours, just fifty-three games in nearly four seasons. That hernia is haunting me.

There's a few half-hearted offers before Micky Adams brings me to Leicester for talks and offers me eight grand a week. Brilliant. Where do I sign? First, I have to do a medical.

My groin is still killing me and the scans soon show why. I fail the medical and Micky makes it clear that he can't take a chance on me. For that sort of money he needs me on the pitch every week, not in the treatment room. His medics don't think they'll even get a season out of me. My chance to sign for Leicester has gone.

It's time to take my destiny into my own hands. I ring Dave and tell him to make contact with the Tranmere manager Brian Little and set up a meeting. I'll offer my services to my local club for two grand a week as a player-coach. I'm so desperate to get a deal that I'm praying the coaching will save my career, and save face for me as well. I can live at home on the Wirral and carry on as a footballer.

Dave sells the idea to Brian. Within twenty-four hours I'm sitting down with him and the chief executive Lorraine Rogers in Heswell, about fifteen minutes from my house. I'm not sure Brian understands exactly where I am coming from and why I want to go from sixteen grand a week at Sunderland to two grand a week at Tranmere, but I make it clear that my ambition now is to get into coaching. He's the perfect man to help me on my way.

In return I can help him with my experience on the field with his very young team, and off it as well. It's a win–win situation as far as I can see.

He agrees, and we settle on a deal that sees me finally

sign for Tranmere on a two-year contract as player-coach, for two grand a week. I'm proper made up with it.

A plan for my future is starting to take shape: a couple of seasons playing with Tranmere working with Brian Little and I'll be ready for management. The mere idea of me as a manager is likely to send most football people running for cover, but I'm not as thick as I like people to think I am.

During the World Cup in Japan, one of the Irish journalists did an interview with me and wrote in his paper afterwards that I was kidding the world. He believes there are two Jason McAteers – the public one who's happy to be a bit of a Scouser thicko and the private Jason McAteer, the real Jason McAteer, who knows it is all a bit of an act and just plays along. When I read that article I thought, *Well done, mate, you've found me out.*

Being at Tranmere is the first time in football that the real Jason McAteer emerges from the shadows of Trigger. I'm the wise old man in the dressing room. I'm the one the youngsters look to for guidance and example. I'm also the most expensive player on the books by a distance. The club need to get value for their money and the youngsters need guidance. I can't be messing around all the time here.

We have some journeymen in the squad, but the real players are the kids looking for a first or second chance in the game. It's a club with a great heart and a great tradition, and I'm determined to enjoy the experience and make the most of it. I need this move to Tranmere to work as much as anyone, more so maybe.

Brian Little's a top bloke but, more importantly, a great coach. You can tell by looking at him at work on the training ground that he has played and coached at the highest level. He deserves a bigger club at this stage of his career, but that's life.

His assistant is a guy called Richard Hill, whom I quickly dislike. He would often throw a Billy-big-time shout at me in front of the players. He's clearly worried by my presence on the coaching staff. He's probably already worked out that I'm a threat to his position, and he's right.

He may be threatened by me but I've a job to do, and I'm not going to let him get in the way. You have to be selfish in this game. Number one is the only number to worry about in this dressing room and I'm not talking about our veteran goalkeeper John Achterberg, who was a hero when Aldo was the manager here and had the club dreaming of success. We've a few other golden oldies around the place. Michael Jackson was at Preston not so long ago and Mark Rankin played for Sheffield United, but it's really about the kids. Ryan Taylor is the best of them and he's already getting a bit of interest from Wigan. Danny Harrison, Ian Hume, Paul Linwood and Gareth Roberts look decent prospects to me as well.

It's only across the Mersey, but Tranmere is different to Liverpool in so many ways. Hilton Hotels have become Premier Inns on the few nights we can afford to stay away before a match. There are no new tracksuits, no swapping shirts, no visits to United or Arsenal or Chelsea. We're back to basics, and you don't get much more basic than Saturdays at Yeovil, Stockport and Lincoln. My journey from Bolton has come full circle – it's all guts and no glamour again.

But I'm not complaining. I'm still a professional footballer.

I'm still getting more in a week than most people earn in a month to kick a ball around a football field.

I've gone back to the past, and that past has followed me. Everywhere we go, there are players who want to kick me, who want to bring this World Cup and Premier League 'name' down to their level in League One, regularly reminding me about where I'm at. The first competitive game for Tranmere is away to Peterborough and the crowd at London Road boo me every time I get on the ball, from start to finish.

It's the same everywhere we go. The worst offenders are the fans at Brentford and their manager Martin Allen. I get abused every time I go near the ball – but our experienced winger Paul Hall is racially abused by fans from start to finish. I'm stood on the sideline listening to it, and it's disgraceful stuff. At Bristol City they spit on me and throw stuff onto the pitch. I'm starting to wonder if I really want to carry on playing, and I'm only a few months into a two-year contract.

The difficulty for me is the expectancy around my move to the club. Aldo had come here at the end of his career, and he delivered goals as a player and cup runs as a manager. He was a goal scorer, I'm not, but it's almost like the fans expect me to score as many goals as he did. I'm not the same player, I'm not going to win matches on my own.

Even the energy is going from my legs now. I need to sit in the midfield and let the kids do the running, point them in the right direction. That's not what the fans want. They want the Duracell bunny, not a clapped-out footballer. Some idiots on the phone-in shows start to question if I'm arsed about playing for the club. Others question the money I'm on and the return the club is getting for their investment. They don't know that I've taken a drop of fourteen grand a week to come here, they don't know that I'm on two grand a week, not ten. I'm not pillaging their money – their club doesn't have any money.

Aldo's success should be the blueprint for the club, but we just don't have the resources to compete at that level anymore. The club will most likely never have the resources to do that again. Signing Jason McAteer as a player-coach isn't going to change that.

We do manage to get to the League One play-off semi-finals at the end of the 2004–05 season, my first at Prenton Park. We lose the first leg away to Hartlepool 2–0 and I get a knee to the head at a corner in the second leg back at our place. I get knocked out and when I come around the physio Les Parry insists on taking me to the sideline. The doc is over to me, and I'm throwing up all over the place. I want to get back on the pitch, but he's not having any of it. He asks me the score. I don't even know who we're playing. Brian tells me I'm coming off, and I'm gutted. It's the biggest game since I signed for Tranmere, and I'm no use to anyone. We do get it back to 2–2 but we lose on penalties.

With no promotion, Lorraine has to cut the budget again, and Brian is told to let players go. It's heartbreaking watching Brian tell some of them he has nothing to offer them. The likes of Ian Hume move on. Wigan offer a million quid for Ryan Taylor and the club has no choice but to sell him in a bid to try and service the club's debt, never mind reduce it.

Less than a year into life at Tranmere I finally get the chance to raise some money for the Tsunami victims in

Indonesia with a big charity match at Anfield. It's something I've wanted to do ever since I sat in horror and watched the news reports from the Indian Ocean on 26 December.

I'd watched a BBC documentary on the tragedy and it really hit me hard. It's easy to put your hand in your pocket and give twenty or fifty pounds to Comic Relief but this needed something more to be done and I want to do it.

As a father, my heart went out to the kids who were left orphaned and homeless that day. Harry was only four at the time and it really affected me. I want to do something for them.

Eventually we organise Tsunami Soccer Aid and a big All Star match at Anfield on 27 March 2005, featuring the likes of Nicky Byrne, Brian McFadden, Paddy McGuinness, John Barnes, Kenny Dalglish, Kevin Keegan, Alan Hansen, Aldo and Ian Rush. It was sold out.

The game is a phenomenal success thanks to the people of Liverpool and fans from across the world. It raises more than £500,000 and it all goes directly to the people affected by the Tsunami in Banda Ache, Indonesia. The money builds 300 homes and provides for more than 1,600 people.

I visit Indonesia to see the benefits for myself and I meet these two children who lost their mum when the wave struck. Little Samsul was holding his mum's hand when she was swept away. The power of the wave pulled them apart and he never saw her again. His spirit is amazing. He is getting on with his life, as is his community, but the reminders are everywhere. In the middle of a housing estate we see an oil tanker, lifted out of the sea by the force of the wave and dropped miles inland.

The money raised by Tsunami Soccer Aid will benefit this community for generations to come. It's the least we could do.

Early in the 2005–06 season I'm forced off with an injury at half-time, and I'm in the shower, bollock naked, when Richard Hill follows me and starts giving me an earful. He squares up to me in the shower and John McMahon, one of the other assistants, has to step in between us.

When Brian finds out, he's fuming. John moves up to be Brian's assistant and I'm officially promoted to the role of first-team coach.

I'm loving it, but I can see the pressure is telling on Brian as things start to go wrong during the season. The crowd is on his back and giving him stick from the terraces, some of them too young to have a clue what they are talking about. Tranmere's home games are a funny place to be because we often get Liverpool and Everton fans over when their teams are playing away. It makes for a very strange atmosphere and Brian seems to be bearing the brunt of the fans' anger.

The financial problems aren't helping him either. He wants to coach a football team, but the boardroom problems take up more and more of his time, and I'm not sure he has the stomach for all the politics. I can tell he's getting bored with everything that's going on behind the scenes, but things on the pitch aren't much better.

Brian gets sacked on 5 May 2006, with two games to go and nothing left to play for. Lorraine asks John McMahon and myself to take charge on a caretaker basis. To be fair to Brian, he rings me and wishes me the best of luck with it, offers me advice on who to play and who to watch out for.

He also tells me that I'll really enjoy it, that I'll get a taste for it, and that I will want more of management when I get my feet under the table.

He's dead right. We throw the kids in and I drop myself to the bench, only coming on for the second half of the final game of the season against Doncaster Rovers. We lose, and my final act that season is to take the drug test – and it takes me a good hour to wee after the game!

I'm loving this management lark though, just as Brian predicted, so I ask Lorraine for a meeting and make it clear that I want the job and am even prepared to rip up the one-year playing contract I'd agreed with Brian if they appoint me as manager. She promises they'll consider me for the role, but says nothing more about it until she tells me they're considering three people and asks for my opinion on Craig Levein, Ronnie Moore and Martin Allen. What about me?

I explain I know nothing about Craig Levein except by reputation, Ronnie Moore is outside of my circle and that I'd walk straight out if Martin Allen got the job, based on my experience that day at Brentford.

Ronnie played for the club, so they plump for the devil they know, and I have at least one more season with Tranmere to look forward to. His assistant John Brechin, Brechs to us, is a good guy, but I feel with me staying around at the club, Ronnie seems just as insecure as Richard Hill was with me around the place.

He has me in and out of the team, but I'm doing my coaching badges and managing the reserves, and I'm happy out with that. I know it's coming to an end for me as a player so anything that happens with the first team – starting or on the bench – is a bonus at this stage of my football life. My kicks now are coming from my work with the reserves and I really want that job full-time when the season ends.

Ronnie doesn't agree. He calls me into the office before the break for the summer and tells me he's letting me go. There's nothing here for me. I'm no longer any use to him as a player and he can't afford to keep me on as a coach. He has his wish. I've forgotten more than Ronnie Moore has ever done and he's bringing the curtain down. It's all over. I just shrug my shoulders, say 'fair enough' and walk out on life as a professional footballer as quickly as I had walked into it all those years earlier at Burnden Park.

The light bulb Phil Neal switched on the day he offered me terms to sign as a professional for Bolton Wanderers when I was about to emigrate and start a new life in America has gone out. Ronnie Moore has switched it off in a dingy little office at the Tranmere training ground.

I go home and, once more, I cry my heart out.

Football is finished with me.

I know that when I wake up tomorrow morning I will have nothing to do and all day to do it. No training, no coaching, no game.

How the hell am I going to cope with life back in the real world?

Chapter Twenty-seven

All I want to do is sit in the bath. I've no contract, no job and no future. Harry and his mum are gone, forever this time. There's nothing for it. It's time to end it all.

The morning after the life before.

There's no reason to get up now, no job to go to, no real job anyway. The first holiday is an easy one. I've done that every year when the season ends. The second holiday never ends.

There's bits and pieces of TV work on offer, but nothing else. No coaching and no coaching courses. No football and no invites to play football. From 50,000-sellout crowds to nothing and all in the space of a few short years.

I have sweet FA to do and all day to do it. So I start sleeping in. I start having baths. Wake up, run the water till it's really hot and get in. Let the water go cold, get out for a few hours and then have another bath. Three baths a day, every day. Mental stuff.

Harry and his mum are gone. The relationship never really survived the sudden deaths of her parents. When you're on the outside of something like that, there's nothing you can do.

August 2007 arrives, and the football season starts – and it gets worse by the day. I've no training ground to go to, no dressing room to sit in, no one to talk to, no one to laugh with and joke with and mess around with.

I'm falling into a state of depression and there's nothing I can do about it. I can't recognise it for myself and I can't fight it. I can't even see it happening in front of me.

My mum has spent twenty years working with the drugs services. She has seen all these symptoms before. She knows what's going on. She knows it's not right to spend your day in the bath. She knows it makes no sense to do nothing more than go round to your mum's or ring your mates when you get bored with the bath, only to find there's none of them free to come and talk to you in the middle of the day.

My head is up my arse. The lowest point comes when the 2007 season starts. Tranmere are back in action and they don't want me. Liverpool haven't wanted me for years. Sunderland have all but forgotten me. I'm gutted now just looking at the results on the teleprinter. The game that made me has forgotten me. Quick as that.

There's an easy end to it. It's a dusky Friday afternoon and I'm driving through the Birkenhead Tunnel. I'm supposed to be on my way to see Harry at his mum's, but my mind has somewhere else it wants to send me.

The lights are coming towards me, welcoming me home. It's time. Time to cross that central isle, cross into those oncoming cars and bring it all to an end. That's all I want to do now – all I have to do. Throw the car across the lanes and end it in an instant. I've had enough. I don't know what I am doing with my life. I don't know what I want to do with my life. I don't know where I'm going, and I can't see any future.

It's all about me now, and even I don't want to know me. I don't like me anymore. I'm totally selfish, and I don't care. I want it all to end and those lights can end it for me.

If I just swing this car across the road I'll smash into the oncoming cars and the wall and they will end it for me.

Harry saves me. His face appears in front of me and I start to think about him. *Who's going to tell him his dad has died in a big car crash? What will they say to him? Will he learn someday that his dad caused the crash? That his dad thought so little of himself that he killed himself on his way to see him?*

He can't grow up without me, I can't do that to him. I can't kill myself or hit another car and kill some other kid's mother or father or even a son or daughter. I can't do it.

What if I am never able to hold Harry in my arms again, never able to touch his hand, to kiss his cheek, to smell him and tell him I love him? I'm flicking between a depressed state and a conscious state. That's what happens.

In my depressed state I can't think about the consequences. I'm just thinking, *Fuck it, I am going to do this. I'm going to hit those cars and that wall and make it all look like a really big accident.*

Then I think of Harry again. Harry and the thought of hurting or maybe killing someone else. And I snap out of it. Just in time.

It's not the first time I've wanted to end it all. It's happened a few times in the last two or three months, mostly in the bath. I'd be lying there with the water starting to freeze over and I'd think about going under the water, holding my breath and ending it all.

I've become a quitter. I want to quit life.

The Birkenhead Tunnel isn't that long. Thankfully. By the time Harry's face fills my mind I'm running out of tunnel. He's saved me, but I can't face him now. There's only one person I can turn to, only one person I can talk to – my mum.

She knows there's something wrong when I start banging on her front door late at night. I'm bawling, crying uncontrollably. Everything's finally come to a head. What the fuck am I going to do? Why is my life such a mess? How have I got to this point?

My mum knows I'm having a breakdown and she knows just the woman to help me. In her line of work they all have counsellors who counsel them, if you know what I mean. My mum's friend in work is a woman called Jane. It's not normal for a counsellor from my mum's work to see me because she knows me. But she also knows, from my mum, how desperate my situation is and how close I have come to ending it all.

She's prepared to help me and the first night I'm with her, she gets me to do this twenty-question test to determine my state of mind. They are all yes or no answers and my answers suggest I am clinically suicidal.

I go to see her three times a week for about six weeks. I'm having a total breakdown. It's like being dropped in the rainforest and you have to get yourself out, but you have to do it in an hour and you are panicking. You are running around and everywhere you go looks the same. You think you won't get out of here.

I can't sleep. I'm waking up at four o'clock in the morning in this big empty house and I can't sleep. I'm walking from room to room, all on my own.

A few times I ring one of the physios at Sunderland, a friend called Gordon Ellis who'd always put me wise in the past. I lean on him now. I'd be awake at four or five in the morning and I'd pick up the phone and just ring Gordon and he'd be good enough to listen and talk to me and put me straight until the next time the panic kicks in.

It's like a madness and it's suffocating. Jane is looking out for me and looking after me. She can't give me the answers, but she can explain things for me and she can talk me through all this.

I start to read. I buy loads of books on everything from co-dependence to coming out of depression. Jane tells me it's important to keep busy, to keep active. Low and all as I am, she tells me to take any bit of TV or media work that comes my way. I'm trying to turn down work and she's trying to fill my diary.

My own idea is to get back with Harry's mum. A family environment will sort me out. I can't tell Harry's mum what happened in the tunnel, or what I'm acting like.

Jane encourages me to see Harry as often as I can, to bring him to matches, to do things together, anything to keep me out of that big house and away from time on my own.

It's not easy. My mum tells me I am too moody and snappy around him and he's bound to pick up on it. I'm guilty of road rage and snapping if things don't go to plan, even in his company.

But soon the time with Harry starts to make a difference. I'm listening to Jane now, letting her fill my diary for me and keeping busy, doing what she says. Seeing Harry more really helps me. It's giving me more focus.

Jane doesn't say anything, but I don't think she approves of me and Harry's mum getting back together. I get the sense that she knows I am only doing this for myself, for the sense of comfort that a family life would bring, and it's probably not a part of her plan to help me conquer this depression.

The fact I am hiding my depression from Harry's mum *isn't* a good idea, but I don't care. I don't want her to know. I know it's a lifestyle – a family – I want, but deep down, I know that there's no going back.

Jane has been like a rock. I've questioned some of her advice at times and I've been wrong. She's too wise, too good at what she does to do anything other than encourage me and point me in the right direction. She knows it has taken me time to see what is right for me and me alone, but I know she is proud of me for getting there.

I'm working again, taking jobs when they come in and socialising with other former players.

I've started to answer the phone again as well. When I stopped playing I went AWOL as far as the lads were concerned. Don Hutchison has become my best mate from football but I blank him when he tries to make contact. I fall off the face of the earth as far as he is concerned. And he's not the only one.

Babbsy and Aldo still regard themselves as my mates, but to me they are just reminders of my recent past and I don't want to know them. I ignore their calls, text them to say I'm busy, anything to avoid contact with players from my previous life.

Aldo doesn't give up. Neither does Phil or Hutch. There's a golf tournament for former players organised by Aldo in the Algarve every autumn, and he insists I play in it. Babbsy gives me a set of golf clubs and they get me out onto the golf course.

The laughter with the boys is just what I need. Hutch is on fire one particular night in Portugal. A fella has come over to chat with us and talk football. An hour later, he's still going on. We've realised he's a big time Charlie and a bit flash, which is doing Hutch's head in. Hutch compliments him on his shoes which turn out to be a pair of £300 Gucci loafers. 'Are they waterproof?' Hutch asks with a glint in his eye. I know something's brewing. 'For £300 I hope so,' says the fella. With that he hands Hutch a loafer to have a look at. Hutch pours his gin and tonic into the shoe and drinks it in one go. 'They sure are,' says Hutch, and the lads are rolling around with laughter. And the fella leaves with a right face on him.

It's just what I need, something to laugh about, something to concentrate on, something to obsess about, something to get me out and about and talking to people.

Jane also realises quite quickly that golf is my new escape from it all. I could have turned to drink or drugs or gambling, like so many former footballers when it all came to an end. I had the opportunity but, thankfully, I didn't go down any of those roads. It would have been easy to get hooked on pills, but I didn't.

Jane is helping me find myself again, the real me, the one who can exist without football, without fame, without all the trappings and the pitfalls of life in that goldfish bowl.

Funny thing is, I'm still struggling to come to terms with the fact that Jane is my counsellor. When I first went to her I told her never to ask me for money. I gave her a blank cheque and told her to take whatever she wanted out of my bank account when the time was right and not to even tell me about it. Naturally enough, this arrangement seems a bit strange to a professional counsellor and she asks me why. I explain that in my own head I don't want to feel that I am paying for her help. I need to believe that she is helping me because she wants to help me, not because I am paying her.

I know now that therapy is a process and I need Jane to help me through the process but I never wanted to feel she was only doing it because I was paying her.

She does cash the cheque eventually, and she gives me a bit of a fright when she finally presents it to her bank. I have two bank accounts. One goes back to my days as a student graphic artist and that's still the account for my day-to-day expenses.

No matter what I am earning, I always put a set amount into that account and live off it. Even when I was on big money at Liverpool, that's how I lived. Even now when money comes in from TV or radio work, that set amount still goes into the account. There's always a float in it. Some weeks I will spend all of the money, other weeks I won't, so there is always a bit of cash in it.

This one night, I go to the bank machine and it tells me there's only a small amount left. It's never that low, so I get a statement and, sure enough, there's a cheque gone from the account.

I tell my mum and she tells me, rightly, to cop on and realise that it's the best money I will ever spend. She's correct. Jane saved my life. It is money well spent.

Even though I have left that depressed state of mind behind me, I do still worry it will happen again. I am in a totally conscious and self-aware state and I can deal with anything.

I can deal with problems. I can deal with life, good and bad. But I know I'm a worrier. I've always been a worrier. I always worried as a footballer. Was I ever going to make it? Will I be in the team on Saturday? Will Jack or Mick pick me for Ireland? Experience in football helps. You have your team-mates around you and they help you through it. Then football forgets about you and you're on your own.

You're left to cope without twenty other blokes sitting beside you in the dressing room. I've had to learn not to get depressed. I can get down like everyone else, but I know how to handle it, how to react.

Now if I'm feeling down, I can cope. I can ring Aldo and go for a game of golf and talk it over. I can get through it. I'm stronger. Thanks to Jane and, in a strange way, thanks to life, I've found myself. But it's taken me a long, long time.

When I was at Bolton I was young and immature and everything was new. I didn't know the industry, I didn't know how to handle things. I was ready to do anything I could or had to do to keep hold of the dream.

I'd not grown up in a professional football environment like those around me, and it was all new and fresh and challenging. Then I moved to Liverpool and I lived the dream. I'm in the dressing room of the club I've supported all my life and surrounded by superstars, some of whom I still idolise.

They want me to be Trigger and I was always going to be Trigger – even when they insisted on calling me Dave because they already had their own Trigger in Rob Jones. I found this niche for myself and I wasn't letting go.

I was the funny guy, the joker. I was everyone's mate and I wanted to be everyone's mate. Everyone. When they went out, they wanted me out. When they wanted a laugh, they wanted me to make them laugh. I was wanted at last, and I wasn't going to let anyone down. I played up to it and it worked for me. It made me popular. It made me part of the team. And, yes, I bought into it. I started to believe it. I was Trigger with Ireland. I was Dave with Liverpool. I was the court jester twenty-four-seven, and it was never going to end.

And that's where the problems started.

Of course, I wasn't Merlin the Magician. I couldn't make my football career last forever, no matter how much I wanted to. The character I created still comes out from time to time – when we play Legends football matches nowadays it is expected of me and I slip right back into character and it's brilliant – but that's not the real me. I have to be me most of the time and, at last, I am happy being me. I've two amazing sons, a rock of a mum who stood up to me when I needed someone to stand up to me and shout stop, and I have the funniest, most beautiful wife a man could ask for.

I'm the lucky one and I know it. I have seen footballers go down the destruction route and nobody has cried stop until it is too late. My mum saw the signs and took action and I like to think I'd do the same for my boys and my own family if the need arose.

It may not arise because my boys may not end up as professional sportsmen. They may never be exposed to the life that got me here. It is all down to circumstance and factors affecting your upbringing. If I had ended up as a graphic artist or a sports shop salesman, maybe none of this would have happened.

When you're a footballer you are living in a bubble, in a world that's not real, and you are expected to be able to cope with it. The game and the business sucks you into a really insecure and artificial lifestyle. You are loved one minute and hated the next. You are left to fend for yourself on a roller-coaster of emotion. You have to live for the moment. That's football.

Every day you get up and you go training and you have a laugh with your mates. You go home and have a sleep, you eat and watch telly, you go to bed and then you get up and do it all over again with the same bunch of mates. The only change to the routine is when match day comes around and that's a routine all of its own. It's the same for as long as you are in the game, no matter what dressing room you are in and who your mates are at any given time.

You end up, if you are lucky like I was, in a seventeen-year routine and, within that routine, you have to deal with emotion, pressure, adulation, injury, disappointment, flagellation, the kind of things that no other job will subject you to.

And then the game abandons you, the routine ends and you are left to your own devices. The club won't prepare you for life outside the bubble, and it certainly doesn't prepare you for life when your particular bubble has burst. All you can do is try to surround yourself with good people. I've always believed in angels – and by angels, I mean people who are around you when you need them, there for you when you have to have someone to lean on, someone to protect you and look after you.

Gordon Ellis at Sunderland is one of those people. So is Mick Byrne from the Ireland camp. I didn't tell Mick about the tunnel and the suicide bid and the depression, but he was there for me at other times, he was my angel when I needed him.

The one incident that stands out with Mick was when my partner miscarried just before the Euro 2000 qualifier against Croatia. I flew into Dublin on the Saturday night then flew back on the Sunday morning when we lost the baby. I then came back over on the Monday night and Mick was waiting at the bottom of the steps on the runway as I got off the plane with the biggest hug in the history of hugs. I just started crying and he kept reassuring me that everything would be okay. How he got on the runway, I'll never know.

The lads were at the movies and Mick and Tony Hickey brought me straight to the cinema, but I was in a daze of my own for the next two or three days. Only for Mick, I don't know how I'd have got through it, but that was typical Mick. He was always there for me. Always an angel.

Chapter Twenty-eight

Barnesy cycled into work but there's no way he's leaving by the same mode of transport. There's dozens of photographers waiting outside the training ground. He can't cycle out that gate and make the 'On Your Bike' headlines too easy for them. We've got to get this bike into the boot of my Range Rover.

There are times when I just love revenge. I have to admit that it takes me a long time to forgive someone who crosses me and I never, ever forget. Ronnie Moore knows that. I wasn't impressed with the way he went about ending my time at Tranmere and I've always had a feeling that, one day, I would get a chance to avenge it.

The opportunity does indeed knock when Rovers start to struggle under Ronnie. Living in the area, I know the knives are out for him as far as the fans are concerned and that the chairman Peter Johnson won't be shy when it comes to taking action.

Peter has about six million quid invested in the club and he is anxious for a turnaround in fortunes. If he wants to sell, and I'm led to believe he might, the team has to be performing on the pitch. As it happens, I know someone who might be interested in a move back to England and a start in coaching – someone called Robbie Fowler who's well known around these parts. So I just happen to have a word with Robbie about coming back from Australia and going to Prenton Park as a player-coach.

Robbie could be the new John Aldridge as far as the Tranmere fans are concerned. And a dream ticket with John Barnes as manager and Robbie as coach would definitely sell the idea to Peter Johnson. I'd go along for the ride as well, of course.

I set up a meeting between Robbie and Peter and let this gem of an idea take on a life all of its own. John's contract as the manager of the Jamaican national team is coming to an end and there's no sign of a renewal, so he's up for it.

We meet in Peter's house in the summer and his only concern is about how genuine John and Robbie are about coming to Tranmere. I set up another meeting with him on my own and convince him that this is good for Tranmere and good for his hopes of getting a return on his huge investment in the club.

He knows I have the club's best interests at heart, and even when Robbie gets a massive offer to go and play in the A-League in Australia – and accepts it – Peter sees enough in John as manager and me as his assistant to go for it.

Ronnie is still officially in charge at this stage, but Peter tells us the deal is on and he will sort it – which is exactly what he does by sacking Ronnie and replacing him with John Barnes and myself!

We're introduced to the press as manager and coach. I knew going into the talks with Peter that I'd never persuade him to give me the manager's job on my own, even though that's what I really want. My best bet is to get someone like John in there and get on the ticket with him. We're good friends from Liverpool and I know how much he wants to make this happen. John wants to manage and I'm happy enough just to get back in there as his right-hand man. The problem is how other people see us.

Everyone wants to know what the two of us are going to do. How we are going to work things out? Who are we going to buy? They all see us as some sort of dream team, Liverpool old boys working together for Tranmere Rovers – but the truth is that John is his own man, far more so than I ever envisaged going into this relationship.

I'd never act inappropriately and I'll always stand by my manager, but John is always the boss in this relationship, even though people think he listens to what I have to say when it comes to the big decisions. He's a fantastic coach; my only criticism of him is that he is too nice, believe it or not. Coming into the job, I really believe we will get it right at Tranmere and before we know it, Liverpool will be offering us a deal as number one and two at Anfield.

That's the dream when I came back to my local club, but the first satisfaction comes with the fact that our arrival ensures Ronnie Moore gets sacked. Sorry.

Reality doesn't take long to kick us in the balls, however, when we start work ahead of the 2009–10 season. When we sat down with Peter Johnson to sort all this, the budget for the year was set at £1.8 million, but within our first two weeks at work Peter tells us they've had to slash £850,000 off it.

We're not fourteen days behind the desk and already our budget is cut to just below a million. We've twenty grand a week to spend on everything from players to diesel for the minibus to get us all to training.

It's a long way from the Premier League, Anfield and Melwood. I can remember putting that first Liverpool pay cheque for twenty-five grand on my bedside locker and not cashing it for weeks. Now I'm on a salary of thirty-two grand a year. It's a decent salary, just not what I've been used to.

We've lost five or six first-team regulars from the previous season, including the captain and the goalkeeper Danny Coyne. Steve Jennings has gone as well. Some have left for six hundred quid a week more somewhere else; others have gone for two hundred quid more in their weekly pay packet. Some have gone just because we couldn't afford to offer them anything.

We start to pull in favours from Liverpool and Everton. Rafa Benítez, to be fair to him, is as good as gold. He offers us Martin Kelly on loan but then Martin Škrtel gets injured and he has to call young Kelly back before he's even played for us. Sam Allardyce sends the young Irish kid Gavin Gunning down from Blackburn, but that doesn't really work out. And the best player on the training ground can't play – that's John Barnes!

The young lads we do sign love it with Barnesy as their boss. They love playing and training with a legend of the game, and John is quick to ask their opinion on everything but, for me, he doesn't get enough respect back from them. He trusts them to the limit, but they don't pay him back where it really matters, on the pitch.

It's all a learning curve and we have to learn very quickly in an environment that is more Marine than Liverpool. Egos are parked. I'm the bus driver now as well as John's assistant, and drive all the lads to training in a clapped-out white LDV van. There's no airs and graces about this job. We're all in it together and Barnesy is not one to refuse to get his hands dirty.

We've a load of kids in the squad and John works hard to do his best for them. He's getting slaughtered on the terraces because the squad has been weakened so much, but those fans don't realise that his budget has been cut almost in half and the six senior players who've left just can't be replaced.

The one thing John does do is protect his players. He is loyal to them to a fault, and the job ends up costing us money because we bring them out for meals at our own expense. The club just doesn't have the money to pay for bonding sessions, but as I well know from my time with Ireland, you get so much more out of a player if you just make him feel wanted and part of something.

That loyalty is never mirrored on the pitch. Results don't go our way and, as is always the case in football, the longer you have to wait for things to turn around, the more pressure you come under.

Our presence in the dugout probably doesn't help. There's big media interest in us working at Tranmere. Even the *Match of the Day* panel talk about us – and that's unheard of at League One level. Everyone wants to know what John Barnes and Jason McAteer are doing, and it's always the pair of us together. We're being blamed together for the mess, fair enough, but I don't have a lot of say in the big decisions, although John and I do discuss most things.

When Brian Kidd was working with Alex Ferguson at United it was all about Fergie. Sammy Lee was Rafa's coach at Liverpool but people didn't call it the Rafa and Sammy show. Had we been a Premier League club there would have been separation. It would have been John Barnes the manager and Jason McAteer his assistant. We never get that chance. We're getting scrutinised by Gary Lineker, Alan Shearer and Mark Lawrenson of a Saturday night, and I'm shouting at the telly to leave us alone. Let us have a go and let us get on with it. We're not even in the middle of the process here. It's a three-year plan for Tranmere and we're only starting, but the spotlight is right on us.

The attention is amplified as we struggle for points, but we don't see the end coming, just four months into our reign. A 5–0 defeat in the league – we've won just twice in eleven league matches – is followed by a Johnstone's Paint Trophy game at League Two Bury. We're 1–0 up at half-time when the four hundred travelling fans start calling for our heads. Nice one, lads.

We lose the game, but it's back to work the next morning when John has to face the media, twenty-second in the League One table at the start of October, with twenty-six goals conceded. We know the results are bad, but the chairman has said the club are right behind us. John goes into the press conference and tells the media that he has the full backing of the chairman despite the run of poor results. So just ten minutes later the chairman proves a vote of confidence isn't worth anything when he sacks John Barnes – and his assistant!

Peter has allowed John to go ahead and do the press conference knowing that he is about to sack him. I tell Peter he's way out of order but it doesn't matter. We're sacked and I'm out of football again.

It hurts. Some people at Tranmere need to wake up and grow up. A minority of the fans understand that the club can't compete on such a limited budget, but the majority don't get it. They want success but they won't accept that you can't be successful if you lose six senior players and have your budget cut in half on the eve of the season.

It's the same at most clubs – the majority of the fans get it but there's a vocal minority who question the manager's every move.

John got a bike from the club to cycle in and out of training. It's club property, but he's determined not to give it back. He also knows better than to cycle out of the training ground in front of the live television cameras and give every presenter and reporter the perfect 'On Your Bike' moment for one of the greatest players of his generation.

So we're desperately trying to get this mountain bike into the boot of my Range Rover when my mobile rings. It's my mate Paul McDonald. 'Turn the front wheel to the left and you'll get it into the boot,' he says.

I ask him where he is, when he just starts laughing and informs me that he's sitting on his couch at home and that we are live on Sky Sports, robbing a mountain bike and getting away with it.

I turn the wheel the other way, and in it goes. We escape with the bike and head for a local Costa Coffee. I need caffeine!

That Tranmere experience doesn't turn me off football, but it certainly turns me off my local club. John and I had a vision for Rovers but you can't turn a vision into reality in just twelve games. You can't rebuild a club from the bottom up when the owner slashes the agreed budget in half before the season has even kicked off.

I haven't been back to the place, not even to watch one game. It's a great football club with some great people behind the scenes and there are some genuine, proper fans who know what they are talking about, but their opinions count for nothing these days.

They won't admit it, but there's a small minority of fans there who don't deserve even one more minute of my time. Years later they're still giving me and Barnesy stick on social media as they languish in non-league football. They still claim it's all our fault. We ruined their club in twelve games! Seriously, do me a favour.

Tranmere taught me how much football can invade your personal space. My family was at games where the vocal minority were slaughtering us. It was too personal, too vulgar. I don't want them to ever go through that again. The wage I was on doesn't give anyone the right to abuse me in front of my son. No money gives any fan the right to be vindictive and spiteful.

It was hard work. I gave their club 100 per cent every day I was there. I drove the players to training in a battered old minibus. We brought them out for meals and paid for them ourselves to improve team spirit. Barnesy even registered as a player in case of an emergency, with the squad so threadbare. Yet when push came to shove, the chairman listened to the empty vessels on the terraces who made the most noise. Not John Barnes – and certainly not Jason McAteer. He was blind to our vision when it really mattered and those fans turned him against it. They'll have enjoyed watching that news break on Sky Sports.

Maybe there's an element of jealousy amongst certain Tranmere fans. They might not like the fact that a local lad succeeded in football and lived his dream. They might be still angry that I signed for Bolton, their big rivals, all those years ago. Maybe those of an Everton persuasion don't like former Liverpool players around the place. Maybe some think every Anfield old boy is going to do a John Aldridge or a Johnny King for them, get them to cup finals and promotion. It doesn't work like that. I have the scars to prove it.

Maybe I should have gone to Cardiff or Carlisle or somewhere like that as assistant manager. Distance learning might have been a better idea. But like Steve Staunton with Ireland, it is impossible to say no when a team that is close to your heart offers you a job in management. Impossible.

Thanks to that Tranmere termination, the football dream is all but over for me. The idea going to Prenton Park was to use it as a platform to eventually convince Liverpool that they just had to employ Barnesy and Trigger as their dream team. Now the only way I'll get to Liverpool is via the Birkenhead Tunnel.

I do work for the club, but the pressure inside the Liverpool TV studio at Anfield is about as intense as it is going to get for me. Management is all about badges now.

Coaching is all about sitting in a classroom and working on a training field with an assessor at your shoulder. How many exams have you taken? How many badges have you got? The system gives you no recognition in terms of your standing in the game. You could be a World Cup winner with Brazil or an international with Ireland, and all they give you in those coaching departments is half a leg up. Essentially you're the same as the schoolteacher who fancies himself as a football coach – and we all know how that went for Gérard Houllier at Liverpool.

I have tried it. I've gone as far as the UEFA B licence with the FAI in Dublin, but I haven't actually got the badge yet. Twice they've called me for the final class assessment. Twice I was too busy working in the media to turn up. I'll get around to it some day – if I can be bothered. Right now, I doubt it.

Chapter Twenty-nine

Don Hutchison has a problem that needs sorting. John Aldridge has got a team together to play a charity soccer match for Autism Ireland in Dublin against Darndale, a local team with a couple of Gaelic footballers as guests.

There's a bloke called Stephen Cluxton in their midfield, a big-time player with Dublin. He's been giving Hutch stick all through the first half. In the tunnel ahead of the second half we hatch a plan to tackle him.

I slide in nice and early, but Cluxton backs out of the tackle. When I stand up, he hits me with a left hook right on the jaw. It's a nice punch. Down I go. The ref's not having this in a charity game and sends us both off. The photos appear all over the national papers in Ireland.

Years later he's at his stag do in Edinburgh wearing an 'I love McAteer' shirt. My mates get a great laugh out of that one and bombard me with photos on social media. Let it go, lads. It's all part of the game. And good luck to him.

The dark days still come knocking from time to time. If things aren't going right, my head goes – but I can see it coming. I see the signs and I go quiet. I don't take many calls. I don't ring people back. I can't be bothered talking to people for three or four days. I become withdrawn and I'm happy with my own company.

Lucy is really intuitive and most of the time knows how I'm feeling; she understands me. She is my strength. She talks to me, texts me when I'm away from the house, FaceTimes me with Logan, our son. Lucy's my wife, by the way! We married in Limerick in 2013. We first met in Liverpool when she was thirteen!

I'll explain before you get the wrong idea. After I finished as player coach with Tranmere, I had to make some decisions. I was single at the time, but I knew I wanted more kids. I wanted a relationship. And a future.

I'd seen Harry and my mum exposed to the abuse coming from the football terraces and it hurt. I don't want Harry to go through that again. I'd experienced how difficult it is to survive at a club so football started to move off the agenda.

Thanks to my angel, Jane, I learned to live again. I'm out there, playing golf, working in the media, mixing with the Liverpool lads at the Legends games and events. Trigger is back to life. I'm learning to love myself again, learning to laugh again. That is the real key to my happiness.

Being released from Tranmere wakes me up. It is time to decide on my future. What do I really want to be? What do I really want to do? Work in the media? Be a manager? Get into coaching?

Whatever decision I make, it has to be the right one. It's probably the last decision I'll make before I settle down. I'm at the back end of my thirties and that's a squad number that keeps going up. I've got to focus now.

Stevie Mac is great to me. He's home from Spain, finished his playing career and is often local inviting me out and about. I've seen the light again and I'm living my life at last. There's more to do than live in the past and fret about football.

I have a duty to Harry. He's still young and I have to be his dad. I have to be the fun person I know I can be. The man I know I really am – the man Jane and my mum want me to be again.

The Grand National meeting is massive round our way, and Stevie Mac and Robbie own a box at Aintree. They often invite me to go. Eventually I say yes. And they're right. It's a great day.

At the 2009 races, I get talking to a woman called Lucy. Her sister Victoria is married to Stevie Mac. We already know each other having first met in the players' lounge when Macca and I played for Liverpool when she was thirteen. She still has the photo, the starry-eyed teenager with the superstar Irish footballer! That's a joke, by the way! Lucy makes me laugh straight off.

She says things that make me smile. She has a great sense of humour. We've bumped in to each other loads over the years at different dos and events but never really had a good chat like we get to do that day at the races. We get on brilliantly all day, then all go back to a Liverpool hotel for a couple of drinks and the chemistry is bubbling. We're getting on so well that I just have to ask her out. Dinner or coffee, her choice. But first I have to do something. I have to ask Macca for his permission. He's known Lucy since she was just ten years old so is more of a big brother to her.

He's noticed the chemistry between us already today and keeps telling me not to get any ideas!

'Would it be all right if I ask Lucy out?'

He starts laughing and for the rest of the night, it becomes a bit of a joke with the rest of the lads winding me up about it.

Lucy is well used to footballers and the industry. She'd been around Liverpool when Macca was still playing there – as that photo proves. She spent a lot of time in Madrid when Victoria and Steven lived there and even ended up spending a year studying there herself. She was also planning on going back over to Spain to work at some point.

She tells me all this over our first date – in a Costa Coffee. Skinny latte for Lucy, please. Always a skinny latte. We're splashing out here. Big time.

I know she is the one. Straight off. There's something about her. She's interesting. She's different. She's happy to invest in me, happy to share her time with me. She's making me laugh again. I've come through such a lot but she's still interested in me. Everything she says just rolls off the tongue and sounds perfect.

My big thing here is to protect Harry. I don't want him messed around. If I am going to introduce another woman into his life, it has to be right. Lucy is the perfect fit. She's beautiful, caring, loving. She's clever, funny, understanding. She gets me. She gets Harry and how important my relationship is with him. And I get her.

We start dating. There's no star-gazing here. She knows my past as a footballer, but it doesn't matter to her or to our relationship. It has nothing to do with where we are now.

I'm starting to work a lot in the media, with the Liverpool club channel and the likes of Sky and ESPN. I'm an ex-footballer and that's fine with Lucy. She postpones her move to Spain and we spend a lot of time together. We go on holiday, and it works. We start to spend all our time together. After a couple of years we move in together, because by now I'm comfortable that Harry is happy and it just feels like the natural thing to do.

Marriage isn't on the agenda just because it's the next step or the right thing to do. I just want to spend the rest of my life with her and couldn't imagine being with anyone else. Lucy loves Majorca and has been going there with her family for years. There's a walk she goes on with her mum and sister that brings you to the top of the island with a vantage point where you can see all the way to Palma.

We're on holiday there with Lucy's family when I hatch the master plan. I travel with the ring, unbeknownst to her, and I do what a man has to do – I take her father for a pint the day before and ask for his daughter's hand in marriage. I'm dead nervous. I pop the question to Lucy's dad. It's a trial run. He just laughs. 'What took you so long?'

The following day I suggest we go for a walk after lunch. 'Let's do that walk you do with your mum, the one you're always talking about. We can stop off on top of the hill and admire the view. Take a few photos.'

We get to the particular spot. I've the phone out. 'Turn around there and I'll get a pic of you taking in the view to Palma.'

Lucy does look a bit bemused as it's probably not something I would normally mention taking a snap of but she turns and I get ready to whip the ring out of my pocket. It's jammed.

'What are you doing?'

'I'm sorting the camera on this phone. Turn back around.' The box frees enough to remove it from my pocket. I drop to one knee, ready to make the proposal. The tarmac is frying in the mid-afternoon sun. My knee is being burned alive.

Lucy turns around to see just what I'm doing. My skin is burning but there's no stopping me now. 'Will you marry me?'

She bursts into tears. When she calms down, she thankfully agrees to marry me. And yes, I did get the photograph eventually – and a burned knee.

Majorca is an obvious place to get married, but with both her brother and sister getting married there, we decide to go for a change. I've always wanted to get married in Ireland but I just didn't know where. Nicky Byrne is the one to ask. The Westlife singer is a good mate and a good man for a bit of romance and a bit of luxury.

He gives me a couple of names and a couple of choices and off we go on a reccy, a little tour of the west of Ireland. After looking at a few places, we arrive at Dromoland Castle near Limerick. It's so right from the minute we drive through the gate. The castle is magnificent, they have two hotels on site and the obligatory golf course and everything feels good about this venue. The staff just can't do enough for us. Venue sorted.

Now we need a church. Cratloe is only five minutes away, but it's very small and the parish priest is changing, which leads to all sorts of additional issues. I pull a favour with Fr Paddy, the priest who used to say Mass for us on the Ireland trips. He can get us the church but we want to have a look at another few potential venues.

We go into Limerick for a bite to eat and a look at St Mary's Cathedral down by the river. It's perfect, steeped in history all the way down to the bare brick in places. It feels like it has been here forever, the perfect venue for the fairy tale wedding. We need special permission to get married here because it's a cathedral. Time to play the Jason McAteer card. We're in and the invitations go out.

'You are cordially invited to the wedding of Lucy Edwards and Jason McAteer at St Mary's Cathedral in Limerick on Saturday, 5 October 2013, and afterwards to a reception and a knees-up in Dromoland Castle.'

The wedding is everything we want it to be. I never wanted a one-day wedding, a big reception and everyone goes home. I want an event. It turns into a five-day party based between Dromoland and Bunratty.

I look down the aisle as I am waiting for Lucy to arrive, fashionably late, and everyone I want to be here is here. My mum, my family, Lucy's family. My best man and best friends. Liverpool legends John Barnes, Stevie Mac, Ronnie, Aldo, Gary Gillespie. My close friends from Liverpool. My mates from beIN Sports in Qatar and Sky Sports in London. Tony Hickey is down from Dublin. It's just a perfect day.

It's a perfect week actually. We couldn't have been luckier on the day. The weather is 21 degrees – who would have expected that in October in Ireland! The reception is a roaring success from start to finish. The chef and his staff pull out all the stops. We have Connor McKeon and his band followed by a DJ who's flown in from Majorca. Lucy and the girls saw him on the hen do and he's brilliant. Barnesy entertains us with his legendary rapping. It's an amazing day, I couldn't have wished for more.

On the Sunday we relax and spend the day in a pub in Bunratty, being entertained by a traditional Irish musician. Everyone is up for another good party. They treat us like kings. Everyone is here to enjoy themselves. Everyone is happy. Just like the perfect wedding should be.

We make the papers the next day. The reporters waiting outside the church wanted to know if we'd invited Roy Keane. My response was 'He wouldn't come, mate, so I wouldn't waste the paper.' But 'Wouldn't waste the paper, mate' makes for an easier headline.

Lucy Edwards is now Lucy McAteer. I'm working away not long after our wedding and Lucy says she has a present for me when I get home.

Now, I've never been one for wearing undies. Haven't done for years. Commando's been my way – saves on the washing, or not as the case may be! Lucy hates it. She's always on at me to clean up my act and wear underwear like every other reasonable human being.

I get home from Qatar and hug Lucy. Then she throws a pack of Calvin Klein boxers at me and says something like, 'Are they what you'd wear if you wore underpants?'

I'm shrugging my shoulders as I open the box and a little Babygro falls out with 'Dada' written on the front of it. 'That'll never fit me! Are you telling me what I think you're telling me?' She is. We're having a baby!

I start to wear underpants. And we get ready for our arrival at Liverpool Women's Hospital.

The baby is due ten days after the 2014 World Cup final in Brazil. I'm working in Qatar presenting the World Cup coverage. It's a step up from being a pundit, and it's a big move in my media career. The consultant back in Liverpool reckons we'll be okay with the dates, as long as Lucy doesn't go early.

Duncan, who runs things over there, is practically in the same boat. His wife is due within a week of Lucy, but she's living in over there. Lucy and her keep tabs on each other over the phone, wondering whether they'll make it past the final!

Duncan's as good as gold with me – he understands the baby comes first. The World Cup will survive without me if necessary. It does. The first twinges arrive five days before the final. Lucy's on the phone. She's not feeling great and has a bit of a stomach ache. Duncan says to go straightaway, but I insist on waiting until Lucy sees the specialist.

Sure enough, the doc is concerned and wants to keep her in. They have to induce the baby early. I'm back in Liverpool by two o'clock that afternoon and straight into the hospital. I'm quickly a bag of nerves. I can see she's in pain but there's nothing I can do. Her sister, who has stepped in as birthing partner after her mum has fallen ill, takes control and soon I feel calmer. The brilliant midwife tries her best to deliver the baby but it seems to be happy where it is.

A consultant, who looks no more than eighteen, comes into the room. She can see the baby's head and she wants the baby out now. I'm sent to the stands when the most amazing thing happens and our baby arrives into the world at twenty to five in the morning. 'Congratulations, Mr McAteer, you have a son.'

I keep it together until the midwife comes in at eight to say she is clocking off. Then the tears erupt. I start to hug her. She has to go home. I'm almost hanging on to her leg. 'Please don't leave us alone. Please.' She assures me we'll be fine.

Logan is nameless for days. We had discussed all sorts, for a boy or a girl. I want an Irish name. Finn, maybe. Lucy has her heart set on Logan but I'm not too sure. Then Victoria brings her daughter into the hospital. She has a lovely cuddly stuffed lion for her new cousin. The tag is still on – 'Logan the Lion'. It's a sign. Welcome to the world, Logan McAteer. And say hello to one of you new best friends, Lara.

Harry is great with Logan from the moment they meet and that's so important. Lucy has this wonderful family life. She is so close to her mum and dad, to her sister Victoria and her brother James. I keep reminding her how lucky she is to have such a strong family bond. She thinks I'm mad the way I go on about it, but unfortunately her family life is not the norm these days. Dysfunctional is the new norm and don't I know it. Not for the want of trying from my mum but unfortunately other circumstances dictated that.

I don't want our life together to ever end up like that. I love Lucy. I love Harry. I love Logan. I want Logan and Harry to have their father in their lives for the rest of my life and us to always have the family bond that Lucy has known. They can live with me or they can travel with me. My work now is in the media. I'm happy going abroad and working for the different international stations and I really enjoy media work in England and Ireland.

I've patched up relationships with people I fell out with during my playing days, Mr Souness included, and I've also made some fantastic new friends through the media such as Clive Allen and his wife Lisa.

Working within the game has taken more of a back seat for now. But I still love playing with the Liverpool Legends – it's brilliant and a reminder of our former days. We get to go all around the world and we still draw crowds. The club is recognising the contribution of the players to the Liverpool legacy, and they are working hard to bring everyone back together in the name of Liverpool Football Club. I'm on the road with the likes of Robbie Fowler and Didi Hamann. We have a stage show that's been to America and Australia as well as across Ireland and Britain. We have a story to tell and people still want to listen. Thank God.

I have a family to love, and a family who love me to bits. I couldn't ask for anything more.

My relationship with my mum is as strong as ever and she remains my rock and inspiration, my brother lives happily in Australia and my sister and her family live close by, I love them dearly. My dad, well time will answer that question but one thing I know is that I love him.

My life is still very much football it's my true passion and love, ever since Kenny Dalglish lit Anfield up that day I first went – he's my hero. I fulfilled a dream when I signed for Liverpool and that's thanks to Roy Evans who I will stay eternally grateful. Don Hutchison has always been a great friend and we holiday quite often with our sons, Harry and Max. We have the same sense of humor;

he's a messer but he's one of those people who you know won't let you down. He's been a solid friend and one that always makes me laugh.

I now have a great passion for golf; it was there when I needed something to fill my time, it helps me focus and channel my energy into a project I can get better at, when I travel I try and play and have been lucky enough to play some stunning courses all over the world. I've also met some great friends through playing, Matt Bryne has become a great friend and professional Alex Evans is always around for advice and a round.

I'm happy with myself now, and more than happy with my privileged life. I feel thankful. At last. The endless baths and the Birkenhead Tunnel are all but forgotten.

Acknowledgements

We all dream of being or doing something as we grow up – a vet, a pilot, one boy in my school wanted to be a snooker player – but life can point us in a different direction for one reason or another and the dream is lost. Life tried to point me a different direction but with enough belief, guidance and knowledge from others I lived my dream, I got to wear the mighty red colour of Liverpool, the greatest football team in the world. I lived the life of a professional footballer and rubbed shoulders of greats like Barnes, Rush and, for me, the best: Dalglish.

I have many people to thank, like Alan Molden, for seeing my potential and helping me – when time was against me, he helped me believed my dreams could become a reality. Dave Ramsden, my coach at Marine, for the same reason. Bruce Rioch, my manager at Bolton, for teaching me to always be better. Roy Evans, my coach at Liverpool, who wanted my signature. And a big thank you to Mick Byrne and Tony Hickey for being there for me all through the years. Jane, the angel who turned up when the darkest days arrived. I have so many to thank, even the doubters and people who betray your trust, who really just make you stronger and wiser.

This book would not have been possible without the help of a number of people. Thanks to Daniel Givens, of JGA Sport, Claire Rourke for her endless dedication, diligence and support during the initial editing process. To Ciara Doorley, Joanna Smyth and all the team at Hachette Ireland for their faith and patience as this long-term project took life. To Liverpool fans John McKeown and John Robinson for throwing an eye over things and to Sean Ryan and Lynne D'Arcy for help with facts and figures.

The biggest thank you must go to my family. In particular, my mum, Thora, who has been an inspiration to me who makes me proud, someone who I know I can trust and believe in. My dad, who, in his own unique way, drove me to win at all cost. My wife Lucy, who I love dearly, who took on so much and always finds an answer; I'm still learning from her. And my two boys, Harry and Logan, who just make it all worthwhile – without them life wouldn't be the same.

One special thank you must go to my nan who will be watching down on me, I'm sure, with a smile. She was always there for me through thick and thin someone who loved me for who I was, someone who I miss so much.

Finally a big thank you to the fans who have made this journey so memorable and, I hope, worth telling.

x

Photograph acknowledgements

The author and publisher would like to thank the following for permission to use photographs within *Blood, Sweat & McAteer*.

SECTION 1

page 1 all: © author; page 2 top: © Ross Kinnaird/EMPICS Sport; page 2 bottom: © David Kendall/PA Archive/Press Association Images; page 3 top: © Colorsport; page 3 bottom: © Neal Simpson/EMPICS Sport; page 4 top: © Peter Wilcock EMPICS Sport; page 4 bottom: © David Kendall/PA Archive/Press Association Images; page 5 both: © Inpho/Allsport; page 6 top: © Peter Byrne/PA Wire/Press Association Images; page 6 bottom: © Inpho/Cathal Noonan; page 7 both: © author; page 8 both: © author

SECTION 2

page 1 top: © Getty Images/Bob Thomas; page 1 bottom: © Inpho/Billy Stickland; page 2 top: © Inpho/James Meehan; page 2 bottom: © Neal Simpson/EMPICS Sport; page 3 top: © Inpho/James Meehan; page 3 bottom: © Inpho/Lorraine O'Sullivan; page 4 both: © Inpho/Lorraine O'Sullivan;

Index